# PREPARING TEACHERS FOR INCLUSIVE EDUCATION

## Case Pedagogies and Curricula for Teacher Educators

# PREPARING TEACHERS FOR INCLUSIVE EDUCATION

## Case Pedagogies and Curricula for Teacher Educators

*Edited by*

**Suzanne E. Wade**

*University of Utah*

**LEA**

2000

**LAWRENCE ERLBAUM ASSOCIATES, PUBLISHERS**

**Mahwah, New Jersey**          **London**

Lawrence Erlbaum Associates, Inc., Publishers
10 Industrial Avenue
Mahwah, NJ 07430

Cover design by Kathryn Houghtaling Lacey

**Library of Congress Cataloging- in- Publication Data**

Preparing teachers for inclusive education: case pedagogies and curricula
for teacher educators / edited by Suzanne E. Wade.
     p.  cm.
    "This volume . . . is designed to accompany Inclusive education : a
casebook and readings for prospective and practicing teachers"-
-Pref.
Includes bibliographic references and index.
ISBN 0-8058-2509-6 (pbk. : alk. paper)
    1. Inclusive education—United States Case studies. 2. Inclusive
education—Study and teaching—United States—Curricula.
3. Teachers of handicapped children—Training of—United States.
I. Wade, Suzanne E.
LC1201.P74   1999
371.9'046—dc21
                                      99-37806
                                          CIP

# CONTENTS

# PREFACE

This volume, *Preparing Teachers for Inclusive Education: Case Pedagogies and Curricula for Teacher Educators* is designed to accompany *Inclusive Education: A Casebook and Readings for Prospective and Practicing Teachers*. Part I of this volume (chapters 1–5) contains a general introduction to case pedagogies and chapters describing curricula that teacher educators have developed using cases that were designed to prepare preservice teachers for inclusive education. Part II consists of teaching notes that correspond to the cases in *Inclusive Education*.

The chapters in Part I are written by teacher educators who teach general teacher education courses and methods courses in literacy, mathematics, and science education. Based on their own experiences and research findings, these authors describe how other instructors can use particular cases or case-writing activities most effectively to prepare prospective teachers for inclusive classrooms. Hopefully, other teacher educators will find these chapters a useful starting point for incorporating cases on inclusion in their own courses.

Chapter 1, by Wade and Moje, describes the case method and why it can be an effective instructional approach in teacher education. In chapter 2, Wade describes a general teacher education course that was entirely case based and devoted to inclusion. In this course, students critically examined the issues related to inclusion, analyzed videotaped and printed cases, developed and evaluated plans of action for those cases, and wrote cases that they shared in case discussion groups and on electronic bulletin boards. Chapter 3, by Remillard, describes a methods course in mathematics education that used teacher-written cases to introduce issues, dilemmas, and pedagogies related to inclusion when teaching elementary mathematics. In chapter 4, Gess-Newsome and Southerland describe a curriculum developed for an elementary science methods course that relied on a variety of teaching strategies, including journal entries, student

interviews, cases, and adaptation plans in lesson plans, to foster the goal
of science for all. Part I concludes with a chapter by Moje describing how
she used teaching cases in content literacy courses to introduce instructional concepts, inclusion strategies, and the ideas of collaborative teamwork among regular and special educators.

Part II consists of teaching notes for the 14 cases that appear in *Inclusive Education*. As is apparent when reading them, the cases in *Inclusive
Education* are narratives that describe in rich detail the experiences in
inclusive settings of students who have disabilities or who are otherwise
"at the margin," along with those of their parents and their teachers. Most
of the cases pose a problem or dilemma to be resolved, such as the struggles of parents seeking inclusive settings for children with disabilities; a
student's attempt to succeed in the general education classroom; teachers'
concerns for the future success of their students; or attempts by teachers,
special educators, and principals to create inclusive schools. As preservice or experienced teachers read and discuss these cases, they will learn
how to analyze teaching situations similar to the ones they may face in
their own teaching. Additionally, they will be framing problems associated with inclusive education, thinking of alternative solutions, and evaluating those solutions. The teaching notes offer detailed suggestions that
will help teachers prepare for and facilitate case discussions and follow-up
activities. We should note that many of the cases describe situations that
were not in compliance with the Individuals With Disabilities Education
Act (IDEA) (PL 101-476) and other federal and state program guidelines.
Therefore, we urge you to have your students obtain copies of relevant
state and federal guidelines as reference materials. For example, you
could contact the education or special education office in your state for the
most recent guidelines for implementing IDEA.

# CONTRIBUTORS

**Dr. Donna Deyhle** is a professor in the Department of Educational Studies and the Ethnic Studies program, and co-director of the American Indian Resource Center at the University of Utah. Her work focuses on anthropology and education, cultural conflict, racism, critical theory, and education of American Indians. Dr. Deyhle has conducted research and field work on educational issues in cross-cultural settings in Brazil, Peru, Australia, and American Indian reservations in the U. S. She has also taught on-site teacher education courses on the Navajo reservation and at Laguna, Acoma, and Zuni Pueblos. Her work has been supported by a fellowship and a grant from the Spencer Foundation and has been published in *Harvard Educational Review, Theory into Practice, Anthropology & Educational Quarterly,* and *Review of Research in Education.* With colleagues, she co-edited a special issue on critical race theory and education in the *International Journal of Qualitative Studies in Education* and a book titled *Race is. . .race isn't: Critical race theory and qualitative studies in education.*

**Dr. David Dynak** is Chair of the Department of Theatre at the University of Utah and Director of Graduate and Undergraduate Theatre Education programs. Dr. Dynak holds a doctorate in theatre from Michigan State University. His dissertation received the Distinguished Thesis Award from the American Alliance for Theatre and Education. Dr. Dynak has taught in theatre, English, journalism, social sciences, and humanities programs at secondary schools in Michigan and Germany. His work has appeared in *Youth Theatre Journal, Stage of the Art, and Action in Teacher Education.* Dr. Dynak's research interests include teacher beliefs, interdisciplinary instruction, arts-based research, and the use of process drama to connect learners with cross-disciplinary content. He has recently collaborated with Sundance Theatre Lab in the design and implementation of a distance learning

Masters of Fine Arts degree in directing and theatre education for second-ary teachers of theatre, currently the only one of its kind in the world.

**Dr. Julie Gess-Newsome** is an associate professor of science education in the Department of Educational Studies at the University of Utah, where she has also served as the director of teacher certification. Prior to receiv-ing her doctorate from Oregon State University in 1992, she taught high school biology and general science for eight years, and was Wyoming's Biology Teacher of the Year and candidate to NASA's Teacher in Space Program. In 1992, she received a Spencer Dissertation Fellowship and the Outstanding Dissertation of the Year from both the National Association for Research in Science Teaching and Division K of the American Educa-tional Research Association. Dr. Gess-Newsome's research interests include teacher cognition and development as a result of university and teaching experience, with an emphasis on biology teachers' understanding of content as it impacts educational practice. She is currently president-elect of the Association for the Education of Teachers in Science and edi-tor for the Science Teacher Education section of *Science Education.*

**Dr. Tamara L. Jetton** is an associate professor at James Madison Univer-sity. She received her bachelor's and master's degrees in English from Bradley University. She taught secondary language arts for 10 years prior to completing her doctorate in Educational Curriculum and Instruction from Texas A&M University. Dr. Jetton, who studies secondary literacy teaching and learning from a sociocognitive perspective, has published articles in journals such as *Journal of Educational Psychology, Reading Research Quarterly, Review of Educational Research*, and *Educational Psychologist.* She is a presenter at the annual meetings of the American Educational Research Association and the National Reading Conference. Her research interests include the study of literacy strategies for reading in content area classrooms and the study of classroom discourse, both in terms of text and talk. She is coauthor of a chapter in the ing *Handbook of Reading Research,* Volume III.

**Dr. Elizabeth B. Moje**, an assistant professor of Educational Studies at the University of Michigan, holds an M. A. in reading education and a Ph. D. in literacy and language. Dr. Moje, who studies the sociocultural contexts of secondary literacy teaching and learning, has conducted a number of qualitative studies, which have been published in *Reading Research Quarterly, The Journal of Reading, Journal of Research in Sci-*

*ence Teaching,* and *Reading Research and Instruction.* While an assistant professor at the University of Utah, Dr. Moje conducted studies of the use of case pedagogies in her secondary literacy methods courses, published in *Teaching and Teacher Education.* Dr. Moje has also studied adolescents' unsanctioned literacy practices in and out of school, and she continues to write about case pedagogies with colleagues from the University of Utah. She has been supported in her research by a Spencer Postdoctoral Fellowship from the National Academy of Education and a grant from the International Reading Association.

**Dr. Janine T. Remillard**, an assistant professor of mathematics and teacher education at the University of Pennsylvania, received her doctorate in Teaching, Curriculum, and Educational Policy from Michigan State University in 1996. In her research, Dr. Remillard examines issues of teacher learning in the context of educational reform. Her findings inform her work with practicing and prospective teachers who are learning to teach mathematics to all students. She was previously involved in a longitudinal study of the relationship between state-level mathematics and literacy policies and classroom practice in three states. This research involved developing detailed case studies of teachers' encounters with reform. Findings have been published in the *Elementary School Journal* and *Educational Evaluation and Policy Analysis.* Dr. Remillard's interest in teaching mathematics for all students began when she was a full-time teacher in an alternative elementary school. During the summer of 1995, she worked with a group of practicing teachers to develop teaching cases, which she used in her mathematics methods courses while an assistant professor in the Department of Educational Studies at the University of Utah.

**Dr. Sherry Southerland** is an assistant professor in the Department of Educational Studies at the University of Utah, where she teaches undergraduate courses on elementary and secondary science methods, graduate courses in teaching and learning, and doctoral courses on quantitative research methods. Before her appointment at the University of Utah, Dr. Southerland received her bachelor's degree in biology and her master's degree in invertebrate physiology from Auburn University in Auburn, Alabama. Prior to completing her doctorate in science education at Louisiana State University in 1994, she taught natural science and biology at the high school level and served as a forensic scientist for several years. Dr. Southerland's research interests include describing the process of conceptual change in high school biology students, especially as it is affected by language and culture, and preservice teachers' understanding of the nature of science and its impact on their teaching. Many of Dr. Southerland's research articles have been published in the premier journal in science education, the *Journal of Research in Science Teaching*.

**Dr. Audrey Thompson** teaches courses on feminist and anti-racist pedagogy, pragmatism and educational inquiry, African-American and feminist epistemologies, the history of women and schooling, and the social foundations of education. Currently an associate professor of philosophy of education and gender studies in the Department of Educational Studies at the University of Utah, and an adjunct professor in Ethnic Studies, Dr. Thompson completed her doctorate in 1990 at the University of Illinois at Champaign-Urbana. Her published research includes work on pedagogy and performance, the role of caring in education, the conventions of scholarly writing, anti-racist pedagogy, philosophy and literature, and aesthetic education. Her work has been published in *Harvard Educational Review, Educational Theory, and Curriculum Inquiry*, in addition to many other journals and books.

**Ruth Trinidad** is a doctoral student in the Critical, Cultural, and Curriculum Studies program in the Department of Educational Studies at the University of Utah. Prior to pursuing her doctorate, she worked as a bilingual teacher in inner city Los Angeles for seven years, and served as a bilingual/bicultural activist in the community and school. She has also taught ESL and U.S. citizenship classes to Latino/a immigrant communities. At the University of Utah, she has taught courses on multicultural education. Her extensive work with Latino families and her interests in Latina women's issues have greatly informed her current dissertation research, which she is conducting in rural Mexico. This research will focus on the literacy practices and empowerment of rural Mexican women.

**Dr. Beth Tulbert** taught students with a variety mild and moderate disabilities for 16 years before getting her doctorate from the University of Florida in 1992. Her teaching experience included elementary, middle, and high school students with learning disabilities, mild and moderate intellectual disabilities, and behavioral and emotional disabilities. She currently is an assistant professor at the University of Utah in the Special Education Department, where she teaches courses in assessment, research methodology, transition, and curriculum and methods. Her current research interests include effective instructional and service delivery practices for students with disabilities, inclusion, effective assessment practices, and collaboration. Dr. Tulbert's work has been published in *Teacher Education and Special Education, Preventing School Failure, Journal of Educational and Psychological Consultation, International Journal of Special Education, Contemporary Education, Reading and Writing Quarterly: Overcoming Learning Disabilities,* and *Career Development for Exceptional Individuals.*

**Dr. Sofia Villenas** is an assistant professor with a joint appointment in Educational Studies and the Ethnic Studies Program at the University of Utah. She received her doctorate in Social Foundations of Education at The University of North Carolina at Chapel Hill in 1996. Her research centers on investigating Latino home and community education within the dynamics of racial/cultural community politics. Prior to coming to Utah, she conducted research in North Carolina on Latina mothers' roles as educators in the family and community and their racialization as women and transnational laborers. In 1995–1996, Dr. Villenas was awarded the National Academy of Education Spencer Dissertation Fellowship. She has published in the *Harvard Educational Review, Curriculum Inquiry,* and the *International Journal of Qualitative Studies in Education.* With colleagues, she co-edited a book titled *Race is . . . Race isn't: Critical Race Theory and Qualitative Studies in Education.* Her research as well as her experiences as a bilingual elementary school teacher in South Central Los Angeles are the foundations for her studies and teaching in the areas of multicultural and multilingual education.

**Dr. Suzanne E. Wade** is a professor in the Department of Educational Studies at the University of Utah. She received her doctorate in 1984 from the Harvard Graduate School of Education. Her areas of specialization include the teaching of reading and learning strategies in the subject areas, assessment and instruction of reading difficulties, inclusive education, and the use of cases in teacher education. Dr. Wade has published numerous book chapters and articles in journals such as *Reading Research Quarterly, Review of Educational Research, Journal of Educational Psychology, JRB: A Journal of Literacy, The Reading Teacher, Journal of Reading, Journal of Educational and Psychological Consultation,* and *Teaching and Teacher Education.* She has been supported in her work by a National Academy of Education Spencer Fellowship, awarded in 1990, and a Career Development Award from the Joseph P. Kennedy, Jr.

Foundation, awarded in 1994 to design and teach an experimental course for preservice and inservice teachers on inclusive education. In 1999, she was a recipient of the University of Utah's Distinguished Teaching Award.

# I

# CURRICULA FOR PREPARING TEACHERS FOR INCLUSIVE EDUCATION

# 1

# An Introduction to Case Pedagogies for Teacher Educators

*Suzanne E. Wade*
*Elizabeth B. Moje*

Case pedagogies[1] are ideally suited to preparing teachers for inclusive education by helping them understand the needs and concerns of students and parents and by developing the understandings, attitudes, and experience in problem solving that teachers will need to work successfully and collaboratively in inclusive settings. As narrative descriptions of particular experiences, cases present realistic dilemmas and problems in richly detailed, contextualized situations that may be similar to ones teachers have experienced or expect to experience in their future practice. Despite a long and distinguished history in other professional schools such as business, medicine, and law, case pedagogies are relatively new in teacher education and represent a radically different approach (Carter, 1988; Harrington & Garrison, 1992; Merseth, 1991; L. Shulman, 1992; Sykes & Bird, 1992). Instead of beginning with abstract theories and generic

---

[1]We use the term *pedagogies* instead of *methods* to emphasize the potential of case teaching to foster critical and constructivist learning. Consistent with Freirean pedagogy, we view teaching and learning as the development of mutual understanding through a process of shared inquiry, not the transmission of fixed, unquestioned truths from a knowledgeable expert to passive recipients. In contrast, the term *methods* suggests that teaching is strategic, directive, and less open ended, and it exaggerates the teachers' responsibility and authority (Burbules, 1993, p. 128).

prescriptions that students are expected to apply to practice, learning with cases involves "acting, reflecting, [and] deliberating on problematic situations with the aid of various theories" (Sykes & Bird, 1992, p. 12). In other words, theory becomes a useful and meaningful tool for understanding practice, rather than an end in itself (Kessels & Korthagen, 1996).

Many educators also see case pedagogies as a way to foster the development of critical, reflective thinking (cf. Grossman, 1992; Harrington, 1995; Harrington & Garrison, 1992; Harrington, Quinn-Leering, & Hodson, 1996). Critical reflection involves analyzing problems from multiple perspectives; questioning assumptions and beliefs; framing and reframing problems; generating and evaluating a range of possible solutions; and considering the personal, academic, political, and ethical consequences of solutions (Gore, 1987; Gore & Zeichner, 1991; Schon, 1983, 1987; Zeichner, 1992; Zeichner & Liston, 1996). Theoretically, case discussions are well suited to promoting critically reflective thinking because they involve *dialogue*. In contrast to the "banking" view of education in which the teacher deposits a fixed body of knowledge into the heads of learners, dialogue has been described as "the sealing together of the teacher and students in the joint act of knowing and re-knowing the object of study" (Shor & Freire, 1987, p. 14). Others have described dialogue as "guided by a spirit of discovery" in which participants develop greater understanding, insight, and sensitivity (Burbules, 1993, p. 8). According to Burbules, dialogue involves one's ability to reason, "especially our ability to solve problems, to think sensibly toward conclusions, to weigh competing considerations, and to choose reasonable courses of action" (p. 11). These same ideas are captured in Martin's (1985) description of *conversation* as:

> neither a fight nor a contest. Circular in form, cooperative in manner, and constructive in intent, it is an interchange of ideas by those who see themselves not as adversaries but as human beings who come together to talk and listen and learn from one another. (p. 10)

By analyzing complex teaching situations and by articulating, listening to, and possibly challenging a variety of interpretations presented during case discussions, students can become creators and definers rather than simply recipients of knowledge (Harrington & Garrison, 1992; Richert, 1992).

Case teaching also can prepare teachers for collaboration with other teachers, special educators and resource personnel, administrators, and parents—a crucial ingredient in creating successful inclusion in schools.

Discussions and small-group work give teachers opportunities to hone their communication skills, articulate positions, and accept and respond to criticism. Also, most of the cases in this volume are problem based and require teachers to engage in collaborative problem solving. Some are also well suited to role playing situations, in which teachers can work together to generate and evaluate solutions.

## PREPARING FOR CASE DISCUSSIONS

As the site where dialogue most often occurs, whole-class discussions figure prominently in case pedagogies. Good discussions require a great deal of planning on the part of both the instructor and the students. "An Introduction to Cases," which begins Part II of *Inclusive Education,* describes in detail what students should do to prepare for case discussions. In this chapter we share what we have learned from our experiences as instructors and the research we have conducted on our own case teaching.

### Deciding on Your Goals and Selecting Cases

The first and most important decision in selecting cases and planning for case discussions is to decide what you want to accomplish with them in your courses. We begin this process by reflecting on our own philosophy of teaching, just as we ask our students (prospective and practicing teachers) to do. Although our primary goal has been to foster critically reflective thinking, we also have more specific goals that vary depending on the content and purposes of our courses and our students' backgrounds and experience with case pedagogies and with teaching. For example, our purpose in using some cases is to have teachers examine their attitudes toward students with disabilities or students from whom they differ in language, culture, or gender. Other cases can help teachers plan a curriculum to meet their students' needs, plan strategies for solving problems in collaborative situations, or analyze racist and sexist assumptions that might underlie certain educational practices.

To help you select the cases in *Inclusive Education* that are aligned with your goals, we have provided, in the "Teaching Notes for the Cases" (Part II of the present volume), a synopsis of each case and a description of some of the issues that are central to it; we have also provided space for you to note additional issues that you find important. Once you have selected (or written) the cases you plan to use and the issues you want to highlight in each case, we recommend that you think about how the cases might relate to one another. To maintain continuity and reinforce important concepts, you may also want to revisit a case on occasion. For example, at the end of a course, you might return to a case presented earlier to allow class members to assess their growth in understanding an idea or their own professional development. We also have found it important to put the same care into selecting the readings and other media presentations that present course content and serve as tools to help class members make sense of the cases. These include textbooks; journal, newspaper, and magazine articles; works of fiction; documentaries; and movies. These texts can provide students with the content, theories, and analyses of issues that you want the cases to illustrate, enliven, or challenge.

## Creating a Community of Learners

Successful case discussions require a classroom environment that encourages both a sense of community and critical dialogue. These two qualities have been contrasted as "connected knowing" and "separate knowing" by Belenky and her colleagues (Belenky, Clinchy, Goldberger, & Tarule, 1986); as the "believing game and the "doubting game" by Elbow (1973, 1986); and as "inclusive" and "critical" orientations by Burbules (1993). The first is most related to the idea of an inclusive learning community, in which participants in a dialogue are willing to consider, at least initially, the plausibility of what another person is saying by listening and thereby attempting to understand the beliefs, experiences, and emotions of the other. By feeling empathy (which comes from experience), people can attempt to share the experience that has led a person to embrace an idea, realizing of course that such knowledge can only be an approximation. The words Elbow used to describe the believing game—for example, "involvement," "commitment," "willingness to explore what is new," "opening," "flexible," "nonaggressive," "supportive," "cooperative," "listening," "silence," and "agreeing"—reflect his desire to give this stance legitimacy (1973, pp. 178–179).

In contrast, the doubting, critical stance is skeptical, questioning, distanced, and evaluative, testing interpretations and beliefs against evidence, logic, and consistency (Burbules, 1993). Elbow (1973) describes the doubting game as seeking Truth by "seeking error" through the use of evidence and logic (p. 148). Belenky et al.'s (1986) conception of "separate knowing" is similar to both conceptions, equated as it is with being tough minded and skeptical, assuming that everyone, including oneself, might be wrong.

While these two stances may appear to conflict, both are necessary and complementary. Only an environment that fosters trust, listening for understanding, the expression of multiple perspectives, and risk taking allows such inquiry to occur. Building a community in which learning can occur requires "responsibility, directiveness, determination, discipline, and objectives" (Shor & Freire, 1987, p. 16) as well as group solidarity and participant sensitivity (Moje, Enersen, & Dillon, 1993). The first step is to encourage class members to get to know one another. Name cards and simple introductions in which they are asked to tell something interesting about themselves work well in the beginning. Small-group activities prior to whole-group discussions also allow more people to contribute in some way and build group solidarity and confidence by enabling students to practice making a point to a smaller, safer audience (Frederick, 1980). Finally, arranging the room in a U-shaped design encourages interaction among class members.

Having the class establish ground rules for discussions also helps to build a sense of community in the classroom. You might begin by asking class members to describe the kinds of interactions they would like to see occur and what they can do to foster them. They will likely mention some variation on the idea of "active listening" (cf. Rogers, 1987). Instead of focusing on one's own turn and responses, active listening involves consciously working to understand what discussion participants mean, what their experiences might have been, and how they feel about what they are saying. According to Elbow (1986), suspending disbelief and entering into another's way of thinking, even temporarily, forces us to analyze our own ideas more carefully. For further information (and inspiration), see Rogers (1987), Wasserman (1993), Welty (1989), and Christensen, Garvin, and Sweet (1991). The "Introduction to Cases" in Part II of *Inclusive Education* also includes a discussion of how to create a community of learners in classrooms.

Once class members have discussed their roles in fostering a community of learners and in case discussions, the facilitator's job is to make these things happen throughout the case discussions. Sometimes it is helpful during "debriefings" to have class members comment on how the discussions are going and to reflect on the difficulties of active listening, suspending disbelief, and questioning not only other people's assumptions but also their own. Debriefings of this kind may result in class members suggesting pragmatic ways to achieve their ideals and perhaps constructing new, emergent rules.

# Thinking About Your Role as Facilitator

The facilitator serves a critical role in a case discussion: structuring discussion time, deciding on whom to call, and trying to ensure that all participants have opportunities to speak (Garvin, 1991). To the extent possible, the facilitator's job also is to ensure that dialogue really occurs: that class members engage in "an *interchange* of ideas, as opposed to mere *exchanges*" (Moje, Enersen, & Dillon, 1993, p. 23). Without careful direction by the facilitator, case discussions can become story or opinion swapping (Sykes, 1989); or involve "parallel talk," in which other perspectives, although expressed, are not heard (Moje & Wade, 1997). Thus, one of the questions you are likely to ask yourself as you prepare for a case discussion is, "How directive should I be as the discussion leader?"

Christensen (1991) suggested that the ideal relationship between students and teacher is one of *reciprocal inquiry*. The teacher's role is not to be the authority in the classroom and to transmit a prescribed and fixed body of knowledge to students, but rather to foster conditions in which students are encouraged to construct knowledge themselves. Shor and Freire (1987) described the dialogic teacher as one who knows the objects of study at the beginning of the course better than students do, but who *relearns* them through studying them with students. According to Shor and Freire, it is the teacher's openness to relearning that gives dialogue a democratic character.

Emphasizing the relational nature of dialogue, Burbules (1993) also argued that we should not frame our position as teacher or justify our authority solely on the basis of that role. Instead, we should be honest about the knowledge and talents that we possess and the position of authority to which they have led. On the other hand, it is important to understand our students: "what motivates them to enter into the process; what they stand to learn and what they stand to teach us" (p. 33). According to Burbules, we need to be willing to listen to students, not only as a way to encourage them to develop and express their points of view but also as a way to learn something new. By listening, the facilitator also helps to create an environment of respect, interest, and concern in which everyone feels confident and secure.

Oyler and Becker's (1997) concept of *shared authority* is similar. They define shared authority as the middle ground between the authoritarian concept of teaching, in which knowledge and power reside solely in the teacher, and the abdication of authority by the teacher. One way to create classroom interactions that exemplify shared authority is to invite students to participate in creating "the work of the classroom"—both its content (what is to be learned) and its processes (how content will be learned). That is, the teacher is open to hearing students express their needs and to helping them pursue what is important to them. When student contributions do not match the teacher's discussion plans, teachers can view such contributions as "diverse entry points" and seek to create links between what has just been said and their original agendas. Shared authority also involves negotiated evaluation of students' work, in which the teacher and students develop criteria together for evaluating work. In addition, shared authority can involve seeking students' evaluation of the course at certain points to find out what is going well and what students would like to see done differently.

## Getting to Know Your Students Well

An important element in selecting cases and crafting case discussions is knowledge of our students. As Christensen (1991) noted, "the subject matter defines the boundaries of the intellectual territory, but the students' intellects, personalities, learning styles, fears, and aspirations shape the paths they will take" (p. 24). Students also differ greatly in their background, experience, culture, language, and pedagogical orientation. Consequently, they vary in the tools they possess to interpret case events, in the motives they construct for individuals featured in the cases, in the assumptions they challenge and leave unchallenged, in the issues they identify as important, and in the solutions they propose. For example, in our own research (Moje & Wade, 1997), we found differences between prospective and practicing teachers in how they made sense of the cases. Whereas prospective teachers relied on theories from university course work and on their experiences both as students and as student teachers, practicing teachers relied primarily on their teaching experiences. As a result, prospective teachers tended to hold the teachers depicted in the cases as responsible for students' success or failure, whereas experienced teachers tended to view teaching as far more complex and constrained by large class size, administrative mandates, and other contextual factors.

Knowing students well also helps in deciding which students to ask particular questions, what to expect in response, and how to pose questions that students can answer successfully, thus building their confidence as well as their critical reflection abilities. Such knowledge is also helpful when assigning students to role-playing activities and when dealing with controversial issues. Additionally, you may want to use less structured

discussion formats and to vary the format and follow-up activities as the
students become more experienced and confident with case pedagogies.

## Knowing the Case Well
## and Planning the Discussion

If you have selected a case to use from *Inclusive Education*, you may want
to turn to the teaching notes for that case in this volume (see Part II).
These are designed to acquaint you with the case and to plan case activities. We encourage you to view the teaching notes as a resource, selecting
what you find most appropriate and modifying questions and activities to
meet your needs. To begin the planning process, you might want to select
the most important concepts and issues you want students to understand,
referring to the "Issues in the Case" section of the teaching notes for the
case you have selected. Returning to your goals, you might then ask yourself, "Why did I select this case and these readings?" Because major concepts have important subconcepts as well as connections to other major
concepts, developing an outline or visual graphic may suggest one or
more logical patterns that the discussion might follow (Welty, 1989). Such
planning, along with experience in using each case, allows you to be ready
for almost any direction or connection students might make. Careful
preparation thus allows you to be flexible and to guide the course of the
discussion—not in predetermined ways, but rather along the multiple
paths that your students may generate. Because students in your classes
will always be different, bringing with them unique experiences and background knowledge, cases and readings that once seemed so familiar to
you may take on new meanings during a discussion.

The "Questions to Think About" section in each of the teaching notes is
designed to help students prepare for the case discussion. These questions
can be reproduced on a separate page, either as an assignment before class
as students read the case initially, or in class as they review the case. A
short, small-group review session structured around this question sheet
helps students remember and share their interpretations of the individuals
and events depicted in the case. We have found it important to keep small-
group discussions relatively short (15 to 20 minutes) to avoid redundancy
with the large-group discussion. In courses where students read a large
number of cases, you may wish to have students keep the "Questions to
Think About" sheets together in a case discussion notebook, which is
turned in as an assignment at the end of the course. As an alternative to the
discussion sheets, you might assign students to write an analysis of the

case in which they discuss what they see as the major issues in the case and frame the problem as different protagonists in the case might frame it.

The next section of the teaching notes is titled "Discussion Outline." This section includes questions for opening the discussion, covering the major issues, framing the problems in the case, and developing and evaluating plans of action. These questions represent a highly structured approach that we found to be the most successful for us when we were starting out as facilitators. We suggest this format only as a starting point and as one of many different approaches to case discussions. As you become more familiar with case teaching in general, and with the cases you use in your courses in particular, you may want to modify the questions and take different approaches. For example, as we became more confident with case pedagogies, we shifted from an approach that involved laying out all the information in the case, describing the key players, and examining the context of events to an approach that begins with a global question such as, "What is the central problem in this case?" or "What are the major issues this case raises for you?" Sometimes, we also have students work in pairs to compare the case to another one studied earlier. When comparing two or more cases, we provide students with explicit instructions such as, "Make a list of as many similarities as you can in five minutes." Then we ask students to share their findings with the whole class. Along with having discussion questions in mind, we are also prepared with an outline that we can put on the chalkboard that consists of categories for organizing the whole-class discussion. Examples of board outlines are provided in many of the teaching notes.

Role playing and debating are powerful, engaging activities that you may want to use to supplement or replace the structured case discussion questions, most of which probably will be discussed at some point in the activity or in the follow-up debriefing. Thus, in many of the teaching notes, you will find suggestions for role-playing or debate activities. For example, students might be asked to act out a scene from an individualized educational program (IEP) meeting for a student with disabilities or from a collaborative problem-solving session involving school personnel. Following Frederick's (1980) recommendation, we sometimes allow students to decide on their own roles or positions. In a debate, we often have students sit on the side of the room or table that represents their position and face the other side. Then we ask, "Why have you chosen to sit where you are?" For the few students who refuse to take one of the two positions, Frederick suggested creating a middle position. You can also invite students to move to the other side during the debate if they become persuaded by the other side's argument. At other times, we assign roles with the intent of having students understand the perspective of an individual whose position they might not agree with. This also encourages risk taking because students are aware that everyone is playing a role and advocating views they may not hold personally.

We have found that role-playing and debate activities take a great deal of preparation to be successful. We usually have students meet first in small groups with case discussion sheets that structure the discussion by asking them to analyze in various ways the roles or positions they are assuming, to prepare their arguments, and to anticipate counterarguments. (Where applicable, examples are provided in the teaching notes.)

As alternatives for structuring whole-group discussions, Frederick (1980) suggested the following activities:

1. Have individual students state one concrete image, scene, or event from the case that stands out; this should be just a brief description, without analysis, at this point. You could list these descriptions on the board, creating a visual record of the images. To begin analysis of the details, you could then ask, "What themes do you see from all of these images and scenes?" "What connects them?" "Do you see a pattern?" "What is missing?"

2. Ask students ahead of time to write down and bring to class one or two questions about the case and the readings that they want the class to explore. When you collect the questions, which are anonymous (at least early in the term), select some of them for class discussion and read them aloud. Later in the term, you might have several individual students read their own questions and lead the discussion until they feel their questions have been satisfactorily explored. As an alternative, you might distribute the questions to small groups and ask each group to select the one they are most interested in discussing. Or, you could have them categorize the questions they have received to reveal any patterns.

3. Have students find a quotation beforehand that illustrates something in the case or the readings that they feel is insightful or important. This could be phrased as, "Find a quotation that you think best illustrates the major theme of the case" or "Select a quotation that you found difficult to understand." Then, while the student reads the quotation, other students in class would read along in the text silently. Frederick (1980) notes that, because students

are likely to interpret such passages differently, this usually generates a lively discussion.

4. Before moving on to a new topic, have students in small groups generate three "truth statements" about the topic, for example, "It is true about students with disabilities that . . ." and "It is true about girls and science that. . . ." According to Frederick (1980), critical inquiry results as students present their truth statements and other students then question or refute them. The result is an understanding of the complexity of knowledge, a list of questions and issues for further study, and motivation and purpose on the part of students to read the assigned material or do library research on the topic.

One final note: Case discussions seem to work best when they are completed in the same class period. Therefore, estimating how much time each part of the discussion will take is important.

## Setting the Stage

As with any pedagogy, the material conditions of the classroom can make a critical difference in the teaching and learning that occurs. A U-shaped arrangement with a table at the opening for the instructor has worked for us and others (cf. Welty, 1989) because it is more inclusive, encouraging students to look at one another rather than the instructor and to feel a part of the discussion. This arrangement also places you in the center, which facilitates your role as discussion guide because it allows you to move easily to different parts of the room and to particular students. We have also found it essential to have a large chalk or white board for writing down student responses. Writing headings on the board prior to the discussion helps students to see the topics that will be discussed and to feel assured that the discussion will have some direction.

## CONDUCTING CASE DISCUSSIONS

## Keeping Track of and Guiding the Discussion

After all of this preparatory work before class and in the small-group discussions, you and the class are now ready for the whole-class discussion to begin. As the discussion ensues, we have found it helpful to record key words under the relevant headings on the chalkboard as a way to recognize and reward students' contributions and to keep track of the discussion. It also helps students see at a glance the range of issues, problems, and solutions that can be generated for any particular case (Welty, 1989). Board work also helps you follow and guide the discussion to ensure that the case is analyzed at multiple levels and to keep students from jumping too quickly to solutions—a problem we have found in researching our own case discussions (Moje, Remillard, Southerland, & Wade, 1999). Finally, board work also lets you record important comments that you may want to discuss in depth later. If, for example, a student were to make an important observation that was not relevant to the topic during a brainstorming session, you could say, "That's a really important point. Let's record it over here and come back to it later." This technique will help you remember to return to the issue, and it helps students feel that their points have been recognized and will be addressed at some point.

## Bringing Closure to the Discussion

The teaching notes offer a variety of postdiscussion activities, from role playing to action research and library research projects, that are designed to engage students in generating and evaluating possible solutions or studying issues in greater depth. These activities offer an alternative to the closing "minilecture," a common practice in some case pedagogies in which the teacher gives a summary of the discussion and states its "larger meanings" in relation to theory and other cases (Welty, 1989). End-of-the-discussion activities, in which students learn more about relevant issues through library work or action research, or role-playing activities involving collaborative problem solving encourage socioconstructivist learning rather than a reliance on the teacher to define the case's one right meaning and solution. In addition, you might ask class members to write a case analysis. This involves an in-depth discussion of the issues in the case, in which students frame the problem in different ways and from different perspectives, and generate and evaluate possible solutions.

## CASE DISCUSSIONS IN NEWSGROUPS ON THE INTERNET

As part of our study of case discussions, we have been experimenting with case discussions and other forms of dialogue outside the classroom in Internet-based electronic newsgroups (cf. Wade & Niederhauser, 1997). In this way, technology has become an extension of the class—a new forum for community building, undominated dialogue, social learning, and critical reflection. Whereas class time typically emphasizes oral language in both small-group and whole-class discussions, newsgroups involve written conversations with peers about the same cases and complex ethical issues discussed in class. Thus, newsgroups have optimized class time and expanded discussion space by allowing students to continue their discussions in places and at times that are convenient for them.

A newsgroup is an electronic discussion forum that allows participants to read and write messages using computers that are connected to the Internet. Because of the large size of the class (45), we established six newsgroups and randomly assigned students to one of the groups. Each week (at least initially), we posted a question and asked that students respond to it and, later in the week, to the responses of other members of their newsgroup. We selected the Netscape Navigator newsreader because it is widely available and includes a feature that provides a graphic representation of the flow of the discussion as it develops. When a student replies to a question or comment on the newsgroup, the new message is added to the discussion in a way that shows the relationship of the new comment to the existing discussion structure. This helps participants follow the "threads" of the discussion as they develop over time. However, if newsgroups are not possible, e-mail groups can be established.

In evaluating results of the effectiveness of the newsgroups, we found that they were successful in meeting our three goals of building communities of learners, creating a forum for undominated dialogue, and fostering high-quality discussion. However, we also found that access and time were problems that interfered with the success of the newsgroups. Here, we describe what we learned from our research on the newsgroups discussion and the solutions we developed to resolve the problems that arose.

## Building Communities of Learners

Many students developed strong group affiliations, a sense of community within the newsgroups, and a commitment to participate in the online discussions. During in-class newsgroup meetings, students provided support to one another in gaining access and overcoming problems associated with the technology. Later, we saw class members put pressure on their less active colleagues to participate more. Analysis of printouts of the discussions revealed that newsgroup members interacted in supportive ways—

building on one another's ideas, inviting responses, and acknowledging their contributions—which in some cases led to more awareness and to change in their thinking.

## Creating a Forum
## for Undominated Dialogue

The newsgroups became a forum in which most of the participants expressed their views, challenged views with which they did not agree, and seemed to take seriously challenges to their own views. We concluded that instructor intervention in the discussion was unnecessary because students often held their peers accountable for the positions they expressed. Students also told us that they liked the sense of ownership they felt over their online discussions because the instructors were not involved, and that they viewed participation as relatively risk free.

## Fostering High-Quality Discussions

In assessing the quality of the newsgroup discussions, we saw our goals realized over the 10-week quarter, although there were variations from group to group and among individuals. Many of the newsgroup exchanges exemplified well-reasoned, reflective, and thoughtful dialogue that drew on the class discussions, readings, students' teaching experiences, and knowledge from other sources. We and the students attributed the high quality of the discussions to two aspects of newsgroups. First, in contrast to in-class talk, the act of writing gave students the time to compose and edit their contributions before making them public in their newsgroups. Second, newsgroups provided students with an authentic audience that was interested and engaged in discussing the issues. Unlike formal writing assignments in which the audience is often the instructor-as-evaluator, students described writing in the newsgroups as similar to having a conversation among practicing professionals.

Unhappy with the early questions we posted to the newsgroups, which students felt did not stimulate true dialogue, students soon assumed responsibility for deciding on the question or issue they would address weekly in their online discussions. In class, we tried various ways to generate interesting questions, such as having class members meet in newsgroups to agree upon a question, having them brainstorm questions as a whole class, and simply posting a complex concept such as *change* for students to discuss. Eventually, the newsgroups began to engage in ongoing dialogue without a structured question or issue.

## Barriers and Problems With Implementation

Although students clearly valued the newsgroups, they also expressed frustration regarding the problems they experienced. In the beginning of the course, a good portion of class time was devoted to resolving problems with newsgroup access. Although this was important to those who initially lacked the necessary technical skills, those who were successfully online complained about this use of class time. To minimize such problems in the future, newsgroup participation has been integrated into a technology course that students are required to take early in the program. However, even with the necessary technical skills, access remained an ongoing problem. Students who did not have reasonably high-level home computers and university e-mail accounts had to use on-campus computers—a problem for those students who only came to campus once a week for class. In addition, the newsgroup server was not always reliable, and computer lines to the university were often busy. Sometimes messages were very slow to appear, and several times, the server went down and no one was able to read or post messages for a time. Although the alternative, an e-mail discussion, did not have the advantages of the newsgroups described earlier, it was more reliable. In summary, if the necessary technological supports are available, electronic discussions, whether in newsgroups or on e-mail, can be a valuable addition to teacher education courses.

## HAVING STUDENTS WRITE
## THEIR OWN CASES

The following quote from a prospective teacher illustrates how powerful case writing can be for teachers by encouraging them to think about their own teaching:

> You can't always have someone there in your classroom observing you, but if you write about [your teaching] and then have someone else read it, he or she can almost be in that classroom and he or she can see something and say, "Well, you didn't do this, you could've done this, or why don't you try this next time?" So I just think it's a way to help you improve your teaching.

Shulman, Colbert, Kemper, and Dmytriw (1990) found that having practicing teachers write cases increased their sense of professional worth and promoted reflection and collaboration by encouraging them to contribute to the literature on teaching. Similarly, we found that asking prospective teachers to write cases about a teaching experience for an audience of peers challenged them to examine their own practices and to make their teaching decisions explicit. Because the purpose of case writing is to reflect upon one's teaching experience as well as to teach others, it has both a meaningful purpose and an audience. We found that the ensuing small-group case discussions with peers provided case authors with new insights and understandings and engaged them in collaborative problem solving as they searched for and evaluated possible solutions.

One type of case writing that seems particularly well suited to inclusive education consists of case studies documenting the schooling experiences or academic difficulties of particular students (whose confidentiality is protected). This genre of case writing can give teachers the opportunity to appreciate and understand the feelings, concerns, and needs of students, their parents, and other practitioners. Another type involves personal narratives of the experiences of the case writer or other teachers in inclusive classrooms or collaborative situations. A third type of case writing related to inclusion might involve narratives based on research conducted by the case author. These cases might focus on comparisons of schools' criteria for classifying children or on teachers' attitudes toward certain groups of students, for example.

For J. H. Shulman (1991), teacher-authored cases are stories that are

> crafted into compelling narratives . . . [with] a plot that is problem-focused with some dramatic tension that must be relieved. They are embedded with many problems that can be framed and analyzed from various perspectives, and they include the thoughts and feelings of the teacher-writers as they describe the accounts. (p. 251)

To write well-crafted teaching cases, Shulman argued, teachers need support and guidance over time, with opportunities to interact with other case writers. Her approach to teaching case writing involves brainstorming possible ideas for cases, having teachers write successive drafts, presenting the drafts to peers, and providing extensive feedback. She also asks teachers to think about the question, "What is this a case of?" These techniques help teachers think about the meaning and goals of their case, make explicit their rationale and assumptions, and identify crucial details. (See J. H. Shulman, 1991, 1992; see also Richert, 1992.)

In addition to these suggestions, we have teachers analyze existing cases that they find particularly effective and that can serve as models; they then brainstorm elements that contribute to the quality of the cases. Because we usually have case authors meet in small groups for 30 minutes (or on the Internet) with other class members to analyze their cases and generate and evaluate possible solutions to the problems they present, we ask writers to avoid including solutions in the cases. In a frequent follow-up activity in our courses, case authors write formal case analyses based on the ideas generated in the small-group case discussions. As with case writing, structuring successful small-group discussions requires a good deal of guidance. In planning their case discussions, students might find the questions in the "Discussion Outline" in the teaching notes in this volume useful as models.

## ASSESSING YOUR SUCCESS

You may want to follow up the case discussion with some kind of debriefing and/or research designed to provide you with information about the success of the discussion and the case activities you have tried. Results can help you answer questions such as: What went well? What issues were covered and what were missed? Did the discussion meet my objectives? Did it move students to examine larger issues? Did they examine them critically? What might I do differently next time?

To answer these questions, we have found students to be a valuable source of information. Gathering student input can be as simple as asking, during a debriefing session, "How did it go?" and "Is there anything you would like to do differently next time?" or having students write evaluations at the end of the discussion and/or course. For example, we have students meet in small groups midway through the course to write down on one sheet, and then share with the class, what they as a group agreed they liked about the discussions and what they would like to see changed. To diminish the tendency of certain students to dominate discussions, students in one course suggested that everyone receive chits at the beginning of class, which would be relinquished each time an individual spoke in a discussion. Student input can also be as formal as end-of-the-term interviews with individuals or focus groups. Other valuable sources of feedback are peer observations, followed by debriefing with the observer immediately after the class; analysis of transcripts of audiotaped case discussions; and analysis of students' written products.

To research our own case pedagogies, we have analyzed student evaluations, transcripts of case discussions, interviews, and students' written products (Moje et al.,1999; Moje & Wade, 1997; Wade & Moje, 1997; see also the evaluation sections of chaps. 2–5 of this volume). Questions that guided our research included the following: Do prospective and practicing teachers consider cases to be a valuable teaching approach that contributes to their own professional growth? What tools (e.g., theories, other cases, and kinds of experience) do teachers use to make sense of the cases? What images of teaching and learning do teachers use during case discussions? And, has our use of case pedagogies moved teachers to become critical, reflective thinkers?

Our findings related to these research questions have led us to critically examine and change our assumptions and practice. This kind of self-study has been advocated by Zeichner (1998) as one of the new directions in teacher education scholarship. In the section that follows, we briefly describe our research findings and the kinds of changes we are making in our case pedagogies.

From interviews, course evaluations, and students' comments during debriefing sessions, we found that our students enjoyed reading and discussing the cases and found them helpful in analyzing important issues and in learning to resolve the kinds of dilemmas that might emerge in their teaching in the future. These responses fit with our initial assessments of the case discussions, in which we found students to be actively and emotionally involved and treating the issues seriously. However, in our first study (Moje & Wade, 1997), in which we analyzed case discussion transcripts, we found little evidence of critical, reflective thinking. Both prospective and practicing teachers tended to locate the problems in the cases either in the teachers and their methods or in the pupils, their parents, and their culture. Rarely did they question the case teachers' goals, the curriculum, or institutional arrangements such as tracking. Many of our students also viewed differences in children's abilities as fixed and innate, rather than as learned and changeable. Furthermore, they tended to view teaching as the act of applying correct techniques in the appropriate circumstances, and believed that good teachers had a well-stocked repertoire of such tools. This view of teaching was apparent in the solution-oriented approach they took to the case discussions: They were often quick to recommend management strategies to control student behavior or to find methods that would serve as "props" to accommodate rather than develop students' abilities. Even when many issues were raised and discussed, some students offered the same ideas repeatedly, apparently unaffected by the expression of alternative perspectives. We concluded that, although the discussions were animated and even complex, they did not reflect much critical thinking.

These findings should not be surprising. From the literature, we know that knowledge tends to be viewed as technical and fixed by teachers and members of the larger society, and ability is seen as fixed, stable, and unchanging (cf. Apple, 1990; Dewey, 1910/1991; Schon, 1983). Furthermore, attempts to promote critical reflection by other means, such as journal writing and action research projects, have not been particularly successful (for a review, see Sibbett, 1996).

As we analyzed the case discussion transcripts and discussed our findings with colleagues, we began to reexamine our objectives for our use of particular cases, our larger teaching goals (e.g., what does critical, reflective thinking really look like?), and our own ideologies of teaching and learning (Moje et al., 1999). For example, we began to question the objectives of the methods courses we were teaching, with their emphasis on strategies for teaching content or literacy. We have also had to ask ourselves what it means to change, and what we can realistically expect of our students in any one teacher education course.

While grappling with these difficult questions, we discovered ways to change our case pedagogies to better meet our goals. For example, to foster critical reflection thinking, we provide students with more tools for making sense of the cases, such as careful analysis of readings that critically examine issues related to ability, curriculum, testing, and tracking as well as race, culture, class, gender, and language differences. We also raise these issues explicitly during case discussions. Similarly, we explicitly explain and model what it means to frame and reframe problems, showing students how each way of framing a problem can lead to different solutions with different consequences for pupils. With better understandings of our students' conceptions and beliefs provided by research findings, we are better prepared to guide discussions toward our goal of critical reflection. After case-related activities, we also give more attention to debriefing, which gives students opportunities to distance themselves from the case and reflect on it analytically. Likewise, we debrief with students about the case activities themselves, discussing their purpose and value. Finally, as described earlier, we have been experimenting with electronic case discussions in Internet newsgroups as a way to extend dialogue beyond the classroom. Current research that we are conducting on these various case discussion formats has revealed a good deal more critical, reflective thinking among many prospective teachers (Wade & Moje,

1997). Thus, similar to what we expect of our students, we too are engaging in critical, reflective practice, as we research what our students are learning from case pedagogies and examine our own assumptions about what it means to teach and to learn.

## CONCLUSION

We hope this chapter is a useful resource as you think about your goals for using cases, foster a community of learning in your classroom, and plan case discussions and related activities to achieve your goals. We encourage you to engage in research on your case teaching; our research has helped us become more confident as discussion facilitators and pushed us to try new pedagogies to better meet our teaching goals. At the same time, our own learning continues, as we examine the content and curricular materials of our courses and study our students' thinking and conceptual understandings.

## REFERENCES

Apple, M. W. (1990). *Ideology and curriculum* (2nd ed.). New York: Routledge.
Belenky, M. F., Clinchy, B. M., Goldberger, N. R., & Tarule, I. M. (1986). *Women's ways of knowing: The development of self, voice, and mind.* New York: Basic Books.
Burbules, N. (1993). *Dialogue in teaching: Theory and practice.* New York: Teachers College Press.
Carter, K. (1988). Using cases to frame mentor-novice conversations about teaching. *Theory into Practice, 27,* 214–222.
Christensen, C. R. (1991). Premises and practices of discussion teaching. In C. R. Christensen, D. Garvin, & A. Sweet (Eds.), *Education for judgment: The artistry of discussion leadership* (pp. 15–34). Boston: Harvard Business School.
Christensen, C. R., Garvin, D., & Sweet, A. (Eds.) (1991). *Education for judgment: The artistry of discussion leadership.* Boston: Harvard Business School.
Dewey, J. (1991). *How we think.* Amherst, NY: Prometheus Books. (Original published by D. C. Heath, Lexington, MA, 1910).
Elbow, P. (1973). *Writing without teachers.* New York: Oxford University Press.
Elbow, P. (1986). *Embracing contraries: Explorations in learning and teaching.* New York: Oxford University Press.
Frederick, P. (1980). The dreaded discussion: Ten ways to start. *Improving College and University Teaching, 29,* 109–114.
Garvin, D. (1991). A delicate balance: Ethical dilemmas and the discussion process. In C. R. Christensen, D. Garvin, & A. Sweet (Eds.), *Education for judgment: The artistry of discussion leadership* (pp. 287–303). Boston: Harvard Business School.
Gore, J. (1987). Reflecting on reflective teaching. *Journal of Teacher Education, 38,* 33–39.
Gore, J., & Zeichner, K. M. (1991). Action research and reflective teaching in preservice teacher education: A case study from the United States. *Teaching and Teacher Education, 7,* 119–136.
Grossman, P. (1992). Teaching and learning with cases. In J. Shulman (Ed.), *Case methods in teacher education* (pp. 227–239). New York: Teachers College Press.

Harrington, H. L. (1995). Fostering reasoned decisions: Case-based pedagogy and the professional development of teachers. *Teaching and Teacher Education, 11,* 203–214.

Harrington, H. L., & Garrison, J. (1992). Cases as shared inquiry: A dialogical model of teacher preparation. *American Educational Research Journal, 29,* 715–735.

Harrington, H. L., Quinn-Leering, K., & Hodson, L. (1996). Written case analyses and critical reflection. *Teaching and Teacher Education, 12,* 25–37.

Kessels, J. P. A. M., & Korthagen, F. A. L. (1996). The relationship between theory and practice: Back to the basics. *Educational Researcher, 25,* 17–23.

Martin, J. R. (1985). *Reclaiming a conversation: The ideal of the educated woman.* New Haven, CT: Yale University Press.

Merseth, K. (1991). *The case for cases.* Washington, DC: American Association for Higher Education.

Moje, E. B., Enersen, D. L., & Dillon, D. R. (1993). Proposing new directions: Research dialogues. In D. R. Dillon (Ed.), *The scientist-practitioner model and practice* (pp. 21–37). West Lafayette, IN: Purdue University Office of Research and Development.

Moje, E. B., Remillard, J., Southerland, S., & Wade, S. E. (1999). Researching case methods to inform our teaching. In M. Lundeberg, B. Levin, & H. Harrington (Eds.), *Who learns what from cases and how? The research base for teaching with cases* (pp. 73–94). Mahwah, NJ: Lawrence Erlbaum Associates.

Moje, E. B., & Wade, S. E. (1997). What case discussions reveal about teacher thinking. *Teaching and Teacher Education, 13,* 691–712.

Oyler, C., & Becker, J. (1997). Teaching beyond the progressive-traditional dichotomy: Sharing authority and sharing vulnerability. *Curriculum Inquiry, 27,* 453–467.

Richert, A. E. (1992). Writing cases. In J. Shulman (Ed.), *Case methods in teacher education* (pp. 155–174). New York: Teachers College Press.

Rogers, C. (1987). Active listening. In C. R. Christensen (Ed.), *Teaching and the case method: Text, cases and readings* (pp. 135–136). Boston: Harvard Business School.

Schon, D. A. (1983). *The reflective practitioner.* New York: Basic Books.

Shor, I., & Freire, P. (1987). What is the "dialogical method" of teaching? *Journal of Education, 169,* 11–31.

Shulman, J. H. (1991). Revealing the mysteries of teacher-written cases: Opening the black box. *Journal of Teacher Education, 42,* 250–262.

Shulman, J. H. (1992). Teacher-written cases with commentaries: A teacher-researcher collaboration. In J. Shulman (Ed.), *Case methods in teacher education* (pp. 131–152). New York: Teachers College Press.

Shulman, J. H., Colbert, J. A., Kemper, D., & Dmytriw, L. (1990, Winter). Case writing as a site for collaboration. *Teacher Education Quarterly,* 61–78.

Shulman, L. (1992). Introduction. In J. Shulman (Ed.), *Case methods in teacher education* (pp. xiii–xvii). New York: Teachers College Press.

Sibbett, J. (1996). *Reflection in practice: An exploratory study of student teacher reflection.* Unpublished doctoral dissertation, University of Utah, Salt Lake City.

Sykes, G. (1989). Learning to teach with cases. *Colloquy, 2,* 7–13.

Sykes, G., & Bird, T. (1992). Teacher education and the case idea. In G. Grant (Ed.), *Review of research in education* (Vol. 18, pp. 457–521). Washington, DC: American Educational Research Association.

Wade, S. E., & Moje, E. B. (1997, March). *Verbal interaction patterns in case discussions associated with critical/reflective and technical/rational thinking.* Paper presented at the annual meeting of the American Educational Research Association, Chicago.

Wade, S. E., & Niederhauser, D. (1997, November). *Electronic discussions in an issues course: Expanding the boundaries of the classroom.* Paper presented at the Utah Association of Superintendents and Curriculum Developers Annual Conference, Park City Utah.

Wasserman, S. (1993). *Getting down to cases: Learning to teach with case studies.* New York: Teachers College Press.

Welty, W. (1989, July/August). Discussion method teaching. *Change,* 40–49.

Zeichner, K. M. (1992). Conceptions of reflective teaching in contemporary U.S. teacher education reforms. In L. Valli (Ed.), *Reflective teacher education* (pp. 161–173). Albany: State University of New York Press.

Zeichner, K. M. (1998, April). *The new scholarship in teacher education.* Division K Vice-Presidential Address at the annual meeting of the American Educational Research Association, San Diego, CA.

Zeichner, K. M., & Liston, D. P. (1996). *Reflective teaching: An introduction.* Mahwah, NJ: Lawrence Erlbaum Associates.

# 2

# A Case-Based Curriculum on Inclusive Education for Teacher Education

*Suzanne E. Wade*

"Teaching Diverse Students in Inclusive Classrooms" is a course developed at the University of Utah to address issues of diversity and inclusive education. It covers not only debates related to inclusive education but also attitudes, curricula, teaching approaches, and assessment practices that foster learning for all students, some of whom might otherwise fail for reasons related to differences in language, culture, ethnicity, economic status, gender, and ability. Additionally, this course examines collaborative partnerships that can provide the knowledge and resources necessary to the success of inclusion efforts. In particular, this course addresses the following questions:

- What are the assumptions and values underlying the inclusion movement?
- What are the different forms inclusive education might take?
- What are the potential benefits and limitations of inclusive education?
- How can teachers create a learning environment in their classrooms that promotes the academic achievement of all students and the acceptance of differences?

- How can teachers adapt their curriculum, instruction, and assessment practices to meet the needs of diverse students?
- What are some problems that may arise in inclusive settings? What are different ways these problems can be understood? What are possible solutions to these problems and their potential consequences? How can teachers, special educators, other school personnel, parents, and students work together to share knowledge and resources and collaboratively solve problems?

## OVERVIEW OF THE COURSE

The curriculum described in this chapter was developed for a one-quarter, three-credit-hour course serving both prospective and practicing teachers at the elementary and secondary levels. To address the questions just listed, I rely primarily on case pedagogies, which are described in detail in chapter 1 of this volume. This curriculum was field tested and refined over a 4-year period in seven iterations of the course. Although it was developed for a 10-week course, the curriculum described in this chapter has been expanded for use in a semester-long course.

### Assigned and Recommended Readings

In all case discussions, students are asked to use the assigned readings, readings from other courses, and their experiences as tools for understanding the cases and constructing knowledge of teaching and learning. Some of the assigned readings and most of the cases that are described in this chapter appear in *Inclusive Education: A Casebook and Readings for Prospective and Practicing Teachers*, which is the companion book to this volume. In addition, Part II of the present volume consists of teaching notes to help you use the cases that appear in *Inclusive Education*. Additional recommended readings and teaching cases are described in this chapter.

### Course Expectations

Students are evaluated on the following criteria, which I outline in the course syllabus:

- *Professionalism and participation.* This involves attending class regularly, being prepared for class, attentive listening, thoughtful contributions to class discussions, sensitivity to other individuals and to equity issues, and handing assignments in on time. It also involves participating with other class members in discussions on the Internet newsgroups, which are described in chapter 1 of this volume.

- *The case discussion notebook.* This consists of case discussion sheets that are handed out for each case discussion, including several videotaped cases. These sheets contain "Questions to Think About," which appear in the teaching notes in this volume. For the print and videotaped cases that are available elsewhere, I have included questions in this chapter that could be developed into case discussion sheets.

- *Written case analyses.* These consist of three parts: (a) an in-depth discussion of the issues in the case and different ways the central problems in the case can be framed; (b) an action plan that involves a critical discussion and evaluation of possible solutions to those problems, an explanation of why each solution might solve the problem or meet specific goals, what resources or support would be needed for the plan's success, what risks or negative consequences might result, and what alternative actions could be carried out if the plan was not working; and (c) a personal reflections section in which students discuss what impact the case and the issues it raises has had on them as teachers and what they will take from the case into their teaching careers.

- *Position and/or critical analysis papers.* In the position paper, students are asked to imagine themselves in a real or hypothetical situation involving a school district's policy regarding inclusion and to describe the position they would take. This paper also requires an extensive rationale for their position, based on appropriate course readings, research, cases, and experiences. In the critical analysis paper, students are asked to critically examine and evaluate the arguments made by the authors of one or more of the readings, the nature of the rhetoric used to make the argument, and the authors' underlying assumptions and beliefs.

- *Special projects.* Completed individually or collaboratively, the special project may involve one of the following: (a) a student-authored case and case analysis; (b) a library and/or action research project such as shadowing special education teachers in several schools, interviewing teachers and administrators regarding an issue or policy related to inclusion, analyzing classroom interaction patterns among students, or conducting survey studies to assess students' attitudes and feelings about being in various types of pull-out programs and general education classes; (c) a readers' theater or improvisation based on one of the cases or on students' experiences, followed by a written analysis of the situation; or (d) some other project of the students' choice. Special projects are presented on the last day of class.

# THE CURRICULUM

The curriculum of the course is described sequentially by topic. For each topic, I outline the activities for each class meeting, focusing on how cases have been used to achieve specific purposes in the course. Because detailed guidelines for using each of the cases in *Inclusive Education* appear in the teaching notes, in this chapter I provide only a brief summary of each case to give the reader an idea of how it fits into the overall curriculum. For the videotaped and print cases that are not included in *Inclusive Education* and therefore do not have teaching notes, I describe in some detail how I have used them in this course.

## Developing a Professional Community

Before cases are introduced to the class, I spend time developing a professional community, that is, a collegial atmosphere that is conducive to critical thinking and problem solving. As Christensen (1991) noted, effective case discussions require that students "become profoundly and actively involved in their own learning, to discover for themselves rather than accept verbal or written pronouncements" (pp. 16–17). This requires a classroom environment in which it is safe to learn from one's peers, to experiment and explore; to err; and to challenge assumptions, beliefs, and interpretations. For specific suggestions on how to accomplish this, see chapter 1 of this volume. You might also have students read "An Introduction to Cases" in *Inclusive Education*, which discusses students' roles in case discussions and what students can do to support one another.

## The Debate Over Inclusive Education
## for Students With Disabilities

This topic covers several class sessions and involves readings, several videotaped and print cases, minilectures, and discussions. The goal of this segment of the course is for teachers to understand the history of special education, including landmark legislation; to examine critically how definitions of inclusive education differ and what each entails; and to understand why some people favor and others oppose full inclusion. For an overview of the history and issues regarding inclusive education, see chapter 1 in *Inclusive Education.*

I introduce the topic of inclusive education by showing the videotape "Sean's Story: A Lesson in Life" (Read, 1994), an ABC production that first appeared on *Turning Point.*[1] "Sean's Story" is a case within a case, introducing the debate over inclusive education at both an individual level and a policy level. It is a documentary about a young child with Down syndrome who is enrolled for the first time in a general education classroom. It tells of the struggles of his mother and teachers to make it a successful experience and of the concerns of another parent who wants her child with disabilities educated in a separate school. It is also a documentary about the Baltimore School District, which became embroiled in a battle with teachers and parents in 1993 when it mandated a policy of inclusion.

The structure of the case discussion of "Sean's Story" (1994) is similar to the one used with many of the cases. Before viewing the case, students receive a case discussion sheet listing questions to think about, which they complete while viewing the video and discuss afterward in small groups in class. Because they are asked to compile the case discussion sheets into a notebook to be handed in as an assignment later in the course, I have found students to be conscientious in completing them in the small groups and adding to them during the ensuing whole-class discussions. The following questions are included in the case discussion sheet for "Sean's Story," and could be adapted to any case of a similar nature:

- What are we told about Sean? His parents?
- Why did Sean's parents struggle to get him into a regular classroom?
- Why did some of the other parents of students with disabilities prefer separate special education settings?
- What concerns did teachers and parents of nondisabled students express when students with disabilities were placed in mainstream classrooms?

---

[1]"Sean's Story: A Lesson in Life," which aired on September 7, 1994, is available from ABC by calling 1-800-913-3434. A good alternative to "Sean's Story" is a 30-minute videotape entitled "Educating Peter," available from HBO, which tells a similar story of a boy with Down syndrome who is enrolled in a general education classroom.

- What support was provided to Sean in the general education setting? What adaptations were made? Were these effective?
- What do you think were the benefits to Sean? What were the limitations? What were the effects on the other students?

In the whole-class discussion that follows small-group work, I focus on
broader, more interpretative and evaluative kinds of questions, such as the
following: What are the major issues this case raises regarding inclusive
education? What position regarding inclusive education do you think
underlies the video? Why? What evidence is there for your conclusion?
What is your position at this point regarding the best placement for Sean?
What would be the best placement and program for him later, when he
enters secondary school?

Another excellent video that can be used to introduce the debate over
inclusion is a 15-minute segment from the *McNeil-Lehrer Newshour*[2]
(1994). In addition to covering a number of issues and views on the topic,
it also presents examples of children with physical disabilities who have
been successfully included in general education classrooms. As a supplement or alternative to these videotaped cases, you might use case 1 of
*Inclusive Education,* titled "One Parent's Struggle for Inclusion." One
purpose of this case is to understand the goals of a parent of a child with
disabilities; it also illustrates some of the barriers parents have faced in
their efforts to include their children and provides examples of how parents, teachers, and other students have worked together successfully and
unsuccessfully to solve problems and provide support.

You may want to extend the debate by including the issue of gifted
and talented programs. Two authors who take opposing views are Clark
(1996), who argued for maintaining separate programs, and Sapon-
Shevin (1996), who argued for inclusive education and the merger of
general education and gifted and talented programs.

To conclude the debate over inclusion, I have students engage in a role
play in which they are assigned to one of two positions that are contrasted
in an interview (O'Neil, 1994/1995). This interview consists of a series of
questions addressed to a proponent of inclusive education, Sapon-Shevin,
and a proponent of the continuum of educational placements, Kauffman.
After having read and analyzed this article and a number of others that
take different positions regarding inclusive education (cf. the 1994/1995

---

[2]This segment of McNeil-Lehrer Newshour aired on June 2, 1994, and can be obtained by calling
1-800-344-3337.

and 1996 issues of *Educational Leadership*; Fuchs & Fuchs, 1994; Shapiro, Loeb, & Bowermaster, 1993; Stainback & Stainback, 1996; Taylor, 1988), students in class are randomly divided into two teams: one that will argue Sapon-Shevin's position and one that will argue Kauffman's. Random assignment to groups requires students to examine thoroughly the rationale and underlying assumptions of a position they do not necessarily hold; it also begins to create an atmosphere of exploration, risk taking, and challenge in the classroom because students are aware that they are playing a role.

To prepare for the role play, students spend from 15 to 20 minutes in their teams (subdivided into small groups in large classes) reviewing the interview and related articles and preparing to argue their positions. Students then reconvene into the two teams, positioned to face each other. As the facilitator, I go back and forth from one team to the other, asking questions that are similar to those posed in the article (O'Neil, 1994/1995). For example:

- Mara (Sapon-Shevin), you're a supporter of more inclusive schools. How do you define inclusion, and what's your rationale for wanting schools to be more inclusive?
- Jim (Kauffman), what's your problem with this position?
- Mara, what's your objection to Jim's idea of a continuum of educational placements?
- Jim, how do you respond to that?
- Jim, the idea of inclusion came from parents of students with disabilities in the first place. Are they misguided?
- Mara, what would you say to parents who want a special class or a special school for their child? Shouldn't choice be more important than inclusion?

A way to conclude the role play is to ask students to come "out of character" and discuss who had the most convincing argument. I also ask them to critically analyze each position by thinking of the possible consequences for students and schools. Additional methods for structuring a debate are described in chapter 1 of this volume.

The debate over inclusive education can be concluded with a written assignment. Based on a real example (e.g., the story of the Baltimore School District, which is intertwined throughout "Sean's Story," 1994) or a hypothetical situation, students can be asked to develop a policy on inclusive education for a school district. The assignment asks students to take the role of a teacher who has been appointed to a blue ribbon committee of teachers, administrators, special educators, and parents in a particular school district. The responsibility of this committee is to formulate a districtwide policy regarding the education of students with disabilities. As part of the decision making, students are asked to write papers stating their positions, which must include answers to the following questions:

- What will you recommend?
- What is the rationale for your position? Based on the readings, class discussions, videos, and your own experiences, what do you see as the benefits of this policy for both students with disabilities and students without disabilities?
- What are the potential disadvantages? What are your concerns?
- What changes, support services, assistance, or other resources will be needed to ensure that your policy will be successfully implemented?

With any kind of position paper, instructors need to be prepared for students who may argue a position that is different than their own. On the topic of inclusive education, my experience has been that students tend to favor the continuum of educational placements option because it represents individual choice and decision making on a case-by-case basis. With this in mind, it is especially important in class to encourage students to take a critical stance and problematize each position, particularly those of which they are least likely to be critical. You will also need to consider carefully your criteria for evaluation. Having students help develop a rubric beforehand is helpful and consistent with the idea of shared authority described in chapter 1 of this volume.

## Including Students Who Are Culturally and Linguistically Diverse

You will note that, throughout this volume and *Inclusive Education*, inclusive education is discussed in terms of diversity, that is, concern for the education of all students, including those at the margins, who are at risk of school failure. A disproportionate number of such students are members of racial, ethnic, and linguistic minorities, and many are in urban schools (Wang, Reynolds, & Walberg, 1994/1995). The purpose of this section of the course is to broaden the concept of inclusive education to include issues of cultural and linguistic diversity.

Several of the cases I use in this section of the course are from Part II ("The Casebook") of *Inclusive Education*. In case 4 "Overcoming Cultural Misunderstandings," the case author, Sione Ika, who is from a small village in the Pacific Islands, describes his own struggles to assimilate into the dominant culture in the United States, both as a student and then as an educator. In this poignant account, Sione describes the cultural conflict he experienced as a band teacher in a small village in the western part of the United States, where he and one of his students, an American Indian, were the only people from minority groups in the school. Devastated by the adverse effect of a popular competitive practice in the band, which he had instituted to motivate his top-ranked musician (the American Indian), Sione became an English as a second language (ESL) teacher committed to the ideals of multicultural education. The teaching notes for this case (in Part II of this volume) focus on understanding cultural differences and the dissonance that may exist between the culture of the school and that of some students, as well as on seeking ways to validate the language and culture of underrepresented groups.

"Teachers' Attitudes Toward ESL Students and Programs" (case 3 in *Inclusive Education*) focuses on Sarah, the only ESL teacher in a junior high school, as she attempted to build an ESL program for her mainly Spanish-speaking students and to integrate her students into general education classes. Based on interviews with teachers in the school, the case author describes three groups of teachers: (a) those who wanted students with limited English proficiency to be segregated in a self-contained unit and not placed in any mainstream classes until they were proficient in English, (b) those who thought ESL classes should be eliminated and that students should be immersed in mainstream classes without any accommodation, and (c) those who were more receptive, although not without concerns, to the idea of mainstreaming students with limited English proficiency. This case lends itself well to a role play in which the three groups of teachers interact with Sarah and teachers who are proponents of native-language instruction and bilingual education (see Trinidad & Villenas, this volume). The role play helps students to generate and evaluate different strategies and plans of action Sarah might try in order to reach her goals and to frame the different problems that emerge as Sarah attempts to implement these solutions. This case could serve as a beginning or end point of a research project examining strategies for integrating ESL students into general education classrooms.

In addition, "The Dialogue That Might Be Silencing," (case 2) concerns pedagogical issues related to the cultural dissonance that can occur between home and school. This case involves an elementary mathematics teacher who questions her pedagogy after reading Delpit (1988) and realizing that the three African-American students in her classroom are not responding to her approach. (Use of this case in a mathematics methods course is described in detail in the teaching notes for this case and in chapter 3 in this volume).

Finally, a case I use later in the course that could be used in this section as well is "Small Victories: Pedro's Story" (case 6 in *Inclusive Education*). This case involves a Chicano student in middle school resource classes who has been labeled as a troublemaker by his teachers.

Additional cases are available in Shulman and Mesa-Bains (1993). Recommended readings for this part of the course include Delpit (1988, 1995), Hollins (1996), McDermott & Varenne (1995), McKay & Wong (1996), and Nieto (1996).

## Gender Equity and Sexual Harassment as Issues of Inclusion

Two topics are covered in the section of the course that focus on gender issues and inclusion. The first is gender as a determinant of success in school, particularly for adolescent girls in the subject areas of math and science, as described in *How Schools Are Shortchanging Girls: The AAUW Report* (American Association of University Women, 1992). The topic of gender equity lends itself especially well to action research projects for teachers who wish to examine their own practice. A case titled "'Girl Speak' and 'Boy Speak': Gender Differences in the Classroom," by Weikel (1995), is a helpful starting point for discussing how teachers often respond differently to girls and boys in discussion activities. It can be used to introduce action research projects that analyze student-to-student and teacher-to-student interaction patterns in the classroom. Other activities for this topic include asking students to complete the self-assessment included in *How Schools Can Stop Shortchanging Girls (and Boys): Gender Equity Strategies* (Wheeler, 1993). Students can then be asked: Of the items in the questionnaire, which ones have you been most successful with? Which ones do you want to focus your attention on now? What are some ways you can do this? Do any of these ideas suggest action research possibilities?

The second topic is sexual harassment. Two cases are particularly useful in examining this as an inclusion issue. The first, "'We Are Chauvinists': Sexual Entitlement and Sexual Harassment in a High School" (case 9 in *Inclusive Education*), describes the environment in a high school where male clubs were allowed to engage in actions that were demeaning towards women, including the viewing of videotapes of these actions at schoolwide assemblies. Told from the perspective of one of the teachers who took a stand against the clubs, the case describes her actions and the resulting harassment she experienced from both the administration and some of the students. The teaching notes for this case (in Part II of this volume) include a variety of role plays and other follow-up activities as well as suggested readings.

The second case, "Boys on the Bus: Bad Language or Sexual Harassment?" (Kleinfeld, 1995) describes a sexual harassment complaint, *Mutziger Versus the Eden Prairie School District*, filed against a school district with the Office of Civil Rights, U.S. Department of Education. In this court case, the plaintiff argued that sexual harassment had occurred, and further that the school district had failed to take effective action to protect the plaintiff's child and to prevent a sexually hostile environment towards girls in its schools, thus denying equal educational services to girls as required by Title IX of the 1972 Congressional Education Amendments Act (PL 92-318, 92nd Congress, S. 659). This case, which received national and international attention, involved 7-year-old Cheltzie, the youngest child at that time to bring a charge of sexual harassment. Cheltzie was verbally attacked by two 9-year-old boys, who were students in special education classes, and by a 6-year-old boy, her chief attacker. The case raises a number of issues including whether the incidents constituted sexual harassment or were instances of "bad language," whether the school had done enough to prevent and resolve the problem, whether it was a societal problem that had no place in courts of law, whether students in special education should be judged by different standards, and whether the mother who had filed the complaint was acting in the best interests of her child.

The discussion of this case can be structured as a role play in which students take the part of lawyers arguing the case before the Office of Civil Rights. On one side are lawyers representing the plaintiff, Ms. Mutziger, who will argue that what happened at Eden Prairie is "a national disgrace," and that Cheltzie and the other girls involved in the suit are victims of sexual harassment. Furthermore, because the school district had not done enough to prevent the existence of a sexually hostile environment in its schools, Cheltzie and the other girls should be awarded punitive damages. On the other side are lawyers representing the school district, who will argue that this case does not involve sexual harassment and that, because the school district took reasonable and comprehensive steps to prevent the existence of a sexually hostile environment in its schools, Cheltzie and the other girls involved in the suit should not be awarded punitive damages. In preparation for trial, students could be asked to consider the following questions in their groups:

- Was 7-year-old Cheltzie sexually harassed?
- What is sexual harassment? How is it different from "bad language?" What are the criteria that have to be met to identify something as sexual harassment?
- Does the age of a child matter in determining if a situation is a case of sexual harassment?
- Are special education labels a consideration in determining what actions should be taken?
- Had the district done enough?
- What other issues are pertinent to your side?

After the two teams have presented their opening statements, they can engage in a more open debate. At the conclusion, you might ask students, "If you were the presiding judge, which side would you rule in favor of?" The epilogue to the case can then be read, which explains why the Office of Civil Rights ruled in favor of the plaintiff and describes the terms of the settlement. Any number of activities could follow, including research projects to help students investigate and design policies and procedures for preventing and resolving sexual harassment.

## Creating Inclusive Schools

At this point in the course, we move to curricular and instructional approaches as well as assessment practices that foster inclusive education. To prepare students for this topic, you might have them read two chapters in *Inclusive Education*: pages 8–16 of chapter 1, "Creating Inclusive Classrooms: An Overview," which describes curricular, instructional, and assessment practices that foster inclusive education, and chapter 2, "Weaving Lessons: Strategies for Teaching Mathematics and Science in Inclusive Settings," which describes the components of inclusive education in math and science classes.

I typically begin this segment of the course with a description of a hypothetical urban school that is designated as an elementary, middle, junior high, or high school, depending on the backgrounds of students enrolled in the class. In classes with teachers from both elementary and secondary levels, students could form small groups based on their levels. What follows is the description of the school, instructions for students in role playing, and questions that students are asked to address in small groups prior to sharing results with the whole class:

Woodrow Wilson is an urban elementary, middle, junior high, or senior high school (choose one). Its student population is predominantly minority and low income. Twenty percent have been attending remedial or special education education pull-out programs for some part of the day, and 15% spend part of the day in ESL classes. For a long time, the school has done poorly on all achievement tests. As a result, a new administration has been brought in that believes in site-based management. This approach to school governance gives a great deal of authority to teachers to redesign the entire curriculum and the structure of the school day. Recently, the faculty has decided to eliminate separate pull-out programs and to implement a team approach for each grade level, cluster of grade levels, or subject areas. You have been appointed to the restructuring and curriculum design committee. Here's your job:

- *School Restructuring.* Provide a general description of the school structure including, but not limited to, policy issues such as organizational units, structure of the school day, and how faculty will work as teams and collaborate.
- *Curriculum.* Describe in general terms what curricular and instructional approach(es) you will advocate.
- *Assessment and Accountability.* Decide how student learning will be assessed and reported. How should teachers be evaluated?
- *Support Services for Students.* What services and programs will you implement to foster both learning and counseling?
- *Faculty Support.* How can faculty be given the necessary knowledge and skills to be successful in your newly restructured school, and what resources will they need?
- *Challenges.* What problems do you anticipate in implementing these changes, and how might you overcome them?

This activity is always highly engaging for students, who create restructuring plans that include block scheduling, multidisciplinary and thematic instruction, alternative assessments, collaborative teamwork, faculty planning time, and opportunities for community building and student governance. As small groups report their plans, I record their ideas on the chalkboard under headings similar to those listed above. At the conclusion of the activity, we discuss similarities among the results as well as issues that have arisen from the discussion.

As an alternative to, or in preparation for, this discussion, you might want to use all or parts of *Restructuring in the Classroom: Teaching, Learning, and School Organization* (Elmore, Peterson, & McCarthey, 1996). In three case studies of schools at various stages of restructuring, this book examines the problems and successes of restructuring at the building level and provides glimpses into four classrooms at each of the schools. Each of the case studies could be used as a teaching case, following the format of a typical case discussion. Beginning with the first case study, for example, you could ask students to brainstorm the following:

- What are we told about the community, students, faculty, principal, school, and district?
- In what ways did the school change? What was the principal's role in bringing about the changes? What role did teachers play in decision making?
- What were the effects of the changes on faculty and students?
- What happened after the principal left?

Some of the classrooms depicted in the book can also be analyzed to understand the ways in which innovations such as project learning and cooperative groups may not be adequately implemented and what teachers need to do to make them successful. Questions to help bring closure to this discussion are are follows:

- How did the teachers' backgrounds and beliefs affect their teaching?
- What would be needed in any school to ensure the success of restructuring efforts and changes in curricular, instructional, and assessment practices?

A number of the cases in *Inclusive Education* are also relevant to the topic of inclusive pedagogies and school restructuring. At the classroom level, "Tragedies and Turnarounds," by Linda Nesi (case 5), exemplifies what a teacher can do to help a student who has been labeled as a troublemaker become fully integrated and accepted in her classroom. Besides treating the student, a fifth grader named Tommy, with respect, caring, and consistency, Linda's success was also a result of a motivating, project-based curriculum and cooperative learning activities. Tommy eventually became a leader in Linda's classroom, working as a peer helper with other children at his table. Unfortunately, the tragedy occurred the next year, when Linda left the school and Tommy moved to a sixth grade classroom organized around individual seatwork and lecturing. The case illustrates what a participatory pedagogical approach, such as project learning with cooperative grouping, can achieve for students who might otherwise be disruptive and unmotivated. It also points out that, to have a lasting effect, such innovations need to be made on a schoolwide basis.

Examples of schoolwide restructuring efforts are provided in two contrasting cases. In "Building an Inclusive School: Vision, Leadership, and Community" (case 12), three educators at an elementary school—a first grade teacher, a special educator, and the principal—describe why and how the school moved over the course of several years from a traditional structure, with a dual system of general and special education, to being an inclusive school. Although the transformation was not without problems, the school is a model of what a strong, supportive principal and a faculty engaged in collaborative decision making can achieve. A contrasting case, "Inclusion for All? Dilemmas of a School's Move Toward Inclusion" (case 13), is told from the perspective of one of its teachers. It also describes the reasons behind a school's decision to move toward inclusive education. However, this school experienced less success. For example, some of the teams in the upper grades reverted to a traditional structure of individual classrooms in which students were placed together on the basis of ability and English language proficiency. In addition, classroom management became difficult for some of the teachers, despite placement of the most disruptive students in the nearby cluster school.

## Specific Adaptations for Students With Special Needs

Within the context of school restructuring efforts, I then introduce issues and strategies related to specific curricular and pedagogical adaptations for students with special needs. Chapter 3 of *Inclusive Education*, "Curricular and Instructional Considerations for Teaching Students With Disabilities in General Education Classrooms," provides background information on this topic. Several of the cases in *Inclusive Education* are also relevant. For example, "When She's Ready, She'll Catch Up" (case 8) describes the struggles experienced by a highly motivated high school girl with a learning disability as she tries to learn in her academic classes, particularly her history course. The role playing activity described in the teaching notes (Part II of this volume), which involves a program planning meeting for the student, enables teachers to practice collaborative problem solving skills and to generate and evaluate plans of action that would support the student in her goals. (Use of this case in a content literacy methods course is also described in chapter 5 of this volume.) Similarly, "Small Victories: Pedro's Story" (case 6), described earlier in this chapter, focuses on ways to help a former gang member who has been in resource classes for most of his schooling become a part of the school community and a more successful student. Of particular relevance to this case are two readings: Juarez (1996), "Where Homeboys Feel at Home in School," and Graves, Graves, and Braaten (1996), "Scaffolded Reading Experiences for Inclusive Classrooms." You might also wish to revisit some of the cases (e.g., Cases 1 and 3) to discuss specific strategies for working with struggling students.

## Alternative and Adaptive Assessment

For background reading, chapter 1 of *Inclusive Education*, "Creating Inclusive Classrooms: An Overview," (pp. 16–20) discusses the use of performance-based assessment in inclusive classrooms and describes some of the problems with standardized testing. Two additional references on this subject that you might find useful are Volume 54(4) of *Educational Leadership* (1996/1997) which is titled "Teaching for Authentic Student Performance," and *Reading Assessment in Practice: Book of Readings* (International Reading Association, 1995). Both resources offer information and examples of authentic assessment practices.

A case titled "Leigh Scott," in Silverman, Welty, and Lyon (1992) is especially useful and generates a highly engaging discussion on equity issues related to grading criteria and adapting assessment for students with special needs. In this case, a high school teacher named Leigh Scott gave a quarterly grade of C to Dale, a White student in her social studies class who was also in resource classes. This grade was higher than what he had earned on tests and homework, but reflected what the teacher saw as effort. When another student, Aaron, an African American who was not in resource classes, received a D on his report card, he confronted Leigh, arguing that she gave a higher grade to "a White kid" even though they had identical grades on homework and tests.

I typically begin the discussion of the Leigh Scott case by having the whole class examine issues such as how student learning can be evaluated, what criteria should be used to grade students and the need to make these explicit, subjectivity in grading, ways to include students in grading policies, and the equity of certain grading practices and adaptations. We conclude by generating general grading policies that teachers might employ to prevent similar problems from occurring in their own class-rooms.

We then move on to solve the immediate problem facing Leigh, which is how to respond to Aaron, whom she has agreed to see the next morning. We begin by framing the problem from different perspectives and at different levels (e.g., those of students, the classroom, school, and society). For example, we discuss how differently the problem might be viewed from the perspectives of Aaron, Leigh, and the special education teacher who had been working with Dale. We then explore how each way of framing the problem can lead to different solutions, which have different consequences for the individuals involved and for society in general. This is followed by an evaluation of all the different solutions that Leigh might consider and their possible consequences. A role-playing activity follows, in which volunteers play Leigh and Aaron as they meet the next morning. Because Leigh's role is especially difficult to play, we occasionally stop the role play to coach the volunteer playing Leigh. This technique is invaluable in keeping the problem-solving process going, giving support to the volunteers, and keeping the audience engaged. One of the most successful solutions that emerged from the role playing was the idea of negotiating a contract with Aaron for subsequent quarters to give him a sense of ownership over his evaluation and to motivate him. During the debriefing that concludes the role play, the volunteers come out of character to discuss the experience, and the class evaluates the solutions that have emerged.

## Collaborative Teaming and Problem Solving

A good way to conclude the course is with the topic of collaborative teaming and problem solving among school personnel, parents, and students, which is critical to successful inclusive education. This topic allows students to reflect on their own collaborative experiences throughout the term in small groups, whole-class discussions, role plays, and special projects. Chapter 4 in *Inclusive Education*, "Collaboration as a Tool for Inclusion," provides students with an overview of principles of collaboration, which they can apply to the cases used in this segment of the course. Additional readings might include Friend and Cook (1992) and chapters in Stainback and Stainback (1996).

Three of the cases in *Inclusive Education* are particularly relevant and offer excellent opportunities for collaborative problem solving. In "Help, With Strings Attached" (case 10) a fifth grade teacher describes the conflicts that arose between her and a Chapter I aide assigned to her classroom. These conflicts were a result of pedagogical differences in mathematics teaching and the requirements of the Chapter I program. "In the Best Interests of the Child" (case 11) describes the efforts of two parents to place their son Scott, who has Down syndrome, in their neighborhood school. For years, their efforts were unsuccessful until a new principal, who was an advocate of inclusion, provided the necessary support and resources. A role play can be constructed around a disastrous IEP meeting that took place at one point and that resulted in threats of litigation. "Conflicts in Collaboration" (case 14) focuses on a reading specialist attempting to work with subject area teachers to provide instructional support for students with reading difficulties. This case provides different perspectives on the difficulties of collaboration, as the reading specialist and three classroom teachers describe the problems they encountered. In addition, many of the cases that have already been discussed can be revisited to examine how teachers, special educators, and parents can successfully work together to resolve specific problems.

## EVALUATION RESULTS
## AND RECOMMENDATIONS

Formative and summative evaluation of the curriculum described in this chapter took place in both preservice undergraduate and inservice graduate courses over the course of four years. Data sources included: (a) student course evaluations, (b) audiotape transcripts of case discussions and debriefings with students, and later with research assistants; (c) students' written products including case analyses, critical or position papers, case discussion notebooks, and special projects; (d) transcripts of case discussions on the Internet; and (e) focus group and individual interviews with students at the end of each quarter after grades were turned in, which were conducted by research assistants. Findings are grouped into two main categories: students' assessments of the value of case methods in the class, and evidence that case discussions and other teaching methods helped students to think critically and reflectively about issues related to inclusive education.

## Students' Assessments
## of the Value of Case Methods

Course evaluations and interviews revealed that students found the topic of inclusion and the cases and case discussions engaging and valuable. On the anonymous course evaluation form, the mean rating for the overall effectiveness of the course for the last two years was 6.48 (*SD*-41) on a 7-point scale, with 7 being the highest score. In response to the question, "What were the most valuable things you learned in the course?" the most frequently cited response was that the course presented different positions and issues related to inclusion. For example, one student wrote: "All of the issues on inclusion and the feelings of all parties involved in inclusion. It helped me to make up my own mind." Another student wrote: "Inclusion involves very tough issues. I learned a lot about inclusion that otherwise I would not have. Cases were very helpful!" The second most commonly cited reason that students gave for valuing the course was that they learned about curricular and instructional strategies for including students in the general education classroom. For example, "I feel like we actually learned new ways of instruction for at-risk, ESL, and other diverse groups within our classes." The third most frequently cited category of response focused on case methods: "I enjoyed the case discussions," and "Reading case studies and learning about actual events [were most valuable]." In response to the question, "What did you find least useful or beneficial to you in this class and why?" no single problem was evident. Instead, concerns ranged from redundancy of information that is also presented in other courses and problems of working collaboratively on projects with other students who were described as "lazy."

Interview results were consistent with the course evaluations. When asked during the interview to rate the case methods used in the course on a scale from 1 to 10 (with 10 being the highest), all the students gave a rating between 7 and 10. The following comment is typical:

> I really enjoyed it. I think it became more personal; it got away from a textbook-style way to study an issue. It was a more entertaining and more enjoyable way to study inclusion. . . . I paid a lot more attention.

Similarly, other students commented that the case discussions were motivating and provided "variety." For example, one student said:

> I thought this was a good way to learn because it was different. I've never worked with the case method until this class. I thought it was a great way to teach. Every day it was different. It wasn't like you go in there and you sit and they lecture to you for 3 hours and you're about to fall asleep. . . . It got us involved, especially with the group of people in there—everyone had their different opinions.

In addition to the motivating aspects of case teaching, a number of students commented that the cases were valuable in preparing them for future teaching experiences. The comment below reflects this:

> I believe that it's better to be overprepared than underprepared. And if I've kind of thought through different scenarios; even if I've just looked at how someone else dealt with it, then I'm better prepared if I ever have to step into that kind of situation. That's what I gained from the class.

## The Iterative Process of Teaching, Research, and Change

As described at the beginning of this chapter, my goals for the course were to provide students with the knowledge, abilities, and attitudes that would enable them to teach successfully in inclusive settings. Central to these goals are the knowledge and ability to implement student-centered pedagogies, open-mindedness, the ability to think critically and reflectively about issues and problematic situations in teaching, and the ability to work collaboratively. Results of the research we (the contributors to this volume) have conducted to examine our success in achieving these goals are described in detail in all the chapters in Part I of this volume and in Moje, Remillard, Southerland, and Wade (1999), Moje and Wade (1997), and Wade and Moje (1997). In the next section, I briefly summarize our findings and describe the changes I have made in this course as a result.

Based on students' high degree of engagement and apparent enthusiasm, as well as the multiple images and issues raised by students in the case discussions, I initially believed that the teaching cases were useful in prompting students to think critically and reflectively about teaching. (For a detailed description of critically reflective thinking, see chapter 1 of this volume.) However, as I systematically analyzed teachers' thinking about case discussions over several years, I began to question the extent to which students had learned to think critically about teaching. I found that both preservice and inservice teachers tended to espouse deficit theories of students' cultures and families and to view teaching as a technical act. For example, some teachers seemed to hold unexamined beliefs that students who fail in school are lazy or deficient (thus locating the problem in the student), that there are "best practices" that can be applied to any situation without regard for context, and that the essence of teaching is organizing and controlling behaviors and knowledge. Adopting a technical approach to problem solving, some students were most concerned with organizing the curriculum to find the most efficient way to disseminate it and to maintain classroom control, without changing the conditions that may have contributed to the problem and without evaluating solutions and their consequences.

Based on these research findings, I have restructured the case discussions in several ways to encourage open-mindedness and critically reflective thinking. First, rather than assume that students had carefully read and understood the assigned readings, I now spend more time in class analyzing the readings so that students can use them effectively as tools for understanding and reflecting critically on the cases. Second, I place greater emphasis on the use of small-group work structured around the case discussion sheets, which I have found to be an effective way to have students review the cases and prepare for the whole-class discussion or role play that follows. I have also adopted a suggestion made by several students that the case discussion sheet be distributed prior to reading the assigned case. Finally, I spend more time on "process" issues related to participation in class and to critically reflective thinking. Besides discussing "An Introduction to Cases" (in Part II of *Inclusive Education*) and holding regular debriefing sessions after the case discussions, I also explicitly teach students how to frame problems from different perspectives and to examine the solutions that each way of framing the problem leads to as well as the consequences of each type of solution (see Zeichner & Liston, 1996).

In conclusion, I recommend that you experiment, trying new approaches and conducting research on your own teaching. Results may surprise you, as they did me, requiring me to refine my goals (e.g., What is critically reflective thinking, and what does it look like in a case discussion?), to better prepare students, to restructure my case pedagogies, and, in a continuous cycle, to conduct further research. The rewards are great, as suggested by one student's comment from an interview:

Whenever you're listening to someone else's opinion, you're looking at your own too, and I think it makes you take a step back and critique your own. I think what has to happen is you have to be open enough to see if that person's opinion is really viable and has more validity than yours—to accept that and adapt.

# REFERENCES

American Association of University Women. (1992). *How schools are shortchanging girls: The AAUW Report.* New York: Marlowe.

Christensen, C. R. (1991). Premises and practices of discussion teaching. In C. R. Christensen, D. Garvin, & A. Sweet (Eds.), *Education for judgment: The artistry of discussion leadership* (pp. 15–34). Boston: Harvard Business School.

Clark, B. (1996). The need for a range of program options for gifted and talented students. In W. Stainback & S. Stainback (Eds.), *Controversial issues confronting special education: Divergent perspectives* (pp. 57–68). Needham Heights, MA: Allyn & Bacon.

Delpit, L. (1988). The silenced dialogue: Power and pedagogy in educating other people's children. *Harvard Educational Review, 58,* 280–298.

Delpit, L. (1995). *Other people's children: Cultural conflict in the classroom.* New York: The New Press.

Elmore, R. F., Peterson, P. L., & McCarthey, S. J. (1996). *Restructuring in the classroom: Teaching, learning, and school organization.* San Francisco: Jossey-Bass.

Friend, M., & Cook, C. (1992). *Interactions: Collaborative skills for school professionals.* New York: Longman.

Fuchs, D., & Fuchs, L. S. (1994). Inclusive schools movement and the radicalization of special education reform. *Educational Children, 60,* 294–309.

Graves, M. F., Graves, B. B., & Braaten, S. (1996). Scaffolded reading experiences for inclusive classes. *Educational Leadership, 53,* 14–16.

Hollins, E. R. (1996). *Transforming curriculum for a culturally diverse society.* Mahwah, NJ: Lawrence Erlbaum Associates.

International Reading Association. (1995). *Reading Assessment in Practice: Book of Readings.* Newark, DE: International Reading Association.

Juarez, T. (1996). Where homeboys feel at home in school. *Educational Leadership, 53,* 30–32.

Keinfeld, J. S. (1995). Boys on the bus: Bad language or sexual harassment? In J. S. Kleinfeld & S. Yerian (Eds.), *Gender tales: Tensions in the schools* (pp. 149–155). New York: St. Martin's Press.

McDermott, R., & Varenne, H. (1995). Culture as disability. *Anthropology and Education Quarterly, 26,* 324–348.

McKay, S. L., & Wong, S. C. (1996). Multiple discourses, multiple identities: Investment and agency in second-language learning among Chinese adolescent immigrant students. *Harvard Educational Review, 66,* 577–608.

Moje, E. B., & Wade, S. (1997). What case discussions reveal about teacher thinking. *Teaching and Teacher Education, 13,* 691–712.

Moje, E. B., Remillard, J., Southerland, S., & Wade, S. E. (1999). Researching case methods to inform our teaching. In M. Lundeberg, B. Levin, & H. Harrington (Eds.), *Who learns what from cases and how? The research base for teaching with cases* (pp. 73–94). Mahwah, NJ: Lawrence Erlbaum Associates.

Nieto, S. (1996). *Affirming diversity: The sociocultural context of multicultural education.* White Plains, NY: Longman Publishers.

O'Neil, J. (1994/1995). Can inclusion work? A conversation with Jim Kauffman and Mara Sapon-Shevin. *Educational Leadership, 52,* 7–11.

Read, M. R. (1994, September 7). Sean's story: A lesson in life. *Turning Point.* New York: ABC.

Sapon-Shevin, M. (1996). Including all students and their gifts within regular classrooms. In W. Stainback & S. Stainback (Eds.), *Controversial issues confronting special education: Divergent perspectives* (pp. 69–80). Needham Heights, MA: Allyn & Bacon.

Shapiro, J. P., Loeb, P. & Bowermaster, D. (1993, December). Separate and unequal. *U.S. News and World Report, 115,* 46–50, 54–56, 60.

Shulman, J., & Mesa-Bains, A. (1993). *Diversity in the classroom: A casebook for teachers and teacher educators.* Hillsdale, NJ: Lawrence Erlbaum Associates and Research for Better Schools.

Silverman, R., Welty, W., & Lyon, S. (1992). *Case studies for teacher problem solving.* New York: McGraw-Hill.

Stainback, W., & Stainback, S. (1996). *Controversial issues confronting special education: Divergent perspectives.* Needham Heights, MA: Allyn & Bacon.

Taylor, S. (1988). Caught in the continuum: A critical analysis of the principle of the least restrictive environment. *Journal of the Association for Persons with Severe Handicaps, 13,* 41–53.

Wade, S. E., & Moje, E. B. (1997, March). *Verbal interaction patterns in case discussions associated with critical/reflective and technical/rational thinking.* Paper presented at the annual meeting of the American Educational Research Association, Chicago, IL.

Wang, M. C., Reynolds, M. C., & Walberg, H. J. (1994/1995). Serving students at the margins. *Educational Leadership, 52,* 12–17.

Wheeler, K. (1993). *How schools can stop shortchanging girls (and boys): Gender equity strategies.* Wellesley, MA: Wellesley College Center for Research on Women.

Weikel, B. (1995). "Girl speak" and "boy speak": Gender differences in the classroom. In J. S. Kleinfeld & S. Yerian (Eds.), *Gender tales: Tensions in the schools* (pp. 7–11). New York: St. Martin's Press.

Zeichner, K. M., & Liston, D. P. (1996). *Reflective teaching: An introduction.* Mahwah, NJ: Lawrence Erlbaum Associates.

# 3

# Mathematics for All: Using Teaching Cases to Prepare Elementary Teachers for Inclusive Classrooms and Pedagogies

## *Janine T. Remillard*

*It is essential that schools and communities accept the goal of mathematical education for every child. However, this does not mean that every child will have the same interests or capabilities in mathematics. It does mean that we will have to examine our fundamental expectations about what children can learn and can do and that we will have to strive to create learning environments in which raised exceptions for children can be met. (National Council of Teachers of Mathematics, 1991, p. 4)*

A central component of the current reform agenda in mathematics education is the commitment to providing opportunities for *all students* to develop mathematical literacy. The phrase *all students* is used frequently throughout all three standards documents recently published by the National Council of Teachers of Mathematics (NCTM). In its initial call for change in the K to 12 mathematics curriculum (NCTM, 1989), the council argued for five new goals related to mathematics education. The third of these is "Opportunities for All." In a second document that presented standards for mathematics teaching, NCTM (1991) articulated a definition of *all students* that included students of differing abilities, ethnicities, and genders:

- students who have been denied access in any way to educational opportunities as well as those who have not;
- students who are African American, Hispanic, American Indian, and other minorities as well as those who are considered to be part of the majority;
- students who are female as well as those who are male; and
- students who have not been successful in school in mathematics as well as those who have been successful.

One of the standards for assessment in the third document (NCTM, 1995) is devoted to promoting equity in mathematics assessment.

In presenting this vision of mathematics for all students, NCTM challenged educators to examine the content, pedagogies, and organization of their teaching practices in order to create learning environments that are inclusive and nurturing of all students. This challenge is in concert with efforts in other areas of education. Science educators and policy makers, for example, used the phrase *Science for All Americans* in characterizing their current reform efforts (see Gess-Newsome & Southerland, chap. 4 of this volume). Special educators referred to *inclusive education* to describe their goals of providing rich, nonisolated learning opportunities to all students (National Association of State Boards of Education, 1992; National Center on Educational Restructuring and Inclusion, 1994).

The vision of learning opportunities for all students also presents a challenge to teacher educators, requiring them to prepare teachers to think in new ways about students' learning and to address the varying needs of diverse groups of students in one classroom. Prospective teachers need to learn to recognize equity concerns in their teaching and to make decisions about how to address them. One of my goals as a mathematics teacher educator is to help preservice teachers begin to develop commitments and approaches to inclusive teaching practices.

In this chapter, I describe my use of cases in a mathematics methods course for preservice elementary teachers, and I report on my students' and my own learning from this project. In using cases, I intended to promote students' examination of issues related to inclusion and equity likely to emerge in their mathematics teaching. I hoped that they would develop new perspectives from which to scrutinize ordinary practices for unjust outcomes and develop a broad awareness of the possible ways such issues might emerge in their teaching. I also wanted them to consider and design teaching approaches that promoted inclusion. As I explain later in the chapter, these goals are likely to conflict with traditional approaches to mathematics instruction and teacher preparation.

I begin my discussion of using cases by examining specific issues related to inclusion in mathematics teacher education that have historical and sociological roots. In particular, I explore unavoidable disjunctures between conventional views of mathematics teaching and learning and the assumptions underlying inclusion and case-based methods. Then I delineate the approaches I used to incorporate cases into a mathematics methods course. I describe the processes of planning and facilitating case discussions and share pertinent events from each. Finally, I reflect on my use of cases by describing students' responses to the cases, discussing findings regarding students' learning, and offering recommendations and perspectives for others. My primary aim is to convey the potential of teaching cases in addressing goals related to inclusion in mathematics education, while realistically conveying the challenges that teacher educators are likely to face while using them.

## INCLUSION: THE CASE OF MATHEMATICS

Using cases to teach preservice teachers about inclusion involves two related challenges. First, inclusion is particularly foreign to mathematics education. Second, case-based approaches in teacher education, while becoming increasingly popular, run counter to common views about what is involved in learning to teach. These two challenges require teacher educators and their students to confront firmly grounded assumptions about mathematics, teaching, and learning implicit in common practices.

### Inclusion and Mainstream Views of Learning Mathematics

The view of mathematics that pervades mainstream culture is that it is a body of rules and procedures that must be learned in a linear sequence through repetition. Almost any adult can recall completing pages of addition exercises before moving on to practicing subtraction. This view underlies pedagogical practices that tend to be individualistic and exclusive. In schools throughout the United States, students are typically grouped according to similar abilities for mathematics. Each group receives instruction that is considered appropriate for its level at a pace that the students can manage. The underlying philosophy of this approach is that it permits students to progress through mathematics content at varying paces, allowing those who are able to excel beyond those who are not. With this approach to mathematics instruction firmly entrenched, it is not surprising that those promoting inclusive mathematics teaching have met resistance. Many believe that mathematics is a subject in which inclusion is inappropriate because the content is sequential and is best learned individually.

Calls for inclusive instructional practices from the mathematics education community assume radically altered images of mathematics. The NCTM's *Curriculum Standards* (NCTM, 1989) argue that "mathematics is more than a collection of concepts and skills to be mastered." It is a complex body of interrelated ideas including "methods of investigating and reasoning, means of communication, and notions of context" that do not fall in any particular sequence (p. 5). This view of mathematics content does not support moving students through a series of rules as rapidly as possible. The standards suggest that students should understand mathematical ideas, be able to reason logically about them, and use them to solve authentic problems. Thus, students need to spend time exploring the mathematical terrain in order to learn to operate effectively within it. Inclusion aims to engage all students in exploring, reasoning about, and using mathematical ideas. This aim, however, is likely to conflict with the ideas about mathematics that most preservice teachers have developed from their school experiences. Thus, if they are to seriously consider teaching all students mathematics, these future teachers need to examine their own assumptions and beliefs about the subject and how students learn it.

## Cases and Mainstream Views
## of Learning to Teach

Mainstream views of what is involved in learning to teach are closely tied to views of the subject matter described above. Because mathematics is commonly believed to be a set of ordered procedures, many prospective teachers assume that learning to teach it involves learning how to show these procedures to students. Mathematics methods courses have traditionally been designed to equip prospective teachers with a collection of techniques to apply in the classroom. The new goals for students' learning suggest that teachers must learn to orchestrate exploration and reasoning in a variety of mathematical contexts. In addition to acquiring a repertoire of interesting tasks to present to students, teachers need to know how to foster and sustain students' work on these tasks by assessing their progress and responding appropriately. Thus, learning to teach mathematics includes learning to make pedagogical decisions in specific contexts.

Case-based approaches in teacher education assume that teaching knowledge is contextual and contingent, situated in actual events, and that consequently, it should be developed in similar sites (Kennedy, 1987; Shulman, 1992; Sykes & Bird, 1992). Although this view is likely to conflict with preservice teachers' expectations about what they need to learn, reading, analyzing, and discussing issues that arise in cases can help them consider new aspects of teaching. In the following sections, I describe how I have used cases to broaden prospective elementary teachers' views on teaching mathematics to all students.

## USING CASES TO EXAMINE ISSUES
## OF INCLUSION IN MATHEMATICS

At the time when this chapter was being prepared, the elementary teacher education program at the University of Utah consisted of four 10-week quarters of courses and practica in schools. Students were placed in cohorts of approximately 20 students who proceeded through the program together. The two mathematics methods courses were offered during the first two quarters of the program in conjunction with a 2-day-per-week practicum in an elementary classroom. The first course dealt with assessing children's learning and thinking. The second course focused on planning, teaching, and analyzing mathematics instruction and attended to issues of equity and diversity with respect to gender, race, culture, and ability as they relate to mathematics teaching. It was in this second course that I had students read and discuss cases on inclusion in conjunction with other readings.

The students in the two cohorts I taught in the fall of 1995 reflected the demographics of the university. All but four students were European American. As is typical of many elementary education programs, 85% of the students were female. Most students were in their mid- to late 20s.

### Preparation for Case Discussions

As all teachers know, preparation is crucial for successful class sessions. Yet, with case discussions, one cannot prepare by outlining what will transpire during the session. It is not possible to predict which issues students will raise in response to a case. My preparation for case discussions was aimed at establishing a context in which authentic issues related to inclusion could emerge and be examined. I found two aspects of planning to be central to developing such contexts: selecting rich cases and framing the discussion.

*What Makes a Good Case?*   My first task was to locate appropriate cases on inclusion and mathematics teaching. The cases on mathematics teaching that I knew about focused on mathematical content issues (e.g., Barnett, 1994), rather than inclusion. Therefore, I worked with a group of practicing teachers to write cases about their own teaching. Having worked with these teachers in various capacities, I was well aware that they struggled with how to make mathematics accessible to all of their students. Furthermore, facilitating the development of new cases allowed me to have some influence on the topics they addressed. I met with the teachers several times over the summer to work on writing and revision.

From working with teachers to craft cases and then from using them in a methods course, I learned much about what makes a good case on inclusion. First, cases that are problem based, in that they present a conflict or dilemma, tend to engage students in thinking through critical issues. As I discussed earlier, inclusion is likely to conflict with commonly held views of appropriate mathematics teaching and, if seriously embraced, will probably create conflicts for new teachers. Thus, problem-based cases can prompt prospective teachers to grapple with these conflicts and their resulting dilemmas prior to facing them in their own classrooms. Second, problem-based cases in which the problem can be viewed from multiple perspectives facilitate students' examination of varying points of view and their impacts on educational practices. Considering a range of different perspectives that they may confront in the process of addressing problems in their teaching can encourage teachers-to-be to reexamine their own assumptions and beliefs. Last, good cases reflect the complexity of real life. As we know, dilemmas that emerge in real life cannot be classified neatly into simple categories. The problems teachers confront in dealing with differing abilities, for example, often overlap with issues relating to race, class, or institutional structures. Thus, if well crafted, cases can invite preservice teachers to grapple with problems of inclusion that are realistically messy.

I selected several cases that met these criteria. Three of them involved attending to the needs of students with differing abilities and were written by teachers whose experience ranged from less than a year to 15 years.

The fourth case, which I wrote, involved understanding students of differing cultural and economic backgrounds. In addition, I used several cases that focused on other mathematics teaching issues. Because they did not address inclusion, I do not discuss them here. The two cases discussed most thoroughly in this chapter can be found in *Inclusive Education* as cases 2 and 10. Accompanying teaching notes can be found in Part II of this volume.

*Planning Case Discussions.* Even though it is impossible to predict the exact route that a case discussion will take, I have learned that the most productive case discussions are not free-for-all sessions that allow participants to make points at random. Case discussions that foster students' examination of key issues are structured and carefully directed by the discussion leader (see chap. 1 of this volume). In leading case discussions, I found it was crucial to know what I wanted to accomplish during the session with a particular case and what issues I wanted students to consider. These objectives guided the on-the-spot decisions I made during the discussion.

In planning the discussion context, I began by determining my objective. Because the cases were complex, raising a number of issues, I had to select one objective from among several possible. For each case, I listed relevant issues and then drew on knowledge of my students to decide which to focus on. I then considered various paths I could take in guiding students' explorations of the issue. In assessing the potential of each path, I thought about other issues that might arise along the way and whether I wanted them to figure into the day's discussion. Having outlined a path, I determined the specific tools I would use to direct the discussion, that is, the questions or tasks I would pose to the class. In the final step of planning, I decided how to arrange the notes from the discussion on the blackboard. This record of the group's journey served as a primary tool for focusing the class on the issues.

## "Help, With Strings Attached"

Our first case discussion on inclusion focused on addressing a range of student abilities, particularly those of students who struggle with math. The preservice teachers were already concerned about this issue. Many had worked with struggling students in their field placements and had observed programs designed to attend to these students' needs. I had noticed that the preservice teachers tended to accept the structures they encountered, such as ability grouping and pull-out programs. At the same time, many were aware that grouping students according to ability was considered inappropriate in the current climate of educational reform, but they did not know why. I hoped to push them toward examining the potential consequences that these structures had on the classroom environment and on students' learning of meaningful mathematics. I selected "Help, With Strings Attached" (case 10 in *Inclusive Education*) for two reasons: It raised these issues, and it was written by a first-year teacher whose perspectives on mathematics teaching and learning were similar to those I was hoping to promote in my course.

*About the Case.* In "Help, With Strings Attached," a first-year teacher, Emma Magleby, describes the struggles she experienced as she tried to accommodate a Chapter I aide in her classroom whose views on teaching mathematics conflicted with her own. Officially, the aide's role was to visit the classroom weekly during math to work with students who were struggling academically. The aide expected to tutor each student individually at the back of the room. Because Emma tended to use a variety of cooperative, activity-oriented tasks, she wanted the aide to assist the identified students while they worked, rather than pulling them away from their groups. As a new teacher, Emma was unprepared to manage the sort of philosophical debate this caused. She was frustrated about the impact that the aide's presence had on her students and on the class culture.

*The Discussion Plan.* The case raises several issues related to academically struggling students, school programs designed to meet their needs, and the tendency for these programs to highlight social-class differences. The issue I found most prominent was the potential consequences for students, teachers, and the classroom culture of programs designed to provide extra assistance for specific students. Thus, my objective for the discussion was for the preservice teachers to become aware of intended and unintended outcomes of approaches to working with struggling students as well as the unintended consequences of all of their choices. Because this was to be our first case discussion and because of the multiple issues embedded in the case, I began by clarifying the setting, key players, and case events. I anticipated that this approach, in addition to enhancing students' understandings of the context of the case, would allow for the differing perspectives to surface and be discussed. I planned to have students then frame the central problem in the case and, finally, to describe actions Emma could take to address the problem. See the teaching notes for this case, in this volume, for additional suggestions on structuring the discussion.

*The Discussion.* As we began the discussion, it was apparent that reading the case had prompted these soon-to-be teachers to consider aspects of the work they had not imagined. Few had thought about how organizational structures in a school might figure into their pedagogical and curricular decisions. For the most part, their teaching ideals did not take classroom or school context into account. In describing what they knew about the key players and case events during the initial part of the discussion, the students described the impact that the Chapter I aide had on Emma's teaching. Taking the classroom teacher's perspective, many students characterized the Chapter I aide and program as a "disruptive" hindrance to the teacher, and Chapter I as "a bureaucratic structure that was unable to accommodate Emma's approach to mathematics."

It was not until we moved to the next portion of the discussion that the class began to examine other perspectives. When asked to describe the central problem in the case, several students pointed out that Emma and the Chapter I aide had different goals, suggesting that the conflict was a result of both teachers lacking understanding of the other's program. As one student explained, "They [Emma and the Chapter I aide] had different objectives."

This change in the preservice teachers' analyses of the case helped to focus the discussion on how to negotiate among a variety of conflicting goals. While the recommended plans of action clearly represented the teacher's perspective, they also aimed at improving communication among all the key players. Moreover, many of the students' comments during this portion of the discussion reflected some understanding of the complex choices teachers must make in an effort to respond to all students' needs. Bobbie, for example, asked: "How can you not be stifled by the system without stepping on someone's toes or jeopardizing your students?" She later made the following comment which captures the tension that many students expressed:

> I can't be forced as a teacher to teach a certain way just because everyone else does it. . . . But I do think the point is true that you can't just meet most of the students; you need to meet all of the students. So you do need to adjust your philosophy a little bit.

Students concluded the discussion by working in small groups to develop ways that Emma might accommodate the Chapter I aide in her classroom while remaining true to her goals.

Considering that this was our first case discussion on inclusion, I was pleased with the extent to which the preservice teachers examined multiple perspectives and were mindful of the needs of all students. I noted two equity issues related to the Chapter I program that had not emerged during the discussion: the general premise and design of the Chapter I program, and the large proportion of low-income students qualifying for Chapter I support. I planned to raise these issues in the future discussions.

## "For Some, Ability Grouping Can Be Disabling"

The following week, my students read, "For Some, Ability Grouping Can Be Disabling," a case similar to Emma's in that it was also written by a novice teacher who hoped to foster problem solving and communication in her class. In the case, the author describes how her efforts were thwarted by the ability grouping arrangement in her school.

*About the Case.*    Cassie was a third-year teacher in an inner-city school that grouped students according to ability for mathematics. Her group consisted of the lowest level fourth and fifth grade students, including those who qualified for resource assistance. Many of these students demanded considerable attention academically and socially. In her case, Cassie described compromising her ideals in order to keep students under control, and she questioned whether heterogeneous grouping would foster a more productive environment, allowing the low-ability students to work with and learn from upper ability students.

*The Discussion Plan.*    My objective in using this case was for students to examine how ability grouping, as well as other classroom organizational structures, effects students and teachers. As with the previous case, I also wanted students to consider how various school structures might influence their plans. My students tended to talk about teaching methods as abstract entities that either "worked" or did not, regardless of the particular context. They often tried new ideas in their field placements and then judged them as successful or not, without analyzing factors that led to their success or failure.

I decided to begin the discussion by asking the students to list the factors that exerted an impact on Cassie's math teaching. I expected that the process of generating this list and describing the impact each factor had would initiate discussion about multiple issues in the case. Once this list was developed, I planned to ask the students whether they thought a self-contained, mixed-ability class would address Cassie's problems. To conclude, I planned to have students consider various strategies for teaching students of differing abilities. My aim in this segment was to allow students to consider a range of strategies and to contrast their benefits and drawbacks.

*The Discussion.* Beginning the discussion by listing factors that had an impact on Cassie's teaching allowed the students to clarify the case events while offering different interpretations of them. Some of the students, for example, attributed Cassie's struggles to the rigid structure imposed by the schedule. Others noted that ability grouping concentrated the low-achieving students in one class without strong role models. Still others focused on Cassie herself, her expectations, her skills in managing students, and her inexperience as a teacher. These students accused Cassie of placing unreasonable expectations on her students and not meeting their needs. As I had hoped, the process of articulating these perspectives involved discussing a number of teaching issues, including appropriate and productive teacher–student relationships, the role of classroom community, and the influence of contextual features such as time and flexibility.

In the next part of the discussion, the students focused on issues directly related to inclusion. The students debated the merits and hazards of ability grouping by considering the types of learning opportunities it offers and the impact it has on a students' sense of self. I recorded the issues students raised in two columns on the board; these were labeled "advantages of a self-contained class" and "disadvantages of a self-contained class." Then, in pairs, students suggested various ways to deal with students of differing abilities and listed advantages and disadvantages of each.

## "Is What's Good for One Good for All?"

The following week, students read another case that raised questions about accommodating all students, but from the opposite perspective. "Is What's Good for One Good for All?" questions whether a student who is extremely able mathematically should be expected to participate in class discussions. I selected the case because I believed it would prompt students to consider how mathematical discourse fit into their goals for students. I was aware that most students had found class discussions about mathematical ideas useful to their own learning and hoped to facilitate discourse in their classrooms. At the same time, they spoke frequently about the need to adjust instruction to students' individual learning styles and abilities. I wanted them to examine these ideals side by side and grapple with possible incongruities.

*About the Case.*   The author of the case, Ryan Cole, had 20 years of teaching experience. He had been trying for several years to engage his students in discussions about mathematical ideas and felt he had met with reasonable success. His case described questions about one student, Jacob, who had strong mathematics skills but no interest in participating in discussions. Considering that Jacob's comments during the class discussions were often counterproductive, if not disruptive, Ryan wondered whether allowing Jacob to work independently would both accommodate Jacob and make class discussions more productive.

*The Discussion Plan.*   My objectives for the discussion of Ryan's case wove several prominent issues together: (a) meeting the needs of individual students, (b) the importance of developing a class community, (c) the role of discourse in learning math, and (d) how teachers manage mathematical discourse in heterogeneous groups. I wanted students to explore reasons for including all students in classroom discourse and to consider ways of doing so. I suspected that examining these issues when the student in question was exceptionally able would push the preservice teachers to confront their beliefs about what it meant to be "good" at math.

I decided to open the class discussion with the central conflict in the case—the individual versus the group—by having the students speculate on Ryan's goals for his class and his goals for Jacob. I hoped that this task would draw the students back to the case as they used it as evidence for their claims and that it would provide opportunities for them to refer to other readings they had done on discourse and to discuss goals related to teaching math. Then I planned to pose the question, "Should Ryan continue to try to get Jacob involved in the class discussions?" In soliciting responses to this question, I planned to focus on the goals for students that were implicit in their decisions.

*The Discussion.*   Because I wanted students to examine Ryan's goals, rather than to critique them, I opened the discussion by reiterating that we would focus first on Ryan's perspectives. As I expected, students attended to different aspects of the case as they described Ryan's goals. Some believed that his goals were focused on the type of classroom interactions he wanted to create. Other students claimed that Ryan's goals were related to what he wanted students to learn. These students argued that Ryan wanted students "to be able to explain their ideas," "to know when their answers were right," and "to think and discuss." Most of the students agreed that one of Ryan's goals for Jacob was for him to be a participating member of the class.

When I asked whether Ryan should continue his efforts to get Jacob involved, the first response was, "It depends on what he has tried already." Monica explained that she wanted to know whether Ryan had tried to assess the situation by talking with Jacob individually. Because Monica's comment could fit into the category of possible approaches, I wrote her suggestion under this new heading on the board, but directed the class away from approaches or solutions at this point. I wanted students to consider possible tensions between goals related to each student's mathematical knowledge, their ability to communicate mathematically, and the classroom culture, all of which are at the heart of inclusion debates in mathematics education. In the last 10 minutes of the discussion, we came back to Monica's earlier suggestion. Other students offered strategies that Ryan might use to facilitate Jacob's participation, which drew specifically on his strengths. Others described alternative formats for engaging him in mathematical reasoning.

## "The Dialogue That Might Be Silencing"

The final case I used focused specifically on issues of race and culture in mathematics education reform. The case was one I had written about my experience teaching mathematics to African-American students from poor families. I selected this case because I believed it could introduce my students to current debates about implications of mathematics education reform on minority and underserved populations. Since three-fourths of my students were placed in inner-city classrooms, I expected them to find the problem in the case relevant to their experience.

*About the Case.* "The Dialogue That Might Be Silencing" (case 2 in *Inclusive Education*) raises questions about students' cultural differences in a discussion-intensive mathematics class. It is set in the first grade classroom in which I taught math while in graduate school. Most of my students were from Anglo, working-class families. Three of the students were African-American children bused to the school from a low-income area of the city. Even though the Anglo students gradually seemed to appropriate the tools that allowed them to participate in class discussions, the three inner-city students experienced little success. My concerns for these three students were further heightened when I read "The Silenced

Dialogue," by Delpit (1988), who argues that most progressive teaching practices assume middle-class interactional styles and tend to exclude poor, minority students. As a result, I began to question the appropriateness of my goals for these students.

*The Discussion Plan.*    The case raises several issues related to culturally responsive teaching (Ladson-Billings, 1994) and the political implications of educational practices (Delpit, 1995). My objectives were for students to examine the cultural roots of their mathematical goals for children and to consider ways of making these goals accessible to students from different cultural backgrounds. I also hoped the case would continue to push the preservice teachers to think about an issue raised by Ryan's case several weeks earlier: that mathematical discourse might be viewed as a goal as well as a central vehicle for learning. I began by asking students to describe what we knew about the context, the key players, and the case events, including my assessment of the problem. Then I planned to pose the question, "Is Janine's assessment of the problem accurate?" I saw this question as a way for students to discuss their interpretations of the situation and respond to mine. The final question, "What should Janine do?" would prompt them to consider approaches they might take with similar problems. I was hoping that this question would lead to a discussion of culturally relevant teaching practices. (See the teaching notes for the case in this volume for more detailed suggestions for planning the discussion.)

*The Discussion.*    In describing the key players and case events, the preservice teachers had the most difficulty characterizing the three African-American students. They tended to insert details from stereotypes and their experiences into what they learned from the case. One student supported the claim that African Americans had limited interaction skills by saying:

> I think all of us have taken a multicultural class and read a lot about different ethnic groups' learning styles and how, in a lower class African-American home, African-American kids aren't supposed to answer back if they are asked questions; they just listen.

Another student used her field experience to illustrate:

> I have a kid where if I word the questions, like if I ask him a why question, he's not going to answer it, but if I ask him one small aspect of that why question, he'll answer it beautifully. And he's also Black.

While I was pleased that these students were drawing on their experiences and previous course work to interpret the case, I was concerned that their comments viewed African-American students as deficient without carefully examining the extent to which the teacher's goals assumed the values of White, middle-class culture. I worried about whether the discussion would serve to reinforce their stereotypes, as McDiarmid & Price (1990) warned can happen.

An opportunity to consider how culture influenced the teacher's goals came later in the discussion when the students discussed the accuracy of my assessment of the problem. Several students speculated that cultural conflict would always exist between school and home for many children and questioned whether it was within our rights as teachers to ask students to change. Patty, for example, recalled cultural knowledge she had learned about in previous courses:

> We are told to respect that [cultural difference]. So why are we trying to make these guys speak to us when in their culture they are told to give the answer and that's all. If they are writing it down and doing it another way, why are you trying to make them verbalize it?

Drawing on Delpit's (1995) argument, Anne challenged this view by claiming that teachers are obligated to teach students the problem-solving and communication skills they need "to succeed in today's culture of power."

As the discussion progressed and the students began to consider plans of action, I was satisfied that the range of approaches they offered reflected understanding of the complexity of the situation. Some students suggested learning more about the students to determine whether other factors might be influencing their behavior. Similarly, one student suggested talking with the parents to communicate goals and enlist their support.

Other students suggested specific strategies, including "a little bit more direct instruction," clarifying expectations with the entire class, more explicit modeling, and individual coaching in expected behaviors. One student stated that she would want to gather more information through reading, talking with others, and observing the children and their siblings in all subjects before making a decision.

In reflecting on these suggestions well after the course was completed, I was interested to note that none of the students recommended I abandon my goals for these students or that I make significant changes to my emphasis on mathematical discourse in my teaching. In contrast, a handful of students had argued strongly in the case discussion several weeks earlier that Ryan should not insist that Jacob, a bright, Anglo fifth grader, become involved in the class discussions. In retrospect, I concluded that asking students to contrast the issues in these two cases might have been a fruitful follow-up activity for future discussions.

## LEARNING FROM CASE-BASED TEACHING

As I facilitated the case discussions, I was encouraged by the way preservice teachers thoughtfully examined critical issues and proposed teaching approaches that reflected a commitment to equity. Because I wanted to assess the impact that these discussions had on the preservice teachers' ideas about their teaching and students, I collected and analyzed several types of data. The data sources included students' reflective writing throughout the quarter, the interactions during the case discussions, students' immediate responses expressed during debriefing sessions that followed several case discussions, and interviews of six students conducted by a graduate assistant after the course was over.

In keeping with the view of pedagogical knowledge implicit in case-based methods (that it is socially and contextually situated), I drew on sociocultural theories of knowledge and learning to analyze these data (Smagorinsky, 1995; Wertsch, 1995). From this perspective, knowledge is located in the processes by which learners employ intellectual and cultural tools to make meaning of situations and events; learning is indicated by transformations in these tools and changes in the sense-making processes. Because I was interested in what preservice teachers learned from the case discussions, the questions that guided my study were:

- What tools did preservice teachers bring with them and draw on in their encounters with teaching cases?
- What meaning-making activities did they engage in during the case discussions?
- What tool transformations or changes in their meaning-making processes occurred during the course?

My analyses focused on the interactional activities during the case discussions as well as what the students said during the debriefing sessions and follow-up interviews.

In the following sections, I first characterize the preservice teachers' responses to the case discussions. Then, I report findings from my analysis of their learning.

## The Preservice Teachers' Evaluations of Case Discussions

The preservice teachers' comments during in-class debriefing sessions and interviews once the class was over suggested that they enjoyed reading and discussing cases. Many found the cases useful in thinking about their own teaching because they presented realistic problems that occurred in actual classrooms. As one student explained: "I like discussing them just because they are very realistic and they happened in classrooms" (Rita). Most students agreed that, in addition to making the reading engaging, examining teaching problems as they occurred in authentic classroom situations helped to contextualize their learning:

> We are more likely to learn, more likely to absorb the ideas behind the theory, if we learn it, or experience it, or come into contact with it in a realistic context, as opposed to simply talking about it in class (Jesse).

Another student commented that the case discussions enhanced her learning because "the cases allowed us to gather solutions from peers and teachers in the cases, rather than just the course professor" (Lahr).

Students also appreciated the case discussions because they offered ways to think about the problems they might face as teachers. Most students found that through analyzing the situations in the cases and considering alternative approaches or solutions, they created a repertoire of practical tools that they might later draw on when facing problems of their own. As one student put it, "We might not necessarily come across these problems now, or be able to relate now, but hearing these, we'll some day actually have something in our repertoire and be able to deal with it" (Cathline).

Some students found that the case discussions helped them to view problems and dilemmas as an inherent part of teaching. One student, for example, pointed out, that even though the teachers in the case were "real people who have been through methods classes," they still confronted "real problems, the real inconsistencies, the real idiosyncrasies of being in a classroom with different kinds of kids" (Jesse). These students appeared to interpret the problems in the cases not as the results of bad teaching, but as the artifacts of teachers trying to improve their practices. In this way, they were able to relate to the teachers in the cases and see the problems they faced. As Gina explained, "Since the teachers were having a lot of the problems I was having, [I realized] that everybody is wondering how to teach math better."

Finally, students said that participating in the case discussions forced them to consider perspectives other than their own. At first, many students were surprised to find that their colleagues did not interpret the case events in the same way that they did. Over time, these students found considering alternative perspectives to be one of the most valuable aspects of the case discussions because it helped them to clarify their own positions and to understand those of others. One student explained that, through the discussions, she was "finding out a lot about my own feelings because I'm forced to examine them, and then somebody will say no to them, and we'll sit here and think about them together" (Leesa).

Some students found that examining new points of view led them to rethink and revise their own positions: "It opens your mind, because when I first read something, I'm like, 'Oh, I know this is the way it is.' [But] when we start hearing other people speak about it, then I start getting swayed" (Connie).

In contrast to the positive comments described above, some students expressed concern about the emphasis the cases brought to the class. One student suggested that the discussions' focus on equity drew the class away from its central purpose of "how to teach mathematics" (Jesse). A few students voiced similar concerns in follow-up interviews, offering that the class did not seem like a methods course. This view was not shared by all the preservice teachers. Several students argued that the issues raised in the cases "may interfere with teaching math" and must be addressed (Pamela).

Finally, one student claimed that she found the case discussions more overwhelming than helpful because they introduced a new set of complications to her ideas about teaching. She explained, "I get a little frustrated because I have all these problems in my class and it's like, oh, there are all these problems that I have to worry about, too" (Rose). For students such as these, both the content and the process of the case discussions seemed to conflict with what and how they thought they should learn in a math methods course. I will return to this issue in my analysis of students' learning through case discussions.

## Preservice Teachers' Learning
## From Case Discussions

In addition to examining the preservice teachers' responses to the cases, I was interested in assessing the changes that occurred in their ideas about and knowledge of teaching. While the students' reactions to the case discussions offer one measure of the value of cases, their responses also reflect their ideas about learning to teach. Many prospective teachers believe that the best way to learn to teach is through experience (Weinstein, 1988). It is not surprising, then, that the preservice teachers found the cases useful because they were realistic and brought up problems teachers were likely to face. I was interested in determining whether case discussions could prompt preservice teachers to examine and reconsider their beliefs about students, learning, and teaching. Thus, I focused my analysis of the transcripts on how the preservice teachers made sense of the case discussions and whether their sense-making processes changed over the term.

*Preservice Teachers' Sense-Making Tools.* My analyses revealed that the preservice teachers drew on three types of tools that reflected their dual positions as university students and preservice teachers. The tools used most prominently throughout the discussions were their images of and ideas about teaching and students. These images and ideas represented a set of guiding perspectives that sometimes conflicted with one another. First, they viewed teaching as a technical activity, consisting of procedures, skills, and techniques they needed to master. Second, they viewed teaching as an insulated activity, minimally affected by people or events outside of the classroom. The third image of teaching that pervaded the preservice teachers' work was that it was an individualized endeavor; they placed primary emphasis on individual styles when discussing pedagogical decisions. Fourth, they believed that teachers should be highly responsive to students as individual learners. Finally, they viewed students as individualized psychologically. In discussing students, they focused on their individual abilities and styles, characterizing them as fixed and requiring instructional accommodation. These five images and ideas figured significantly in how the preservice teachers interpreted the issues in the cases.

A second type of sense-making tool used less prominently by the preservice teachers was their experiences in classrooms as teacher candidates and as students. They tended to use their experiences to explain or justify their perspectives during the case discussions. The third tool, employed least frequently by the preservice teachers, was information gleaned from course work. On occasion, students referred to material they had read or issues discussed in other courses.

During the case discussions, the preservice teachers engaged in a variety of sense-making activities in the process of assessing and responding to the cases. These activities involved drawing together and often negotiating tensions among tools that were in conflict with one another. For example, images of teaching as individualized (in that each teacher has her own style) and as responsive to students' individualized approaches to learning have the potential to produce internal conflicts when teachers are faced with a diverse class of students. Through the case discussions, the preservice teachers were asked to examine and address tensions between their ideals as teachers and their understandings of students' needs. Similarly, several of the case discussions required students to consider concurrently their perceptions of the power of the existing teaching context and the power of the teacher to adapt that context.

*Preservice Teachers' Learning from Cases.*   My analyses suggested that making sense of the cases prompted students to develop more complex images of the multiple demands of teaching and to refine their personal goals and philosophies to be responsive to a variety of students. One student, for example, said the case discussions helped her to become "more aware of the many issues teachers need to think about" (Gina). Another said that the cases helped her to "narrow" her philosophy of teaching and required her to test it out in realistic situations (Leesa). Another student described this process as "grounding" his beliefs: "They made us more aware of our own ideas to see if we wanted to change them" (Tony).

My findings revealed, however, that the preservice teachers' images of teaching—the tools that were most prominent in their sense-making activities—did not undergo significant transformation during the course. Rather, the changes that occurred were refinements or adjustments in the way students interpreted the situations in the cases. The example in the following section illustrates these modest changes, hinting at the resiliency of preservice teachers' images of teaching. This finding raises questions about how case-based methods might foster more significant transformations.

*Teaching as Individualized.*   One image that played a prominent role in the preservice teachers' sense-making, and that is particularly relevant to issues of inclusive teaching, is the view that teaching is an individualized endeavor. The notion that each teacher has a style that is her own and that has its own merits was evident throughout the discussions. Preservice teachers, for example, frequently referred to personal preferences and styles when asked to assess particular decisions with claims like, "There is not one right way to teach" and "Each teacher has to develop a style that is right for her." Over the term, the preservice teachers began to emphasize teaching philosophies that were subject to the needs of students, rather than personal preference. Still, many were reluctant to ground their assessments in normative theories or frameworks, arguing that the best choice depended on the situation, the students, and the teacher. Their tendency to use relative and idiosyncratic criteria to assess teaching suggests that an image of teaching as individualized continued to dominate their views.

While I want students to appreciate the contextual nature of teaching, my concern about this stance, particularly with respect to inclusive practices, is that it is likely to promote an uncritical view of teaching. It was my hope that students would learn to assess teaching practices against norms that are mathematically, pedagogically, and socially sound. These findings suggest that the images held by preservice teachers are firmly established and, as others have found, form the tools with which they make sense of their teacher education experience (Feiman-Nemser & Buchmann, 1986; Tabachnick & Zeichner, 1984). From this perspective, significant transformation of preservice teachers' images is improbable, even though cases are thought to have the potential to prompt change by providing students with opportunities to test their ideas in realistic contexts.

Further examination of the data, however, revealed that the open nature of case discussions may have helped to reinforce preservice teachers' images of teaching as an individualized endeavor. My intent was for the discussions to prompt students to examine the viability of their images. Analysis suggested that they interpreted the many opportunities they had to voice their perspectives as an indication that good teaching was a matter of one's opinion. In describing what she learned from the case discussion, Krista explained:

> Several times we never came to a conclusion. I mean, we'd talk about it and we didn't know what the right answer was, and there were a lot of right answers. Finally, our conclusion would be, everybody is different and you have to do it your own way.

While responses such as this did not represent the views of all of the students in the class, I found them informative in analyzing case-based teaching methods. Despite sound theoretical arguments for the use of cases, the opportunities for learning what cases provide are mediated by the preservice teachers' ideas about what they need to learn and how they should learn it. As I described earlier, most preservice teachers expect that learning to teach math involves being given a "bag of tricks" to use in the classroom (Ball, 1989). Because the case discussions did not fit this expectation in content or format, their purpose was open to interpretation. It is likely that the open nature of the discussions communicated to students an acceptance of all ideas, rather than facilitating critical analysis of teaching issues.

## Examining the Role of the Facilitator

This realization led me to examine the nature of discourse during the case discussions and my role in fostering it. Using the transcripts of the first and last case discussions, I coded and categorized each of my remarks according to its intent. Eleven categories emerged that could be grouped into three types of facilitating actions: (a) providing openings for students' ideas, (b) guiding or structuring the conversation, and (c) pushing students' thinking. I was surprised to find that 61% of the remarks I made were aimed at opening the discussion and getting more students' ideas into the conversation. Only 27% of the remarks I made were aimed at guiding or shaping the discussion. Finally, 12% of the comments I made during the two discussions were intended to push students to think more deeply or provide further evidence for their claims.

The proportionally low number of comments intended to push students was surprising, given my interest in encouraging them to rethink their images and ideas. Similarly, the rate at which I made comments intended to get students' ideas into the conversation may help to explain the tendency for the case discussions to be viewed as conversational free-for-alls. These findings and those described earlier led me to the following conclusions about the power and limits of case-based teaching and about the crucial role of the facilitator in constructing opportunities to learn.

## REFLECTIONS AND RECOMMENDATIONS

My experience suggests that case discussions can be valuable tools for prompting preservice teachers to consider issues of inclusion and equity in teaching mathematics. They have the potential to introduce preservice teachers to crucial teaching issues that they are likely to confront in their practice. The realistic contexts that cases present tend to enrich students' examinations of these issues by representing them in their full complexity. Further, they invite students into the processes of analysis and generation of actions in response to real problems. For these reasons, students find them engaging and provocative; well-written cases have the potential to initiate rich discussions that lead teachers to examine a number of important issues.

Rich case discussions, however, were not enough to meet my pedagogical goals. In addition to introducing students to issues related to inclusion, my aims were for preservice teachers to learn to examine their own beliefs and to develop new tools to help them identify unjust practices. I also wanted them to learn to design inclusive teaching practices that were proactive, rather than merely responsive. While students appeared to make small steps toward meeting these goals, significant transformations in their ideas about teaching and learning were not apparent.

Clearly, cases are not a panacea. Like all teaching tools, they are not absolute; nor do they stand alone. Inviting preservice teachers to read and discuss teaching cases does not determine what or if they will learn. Multiple factors influence the capacity of case discussions to contribute to specific learning goals. The issue is further complicated by the fact that assessing the impact of case discussions is not easy. The type of knowledge such methods aim to develop—thinking that is analytical, interpretive, and situationally grounded—is difficult to monitor. Moreover, the rich discussions cases are likely to stimulate and can be misleading to the facilitator. It is possible to assume, as I did, that more transformation is taking place than actually is.

My analysis has taught me that what case-based teaching methods are able to accomplish depends on how they are used. In particular, my experience and research findings suggest two key points about the use of cases that I recommend other teacher educators consider. First, the role that the instructor plays in designing and facilitating case discussions is central to the learning opportunities the cases offer. Therefore, it is important to examine your own role as facilitator by analyzing case discussion transcripts (see Moje, Remillard, Southerland, & Wade, 1999; Remillard & Geist, 1998). Second, a crucial role of the facilitator is to help students process and concretize changes in their thinking stimulated by case discussions. These two points are related to the concerns raised earlier in the chapter about the potential conflicts between the process and content—the how and what—of learning through case discussions and the expectations of most preservice teachers. Thus, my recommendations involve helping preservice teachers engage in a new type of learning.

Even though I was careful to select cases that introduced key issues in their natural complexity, and though I painstakingly outlined my goals and plans for each discussion, I did not give sufficient thought to my role as facilitator and orchestrator of the interactions during the discussions. The clear objectives and plans I developed for the case discussions gave me direction and focus. I now believe that it is also necessary, albeit much more difficult, to examine and assess one's actions with one's objectives in mind while facilitating the discussions. If we want students to think in particular ways, we need to challenge them to do so. If we want students to examine their beliefs and how these influence their judgments, we must engage them in making their beliefs explicit. We need to ask students questions and respond to their remarks in ways that challenge them to think critically and analytically. It is important to avoid merely validating all types of student input to a discussion.

Teacher educators using cases also must help make explicit to students what the students are learning through the discussions and the implications it has for their teaching. Case-based teaching methods are likely to be foreign to most preservice teachers; thus, it is possible that they will not know how to learn from them. Moreover, the idea that teachers should help learners process their own learning is not new. Those who study learning and memory have known for more than a decade that metacognitive abilities, or the ability to regulate and monitor one's learning, can enhance learning (Siegler, 1986). More recently, research on successful teaching practices in urban settings suggests that explicit guidance in using the codes, customs, and interactional styles expected in the classroom can help students who lack these cultural tools participate in types of classroom practices that are foreign to them (Ladson-Billings, 1994; Zeichner, 1996). It is my position that case discussions as a context for learning are foreign to most preservice teachers. Thus, teacher educators must facilitate students' learning from them.

One way that teacher educators can facilitate students' learning from cases is to be explicit about their aims and expectations. By telling students why the discussions are part of the curriculum, teacher educators can help students understand their goals. Moreover, teacher educators can help students participate productively in case discussions by providing them with guidance on how to read and analyze the cases, how to respond to the comments of others, and how to interpret the facilitator's actions.

This type of guidance can be integrated naturally into the facilitator's activities. Often, having the students think through a set of questions, individually or in small groups, prior to the discussion can direct their thinking in a purposeful way while communicating expectations about an appropriate level of thinking. Examples of such discussion questions can be found with the teaching notes in this volume.

Another way for teacher educators to increase students' learning from cases is to ask them to assess their learning after each case discussion. In subsequent courses, I have concluded each case discussion with a debriefing discussion during which the students reflect on the impact that the particular case discussion had on them. Having students share the shifts they experienced in their beliefs can help them solidify their developing perspectives. Drawing attention to questions they still have can help all students examine these issues explicitly. During these sessions, particularly early in their use of cases, it might be helpful to ask students to assess the discussion process itself, providing opportunities for the teacher educator to offer additional guidance in participating in the discussions.

A final way for teacher educators to foster students' learning through cases is to use follow-up activities, like those suggested in the teaching notes. These activities are designed to help students concretize and build on their learning from case discussions by engaging them in using or articulating their developing perspectives. For example, the students might pursue further research, interview a teacher or principal, or engage in a role-play related to the issues in the case. In addition to furthering the students' learning, follow-up activities provide opportunities for teacher educators to assess the students' perspectives and growth.

In conclusion, I heartily recommend the use of cases to introduce pre-service teachers to issues of inclusion and equity. Because these issues are not straightforward and emerge in a variety of complicated situations, cases about real teaching instances provide ideal contexts in which prospective teachers can explore them. At the same time, I encourage teacher educators to carefully consider their learning goals and how they go about accomplishing them. Case discussions do not automatically guarantee learning. Teacher educators must take specific actions directed at facilitating students' learning from cases. Moreover, because the richness of case discussions can be misleading, I recommend that teacher educators develop strategies to continually assess both their teaching and their students' learning (e.g., Moje et al., 1999). To a large extent, we must impose the same level of examination and critique on our teaching that we are asking prospective teachers to bring to theirs.

# REFERENCES

Ball, D. L. (1989). *Breaking with experience in learning to teach mathematics: The role of a preservice methods course* (Report No. 89-10). East Lansing, MI: National Center for Research on Teacher Education.

Barnett, C. (1994). *Mathematics teaching cases: Fractions, decimals, ratios, and percents.* Portsmouth, NH: Heinemann.

Delpit, L. (1988). *The silenced dialogue: Power and pedagogy in educating other people's children. Harvard Educational Review, 58*(3), 280–298.

Delpit, L. (1995). *Other people's children: Cultural conflict in the classroom.* New York: The New Press.

Feiman-Nemser, S., & Buchmann, M. (1986). The first year of teacher preparation: Transition to pedagogical thinking? *Journal of Curriculum Studies, 18*(3), 239-256.

Kennedy, M. M. (1987). Inexact sciences: Professional development and the education of expertise. In E. Z. Rothkopf (Ed.), *Review of Research in Education* (Vol. 14. pp. 133–167). Washington, DC: American Educational Research Association.

Ladson-Billings, G. (1994). *The dreamkeepers: Successful teachers of African-American children.* San Francisco: Jossey-Bass.

Moje, E. B., Remillard, J. T., Southerland, S., & Wade, S. E. (1999). Researching case pedagogies to inform our teaching. In M. Lundeberg, B. Levin, & H. Harrington (Eds.), *Who learns what from cases and how? The research base for teaching with cases* (pp. 73–94). Mahwah, NJ: Lawrence Erlbaum Associates.

McDiarmid, G. W., & Price, J. (1990). *Prospective teachers' views of diverse learners: A study of the participants in the ABCD project.* East Lansing, MI: National Center for Research on Teacher Learning.

National Association of State Boards of Education. (1992, October). *Winners all: A call for inclusive schools.* Washington, DC: Author.

National Center of School Restructuring and Inclusion. (1994). *National survey on inclusive education. Bulletin of the National Center on Educational Restructuring and Inclusion, 1*, 1–4.

National Council of Teachers of Mathematics. (1989). *The curriculum and evaluation standards for school mathematics.* Reston, VA: Author.

National Council of Teachers of Mathematics. (1991). *The professional standards for teaching mathematics.* Reston, VA: Author.

National Council of Teachers of Mathematics. (1995). *Assessment standards for teaching mathematics.* Reston, VA: Author.

Remillard, J. T. (1996, March). Paper presented at the annual meeting of the American Educational Research Association, New York.

Remillard, J. T., & Geist, P. (1998, April). *What an innovative curriculum for teachers reveals about supporting teachers' professional learning.* Paper presented at the annual meeting of the American Educational Research Association, San Diego, CA.

Shulman, L. S. (1992). Toward a pedagogy of cases. In J. Shulman (Ed.), *Case methods in teacher education* (pp. 1–30). New York: Teachers College Press.

Siegler, R. S. (1986). *Children's thinking.* Englewood Cliffs, NJ: Prentice-Hall.

Smagorinsky, P. (1995). The social construction of data: Methodological problems of investigating learning in the zone of proximal development. *Review of Educational Research, 65*(3), 191–212.

Sykes, G., & Bird, T. (1992). Teacher education and the case idea. In G. Grant (Ed.), *Review of Research in Education* (Vol. 18, pp. 457–521). Washington, DC: American Educational Research Association.

Tabachnick, B. R., & Zeichner, K. M. (1984). The impact of the student teaching experience on the development of teacher perspectives. *Journal of Teacher Education, 35*(6), 28–36.

Weinstein, C. (1988). Preservice teachers' expectations about the first year of teaching. *Teaching and Teacher Education, 4*(1), 31–41.

Wertsch, J. V. (1995). The need for action in sociocultural research. In J. V. Wertsch, P. del Rio, & A. Alvarez (Eds.), *Sociocultural studies of mind* (pp: 56–74). Cambridge, England: Cambridge University Press.

Zeichner, K. (1996). Educating teachers to close the achievement gap: Issues of pedagogy, knowledge, and teacher preparation. In B. Williams (Ed.), *Closing the achievement gap* (pp. 56–76). Alexandria VA: ASCD.

# 4

# Teaching Science for All

*Julie Gess-Newsome*
*Sherry A. Southerland*

*[Science for all students:] It's a goal. A goal. That means we should try to achieve it, but we won't make it all the time. As a goal it means that we should actually be taking steps to go toward it. Like maybe spending more time with some students, working with them more, giving them different ways to represent what they know. (Fran, student teacher)*

Science for *all* Americans: The recognition of the need for changes in science instruction began in the early 1980s with the release of the report, *A Nation at Risk* (Golberg & Harvey, 1983), and has culminated in the current movement to create national standards across the content areas, including science. Of the common themes that can be traced across the two most influential science reform documents, the American Association for the Advancement of Science's (AAAS; 1989) *Science for All Americans: Project 2061* and the National Research Council's (NRC, 1996) *National Science Education Standards*, equity of educational opportunities in science stands at the forefront of reform, as emphasized in the following statement:

The intent of the [National Science Education] Standards can be expressed in a single phrase: Science standards for all students. The phrase embodies both excellence and equity. The Standards apply to all students, regardless of age, gender, cultural or ethnic background, disabilities, aspirations, or interest and motivation in science. (NRC, 1996, p. 2)

Clearly, the science education community recognizes the need for teaching methods and strategies that address the unique needs of diverse student populations. We believe that the means of meeting this goal can be encompassed within the rubric *inclusive education*. Characteristics of inclusive science teaching include:

1. the recognition of the unique strengths and challenges that each student brings to the classroom;
2. the design of science lessons that can engage all students in the social construction of science knowledge through inquiry-based lessons;
3. the portrayal of science as a powerful, but limited, way of making sense of the natural world; and
4. the creation of a curriculum that holistically attends both to varying instructional strategies and to selecting content that allows students to use science in a meaningful way.

In inclusive science teaching, we believe that the needs of the individual must be considered and balanced against the needs of the group. As instructors of an elementary science methods course, we are continually challenged to find ways to help our preservice teachers understand and embrace the principles of equity and inclusion and to help them select teaching strategies that will translate such goals into classroom practice. Our task is not simple; we are products of the same educational system that has denied equal science access to women and minorities. In addition, the concept of diversity has expanded: Age, disabilities, aspirations, interests, and motivations have been added to the previously recognized categories of gender, cultural, and ethnic diversity. We applaud the recognition of student diversity and are committed to helping our students become the science teachers called for in the national reforms. However, like other science educators, we face the challenges of meeting this goal while continuing to provide our preservice teachers with the more traditional goals of a science methods course (as described later in this chapter). This chapter describes our efforts toward this end.

Our purposes for this chapter are: (a) to present a curriculum outline for an elementary science methods course highlighting specific aspects (including case discussions) that address issues of inclusive science teaching; (b) to evaluate the success of this curriculum in terms of preservice teachers' attitudes toward and preparation for teaching science in inclusive classrooms; and (c) based on data collected during the course, to present suggestions to refine our focus on inclusive science teaching and to describe the role of cases within such a course.

We base our discussion on our study of three sections of an elementary science methods course taught during 1995/1996. Information we found valuable in our description and assessment included: (a) preservice teachers' written course assignments (used to gain an understanding of how each assignment influenced conceptions of inclusive teaching); (b) lesson and unit presentations (used to search for the ways in which students applied ideas of inclusive teaching in their own planning); (c) transcripts of audiotaped class discussions related to inclusive teaching, including case discussions (used to understand the meanings preservice teachers constructed of teaching science in inclusive classrooms); and (d) transcripts of audiotaped debriefing sessions between the course instructors (used to search for commonalities across sections).

## COURSE CONTEXT

The elementary science methods course was taught during the second quarter of the 4-quarter teacher certification sequence. The three sections of this course met twice each week throughout the fall quarter, with three additional meetings during the winter quarter's student teaching experience. Our students were also involved in four other methods courses in the fall quarter and participated in field experiences two days each week, essentially dividing their time between university and classroom settings. For both their field and student teaching experiences, the preservice teachers were placed in one of three types of schools serving both urban and suburban communities: schools with student populations drawn from predominantly White, middle- to upper-class neighborhoods; schools with student populations that were diverse in terms of both ethnicity and socioeconomic status; and schools that had moved to a full inclusion model of education with student populations drawn from primarily White, lower- to middle-class neighborhoods. Because of the intense course load combined with the required field experience, our students found the fall quarter particularly taxing.

Of 67 students across the three sections, the majority were parents and/or were pursuing education as a second career. The students were primarily women, with a total of six men distributed across the three sections. The majority of students were of European ancestry, with only three students representing an ethnic minority group (Asian American, American Indian, and Middle Eastern decent).

## CURRICULUM OUTLINE

### Course Goals and Overall Structure

We designed the elementary science methods course to provide our preservice teachers with a combination of practical teaching experiences, informed classroom discussions about science teaching and learning, and models of teaching practices informed by a synthesis of science education research. The course included experiences that would allow our preservice teachers to analyze and develop understandings of science teaching; to develop and refine science teaching practices; to further develop understandings of the nature of science and specific science content; and to develop the skills needed to successfully plan, write, and implement an elementary science program. In addition, as course instructors, we sought to move students toward an appreciation and understanding of student diversity and to prepare them to teach science in inclusive settings.

In teaching this course in the past, we have found that the most challenging aspect was to provide the preservice teachers with opportunities to see science as an understandable and useful way of making sense of the natural world while they developed tools to teach science. Toward these ends, each of the first seven weeks revolved around our modeling of inquiry-based science activities while the preservice teachers assumed the role of science learners. After each activity, the lesson debriefing highlighted both the science content addressed as well as the specific teaching strategy modeled. Aspects of science content knowledge, characteristics of the nature of science, and specific methods of inquiry teaching were emphasized in each activity. In addition, discussions of course readings, journal entries, class maps, and science interviews were held during these class meetings.

The last three weeks of the course during the fall quarter focused on student-conducted presentations of their unit plans. The intent of the unit preparation was to provide an additional experience in making personal sense of science content, to develop the research tools needed to thoroughly investigate science topics, and to translate science knowledge into teaching practices that were sensitive to the needs of all students. Again, after each of these presentations, a debriefing session was held to address the content understandings presented and to analyze the consequences of the selected teaching strategies on student learning. The final class sessions, held during the winter quarter, were devoted to emphasizing teaching strategies that addressed inclusive populations, issues related to inclusive teaching, and the role of inquiry methods in inclusive science instruction. These issues were introduced during the first session through the use of three cases.

In the next section, we describe more completely the assignments used in the course as they focused on inclusive science teaching, highlighting the use of cases. These assignments and activities ranged in intent; some were designed to provide a theoretical justification for teaching science for all, others provided specific inclusive teaching methods, and still others required students to reflect on and make sense of both the goals and the means of equitable science education. These descriptions will be followed by examples of student work from each assignment and our overall assessment of the impacts of our efforts related to inclusive science teaching.

## Course Assignments and Activities

*Journal Entries.* These in-class writings were composed by the preservice teachers once a week in response to prepared prompts. Typically, we designed the prompts to directly relate to the specific teaching issues addressed in class that week, fostering student reflection prior to class discussion. Journal prompts typically required our developing teachers to consider their assumptions about students and the act of teaching as these intersected with their specific goals for science teaching. The journal entry from week 5 focused on issues of inclusive science teaching using the following prompt:

> One goal of scientific literacy is for *all* students in our classes—not just a select high-achieving few—to build a core of useful scientific knowledge that they can apply throughout their lives. What is your

view of this goal? Can we expect teachers to reach all students in science? Is the goal of teaching *all* students reasonable or are we setting unrealistic expectations for teachers? How do you intend to meet the needs of all your students in science?

*Reading Discussions.*    Each week, the first 30 minutes of class were devoted to a student-led discussion of assigned readings from *Science for All Americans* (AAAS, 1989). The first of these discussions, completed after reading the preface to *Science for All Americans,* centered on the goals of science literacy and inclusive, equitable science education.

*Science Interviews.*    Regardless of the form of constructivism used to understand learning (Matthews, 1997), it is essential to understand students' prior knowledge frameworks. These frameworks are understood to include not only declarative knowledge but also the historical and cultural backgrounds that students bring into the science classroom. Thus, we argue that the educator must become familiar with what the student knows before organizing instruction. In order to acquaint our preservice teachers with what their students knew about science, each preservice teacher conducted an interview with two elementary students of varying science abilities (as judged by the site teacher educators) prior to the third week of the course. We believe that these interviews acted as an important introduction to the notion that learners bring a lifetime of culturally constructed knowledge into the classroom and that this knowledge often differs significantly across groups and individuals.

The interviews consisted of four parts. Part 1 involved a description of the students in terms of grade level, gender, ethnicity, and the site teacher's judgment of the student's science ability. Part 2 consisted of the students' answers to structured questions provided by the course instructors related to the students' conceptions of science and scientists. Part 3 consisted of preservice teacher-created questions related to a particular science topic. These questions were designed to elicit the diversity of students' understandings and to examine possible alternative conceptions. Part 4 required the completion of two Piagetian tasks. While the assignment of a student to a developmental level has been challenged by sociocultural theorists (O'Loughlin, 1992), our intention was to include a standardized data collection tool from which our students could analyze and problematize issues related to the developmental classification of students.

Our preservice teachers were asked to create transcripts of the interviews to be displayed on the classroom walls, organized by grade level.

After a short introduction during which anecdotes about the interview experience were shared, our preservice teachers generated a tentative list of patterns or hypotheses that might be explored while they examined the interview data. The initial categories generated included: (a) stereotypes of science and scientists; (b) differences among students based on ethnicity, gender, background knowledge, experiences, and grade level; and (c) the accuracy of assigned labels for predicting students' academic abilities. This was followed by the preservice teachers generating and answering questions from the data that were of greatest personal concern and interest. The assignment culminated in a written synthesis of the interview observations and the class discussion, with an analysis of the issues that would influence science teaching and the suggestion of potential strategies that could be used to provide positive science learning experiences for all the students in their diverse classrooms. Through the analysis and synthesis of the students' own research findings, we hoped to highlight issues of diversity in learners within a single grade level and to challenge the assumption that students learn, reason, and understand in the same way as the teacher candidates (Birrell, 1995).

*Class Map.*   Following six to eight weeks of field experience (both prior to and during the quarter), the preservice teachers designed maps of their classrooms that consisted of the physical features of the room and a short description of each student in their classes, including the personal, behavioral, social, and cognitive characteristics that would be important to consider when making teaching decisions. Our goal for this assignment was to encourage our preservice teachers to focus on students as individuals instead of looking at them as a single, homogeneous group. These maps were later used to construct the adaptation sections of the lesson and unit plans.

*Lesson and Unit Plans for Teaching Science.*   Lesson planning and implementation were stressed in two separate assignments in the course. For the first assignment, the preservice teachers wrote and taught two inquiry-based science lessons in their field placement classrooms during the fall quarter. The second assignment involved designing a science unit of at least five lessons in cooperation with one or more members of the class. The unit plans were designed as written resources for student teaching and were presented in abbreviated form to the class during the last four weeks of the quarter. Upon conclusion of the unit presentation, each group was asked to explain how the curriculum and teaching methods employed in the unit addressed issues of inclusion.

Both the lesson and unit plans included five primary parts:

1. A outline that provided specific information about the content that was to be taught, including a content presentation sequence with connections among concepts.
2. An inquiry-based lesson plan that portrayed the targeted science concept in a developmentally appropriate way. Each lesson plan included a rationale, objectives, materials, lesson structure (introduction, body, and closure), and a classroom management plan.
3. An integration plan that related the lesson or unit content to other lessons in either science or across the curriculum, for example, the identification of a trade book that would link the science topic to the teaching of reading skills.
4. An adaptation plan that described how the lesson could be adapted to meet the special needs of particular students. The adaptation plan was the most salient aspect of the lesson with respect to inclusive education. Through the adaptation plans, we hoped to focus the preservice teachers on the needs of individuals and, in doing so, to build both awareness of and attention to the diversity of learners in the classroom.
5. A lesson/unit reflection that stated the preservice teacher's assessment of the implemented lesson, including specific comments about the perceived strengths and weaknesses of the lesson as viewed through the lens of student learning. Additionally, students were asked to consider how the lesson might be changed if presented again and to detail any changes in their personal goals for teaching future lessons.

*Case Discussions.*    For the purposes of our class, we viewed teaching cases as accounts of experiences that could be used to teach a concept or theory (Shulman, 1992). We recognized teaching cases as particularly useful tools in addressing teaching in inclusive classrooms because they represent the complexity of issues faced in the classroom (Doyle, 1990; Shulman, 1992; Sykes & Bird, 1992). Additionally, case-based instruction is credited with supporting the social construction of knowledge (Sykes & Bird, 1992), increasing opportunities for teacher reflection (Harrington, 1995; Sibbett, 1997), allowing the contextualization of learning to teach (Grossman, 1992; Shulman, 1992), and increasing the application of educational theory to classroom practice (Kowalski, Weaver, & Henson, 1990). Our use of cases was designed to build upon these strengths as we supported students in their efforts to teach science for all.

Teaching cases were presented at the end of the course, after many of the more technical aspects of science teaching had been discussed, lesson plans had been implemented, and content and pedagogical concepts had been mastered. Our preservice teachers read three teaching cases written by the previous year's students. Based on the case authors' experiences in teaching science, these cases involved issues related to gender, ability, expectations, and assessment of students' understanding. Class case discussions focused on creating generalizations across cases, suggesting problem-solving strategies, and addressing guidelines for future science teaching practices.

The first case focused on the differential interest and participation of boys and girls during science lessons. While teaching a lesson on the water cycle to first grade students, Emily, the preservice teacher, noticed that while the boys were animated and enthusiastic about the science topic, the girls seemed resistant to participate in the activities or discussions unless an art project was involved. Despite attempts to balance gender participation during the science lesson, Emily was concerned about the evidence of gender-based science interests in her young students.

The instructor-facilitated case discussion used the following types of questions: What were Emily's concerns? How do gender differences related to science participation affect the notion of science for all Americans? Is overt participation in science equivalent to student interest and learning? Is differential participation and interest something teachers should be concerned about? If so, how might you address this issue in your science instruction?

The second case centered on a preservice teacher, Carla, who described how a science lesson allowed Kelly, an underachieving girl, to excel in a classroom activity. Kelly was a fifth grade student in a total inclusion school and was placed in the lowest achievement cluster for math, science, and social studies. During a science lesson involving a scaled representation of the earth's layers, Kelly insightfully used proportional reasoning to determine the appropriate thickness of one layer of the earth based upon the scale used for another layer. To the surprise of her classmates and Carla, Kelly described her reasoning in a clear manner, providing an explanation that assisted the other students in making similar calculations. In the case narrative, Carla noted that she had originally considered eliminating the calculation of scale in the lesson because she had deemed it too difficult for her students. After her lesson, however, Carla realized that this problem-solving activity had allowed a student who was perceived to be of low ability to "shine" in front of her classmates. Carla's case ends with the questions: Do all students, regardless of their achievement level, have an academic contribution to make to a classroom? How can instruction be planned so that all students are challenged but still have the potential to succeed?

The following questions structured the discussion that followed: Do you think this was an effective lesson? Why? What characteristics of the lesson allowed Kelly to participate? What are the benefits of heterogeneous grouping in an inclusive classroom? Who gains from these benefits and how?

The third case centered on a teacher's attempt to help a behaviorally and cognitively challenged learner express what he had learned through a science unit. Josh was a student with reading difficulties who spent most of his day in a pull-out resource class. As "punishment" for misbehaving, Josh was sent to spend the entire day in his regular sixth grade classroom. Joan, his student teacher, viewed this event as an opportunity. The students were working at learning centers on the topic of microorganisms. Josh was positive and enthusiastic about participating in the day's activities and seemed to be interacting well with both his peers and the content. Following hands-on instruction at the centers, the students completed a study guide on the key concepts presented. Joan, recognizing Josh's reading difficulties, worked with him individually to discuss each of the concepts. As Joan explained a concept, Josh attentively nodded his head in understanding. Josh and Joan then participated in a whole-class review and discussion of the study guide. Thinking that Josh had now been exposed to the microbiology concepts on three occasions—at the learning centers, in their individual session, and during the whole-class discussion—Joan felt confident that Josh would be able to succeed in answering the questions on the test. After his initial request for help on the first question, however, Joan discovered that Josh had attempted to answer only one of the many test questions. Joan ended her case with the questions: How could I have better assessed Josh's knowledge? How can I make Josh accountable for in-class work despite his reading difficulties?

Questions we used to start the case discussion included: What evidence can you find of Joan's views of Josh? How could Joan have better assessed Josh's knowledge? Based on this case and your own teaching experiences, what are some of the characteristics, strengths, and difficulties of teaching in an inclusive classroom?

After the third case was discussed, we asked the preservice teachers to draw generalizations across the discussions of the three cases and relate them to the goals of *Project 2061* (AAAS, 1989) and science for all. Questions asked to promote student sense making included: What makes each of these scenarios a case of inclusive science teaching? What challenges associated with inclusive science teaching are described in these cases? How can these challenges be overcome? What challenges of inclusion have you experienced? What benefits—cognitive, social, and ethical—does an inclusive science classroom offer? How can we structure science teaching to meet the challenges and take advantage of the benefits of inclusive classrooms?

*Postreflection on Student Teaching and Discussion of Inclusive Science Teaching.* Three follow-up class sessions were held during the winter quarter when the preservice teachers were student teaching. These sessions were designed to help students solve immediate, pressing problems in their science teaching and to encourage them to reflect on their student teaching experiences, particularly on the strengths, drawbacks, and difficulties of inclusive science teaching. Some organizing questions for the discussions included: How is your science teaching going? In what areas have you excelled? In what areas do you still have room to develop as a science teacher? Which student or students do you feel have benefited most from your science teaching? Who has not? What is your evidence for these answers? Based on your experiences, what factors can enhance or inhibit a student's ability to do well in science? What do you feel is the strongest aspect of your approach to inclusive science teaching? How can you further refine this approach? What school or community resources can you rely upon to enhance your inclusive science teaching?

## HOW DID THIS CURRICULUM WORK?
## EVALUATION OF OUR FOCUS
## ON INCLUSION

The following section includes our evaluation of the students' responses to the various course activities and our understandings of what our students took away from our class: What were their conceptions of inclusion and how did they change during the course? What issues did the students recognize as being related to inclusive science teaching? What teaching practices did they invoke to adequately teach individual students in diverse classrooms? To answer these questions, we observed our preservice teachers, listened to their discussions, and reviewed their work. In this section, we discuss our findings along with both short and extended data clips from our preservice teachers' written work and classroom discussions connected with each assignment to illustrate their views about inclusion and science teaching.

## Journal Entries

Several trends were found in the early journal entries concerning issues of inclusion. First, our preservice teachers tended to understand diversity as "different ability levels coupled with different learning styles" (e.g., low-level students learn best through concrete experiences). This narrow understanding of student diversity was found in responses from all three sections, despite our very explicit and repeated attempts to define diversity in the very broad cognitive, cultural, and behavioral terms outlined in the national reform efforts.

The most common teaching methods invoked for teaching in diverse classrooms included peer tutoring, cooperative grouping, and "hands-on" science instruction. Peer tutoring and cooperative grouping were valued because "students could learn from one another" as the high-ability students "helped the lower achievers"—a consistent implication of the perceived one-way benefit of group work. We were very disappointed, although not surprised, to discover that the preservice teachers could not yet understand that group work supports the social construction of knowledge of all participants (Nix & Spiro, 1990). Hands-on science instruction was typically described as a way of "keeping student interest up and motivation high." Though we agree that student manipulation of materials aids in interest and motivation, our attempt was to convey inquiry-oriented approaches to science instruction as rich and complex learning opportunities, a distinctly different view than was represented by the simplistic hands-on approach so readily suggested by our students.

The final trend we found in the preservice teachers' journals was the blend of idealism and pragmatism with which they approached the idea of science for all, as shown in the following journal entry:

> I don't think science teachers should beat themselves up if a couple of their students don't seem to be catching on [to a science concept]. But they *must not* give up on those students and figure that they're a lost cause. We can expect our students to try, and like our students, we should work toward a goal [of inclusive science for all students]. (Marta)

## Student Interviews

After the preservice teachers analyzed the student interviews in class, they concluded with generalizations about student learning and implications for instructional practice. The tone of this class discussion as well as the students' written summaries suggested that the preservice teachers were sensitive to differences in students' backgrounds and abilities, particularly realizing that ability labels (as provided by the site teacher educator) did not always accurately reflect a student's ability in science. For instance, many students identified as low ability (often defined as resource students) were found to be very capable in and knowledgeable about science during the interviews. This realization and our subsequent discussion caused our preservice teachers to begin to question the practice of labeling, as well as to begin to recognize students as distinct and sometimes surprising individuals.

While the student interviews moved our teachers toward our goals of recognizing the unique characteristics of individual students, other issues were uncovered as we read their summaries. Our preservice teachers often equated science success and ability with a high degree of student engagement and interest, as demonstrated in the following essay excerpt:

> I have witnessed in my STE's [site teacher educator's] classroom that different achievement levels can be nonexistent, and that high achievement is the norm in direct correlation to the way science is handled. The students love what they are doing, and they feel confident and capable, all because of their [high] interest level. (Cheryl)

So, in a manner similar to that in which inquiry instruction was simplified to hands-on manipulation, student success was interpreted as maintaining student interest and increasing personal confidence. Helping students construct highly interconnected, conceptual knowledge about a science topic was rarely used as the metric by which successful teaching was measured. Instead, as seen in the above quote, our students understood science achievement to be measured by students' self-confidence and interest in a topic, not the soundness of the concepts they constructed. Our data analysis helped us to understand that the meanings derived by our preservice teachers about teaching diverse student populations were significantly different than the conceptions that we had tried to convey. While we were generally pleased with some aspects of their conceptual development, we felt that further guidance on these issues was required.

When asked what teaching strategies could be used to build upon the strengths and challenges of an inclusive classroom, most of the preservice teachers mentioned peer tutoring as a way to meet the diverse needs of students. As in the journal entries, peer tutoring and other group work were understood to primarily benefit the low achiever. Gratefully, however, at this same point, we noted signs of continued pedagogical development in the preservice teachers, as many of them began to recognize the importance of varying instructional methods as a necessary tool to facilitate the learning of all students.

## Class Maps, Lesson Plans, and Unit Plans

Because the goals underlying the assignments of class maps, lesson plans, and unit plans were closely intertwined, we will combine our discussion of students' responses to these assignments. As we have mentioned previously, the class map assignment was designed to encourage our preservice teachers to consider the individual needs of the diverse students in their field placement classrooms, particularly as they wrote and implemented their lesson and unit plans. Below are two descriptions of students (Gerry and Darrin) from these class maps:

> Gerry: Until very recently I would have said that he is just on another planet. But consistently he is turning in work that is in the top 5% of the class. He is so, so, so messy and unorganized! His desk always looks like a tornado zone. Emotionally and socially he is immature, so the other class members have little to do with him. (Lori)

> Darrin: Darrin is a good kid, but just can't stay focused. He leaves for [the] resource [room] for math and reading. He just needs a pat on the back every so often. He doesn't ever finish his work, so it's good if he even gets half of the work done. He needs structure. (Rebecca)

We were torn as we read such descriptions. On one hand, we were disappointed to see that the descriptions seemed far from being informed by past multicultural and special education courses that our students had experienced. On the other hand, the descriptions did show evidence that the developing teachers were seriously considering the distinct attributes and needs of individuals in their classrooms.

Using these classroom maps, our preservice teachers often described adaptation plans that only addressed classroom management or issues related to early and late finishers. Some students, however, used these maps to produce relatively sophisticated and focused instructional strategies in their adaptation plans that included modeling, clear explanations, peer-mediated instruction, and collaboration with specialists, as evidenced in the following lesson excerpt:

> For ESL students, I would have them work with a student who speaks their native language, if possible. If they were able to read in their primary language, I could have the activity and questions translated and written in this [primary] language. The school also has an ESL teacher who might have time to provide services for the child. If so, I would ask the teacher to discuss the lesson concept with the ESL students prior to when the activity is given in class. This would require extra planning and coordination with the ESL teacher, but it would be worth the effort. For children in the class whose reading skills will make it difficult to access the conceptual information in the reading, I will have fluent readers read the ending activity and nonfluent readers answer the questions orally. I will also support inventive spelling as we move toward conventional spelling, so that students who have difficulty in writing will be encouraged to share their ideas. (Marta)

In contrast to the adaptation plans in the lesson plans, we were surprised to find that those in the unit plans included far less detail and showed far less evidence of serious consideration. Virtually all of our developing teachers attended only to problems associated with the management of early and slow finishers, showing at best only shallow consideration of selecting or varying appropriate teaching strategies. Missing from all the unit adaptation plans was an explicit discussion of the purposeful selection of science content and teaching strategies that would foster learning in a diverse classroom.

## Case Discussions

While we hoped to infuse our entire course with discussions of and reflections about teaching science to all students, the class activity that most closely targeted this issue was that of case discussions. As course instructors, we hoped to culminate our approach to inclusive science teaching with these discussions. Our findings reflect both on how students make sense of cases and on their developing conceptions of inclusive science teaching.

*How Preservice Teachers Made Sense of Cases.*   In the case discussions held in each of our classes, we were delighted to see the high degree of student engagement. Perhaps because the preservice teachers knew that the cases had been written by former students, they saw the cases as representing something very close to their own teaching situation and placed a great deal of importance on the knowledge constructed from these case discussions. This valuing supports the arguments of Shulman (1992) and Grossman (1992) who claim that one of the strengths of case-based teaching is the degree to which cases allow for the contextualization of learning to teach, that is, situating cases in personal experiences.

The preservice teachers immediately and enthusiastically related to the teaching cases through the lens of their own teaching experiences. With the case of gendered participation (Emily's case), for example, several students animatedly recounted similar incidences in their own science lessons. The pattern of the preservice teachers initially was to situate the case within their own experiences and then, only after these connections were made, to address their attention to the details of the specific case. Other researchers, including Sibbett (1997), have also noted this pattern in the case discussions of preservice teachers.

The case discussions also revealed preservice teachers' orientation toward the act of teaching, which we describe as the positivistic, technical "search for solutions," a tendency also noted by Swanson, O'Connor, & Cooney (1990). After situating the case within their own experiences, the students quickly moved the discussion toward solutions for the perceived "teaching problem" rather than pursuing an in-depth analysis of the problem and issues in the cases. For instance, in the case of Josh, the resource student who participated in the microbiology lesson (Joan's case), many of the preservice teachers suggested that Josh needed to be tested for behavioral disorders, and others suggested that he needed "to be put on Ritalin" to manage his behavior. Still others suggested that "maybe he has a vision problem and needs to be tested." The preservice teachers failed to recognize the multiplicity of issues and problems associated with the case: Once a potential "solution" was suggested, they were ready to move on to the next case.

It is possible that this positivistic, technical search for a solution approach was due to our own naive approach to leading case discussions. As discussed by Moje, Remillard, Southerland, and Wade (1999), leading successful case discussions can be a delicate and difficult procedure. In our methods course, we attempted to structure our discussion to focus on a critical analysis of the context of the dilemma, rather than focusing on the solution. Our students, however, often leapt ahead to offer solutions. As described by Moje et al. (1999), while we knew our students were not critically analyzing the case situation in ways we found productive, we discovered that we had a limited understanding of what such a critical analysis might look like. How far could we expect students to move toward this nebulous goal? How could we scaffold their efforts in such an analysis? While we were seeking critical reflection, as course instructors we failed to visualize what such reflection might look like or how best to urge students toward this goal.

We now recognize that the manner in which we led the case discussions may have allowed for, or at least failed to challenge, the technical approach prominent in students' case discussions. Hand in hand with this "fix it" approach was our preservice teachers' failure to understand the complexity of the classroom and their lack of awareness of the synergistic consequences of a teacher's actions for both the individual and the group. As instructors, we hoped our students would use cases as a means of illuminating the context-dependent aspects of teaching; instead, our students were searching for a solution that would provide a single "best practice." Again, we recognized that our preservice teachers had constructed a different kind of knowledge than we had intended, a difference in large part due to our differing views of the act of teaching: simple versus complex contexts, well- versus ill-defined problems, and uni- versus multidimensional solutions.

## Overall Assessment of Teaching Strategies Related to Inclusive Teaching

At the outset of the science methods course, we found that our preservice teachers had a relatively narrow definition of inclusion, as reflected in their class maps, early journal entries, and adaptation plans. As their early efforts revealed, they rarely addressed issues related to gender, ethnicity, experiential background, or socioeconomic status. Instead, they were primarily concerned with the behavioral and academic backgrounds of their students. The emphasis on issues of behavior and academic potential matches the findings of the research in teacher development, which show that beginning teachers often focus exclusively on issues that will affect them directly as teachers (i.e., behavior and academic ability) in contrast to characteristics that would affect student learning, such as the broader characteristics that we have used to describe diverse student populations (Feiman-Nemser & Remillard, 1996).

There is evidence, however, to suggest that the methods course and the use of cases in particular was successful in partially broadening these incoming views. While many students left our course with initial beliefs relatively intact, several students expressed views of inclusive science teaching similar to those for which we had hoped. Perhaps as a result of the use of the case that dealt with issues of gendered participation in a science class, students began to include gender as a consideration, as represented in a comment by Cindy: "Yeah, it's like that sometimes in my class. The girls just don't talk as much when we're doing science." While we had anticipated that the teacher candidates would use a more robust definition of inclusion by course end, it is our hope that their beginning recognition of the influences related to gender may lead to a broadening to the other facets of diversity in student groups. Perhaps the evolution of this conception must occur gradually, over years, as new teachers work within their own classrooms. Thus, our role as instructors can be to provide an initial sensitization to the needs of diverse student populations through inclusive teaching strategies.

Case discussions and the content of the adaptation section of the lesson and unit plans reflect our candidates' understanding of teaching as a technical act, a pattern also described in other chapters in this volume (see chapter 3 by Remillard and chapter 5 by Moje in this volume). As a result of their somewhat simplified and technical analyses of the situations in the cases, many of our preservice teachers offered similarly simple and technical teaching suggestions. (Again, we understand this technical approach to be due in part to our students' orientation to the act of teaching and our own naiveté in leading case discussions.) Two of the most commonly recommended inclusive science teaching strategies included the use of peer tutoring and cooperative learning. Although such strategies are potentially useful, we noticed that often such suggestions were made without a reflective consideration of how or why they may succeed. In later assignments, there was evidence of a broadening of strategies and an increase in the sophistication of the teaching suggestions. In case discussions, several pre-service teachers voiced the need to use multiple teaching methods to intro-duce and reinforce science concepts. Other suggestions offered included the maintenance of a "safe classroom environment" so that all learners, particularly those students who learned in ways different from the majority, could feel comfortable with taking part in and making contributions to class activities. We were pleased to note that portfolio assessment was also offered as an inclusive teaching practice. Several individuals from all sec-tions explained that this form of assessment helped to remove the compet-itive nature of traditional grading measures and allowed all students to recognize individual achievements made throughout the year.

Although these teaching strategies reflected increased reflection and the beginning of thoughtful pedagogical practices, we were uncomfort-able with what was missing. For example, in addition to modifying teaching strategies to address student diversity, we had anticipated that students would recognize the need for curricular changes in their inclu-sive classrooms. For instance, how can the selection of science topics and multiple methods of presentation affect the learning of students of diverse backgrounds? Our students, however, rarely acknowledged the need for such considerations. Instead, they continually responded to the diverse needs and abilities in their classrooms with isolated teaching strategies. We came to realize that our students were searching for what we understood as "band-aids," isolated solutions to individual symptoms, rather than embedded cures aimed at resolving fundamental problems.

Our preservice teachers' technical conception of teaching was in con-trast to the broader, more reflective conception of teaching that we had hoped to foster. But, as discussed by Moje (chapter 5), gaining a reflective approach to the practice of teaching is a difficult skill, both for our stu-dents and for ourselves as course instructors. As Feiman-Nemser and Remillard (1996) insightfully point out, learning to teach does not begin when a preservice teacher enters a teacher education program. Instead, teachers bring with them a lifetime of historically and culturally situated knowledge about what it means to know, to learn, and to teach. In our sci-ence classes, one aspect of this culturally situated knowledge was the teacher candidates' positivistic, technical view of teaching. This positivis-tic view shaped their understandings of and expectations for teaching. Thus, identifying acceptable solutions became far more important than understanding the dimensions of the problem.

## SUGGESTIONS FOR ADDRESSING
## INCLUSION IN A SCIENCE
## METHODS COURSE

As science educators, we are dedicated to the discussion of inclusive education issues within the content of a science methods course. Without such an emphasis, how can we ever hope to educate teachers who have a commitment to and understanding of what it means to teach science for all? From the outset, we designed our course to help students examine reflectively the practice of inclusive science teaching. In particular, through our use of teaching cases, we hoped that the preservice teachers would go beyond the individual concrete teaching accounts to construct a generalized knowledge that could be applied in their own specific, contextual situations (Kowalski, Weaver, & Henson, 1990). Based on our assessment of the preservice teachers' written work and their conceptions of teaching and learning that were portrayed in classroom discussions, we feel that we partially achieved these goals. However, the *partial* aspect of our assessment requires discussion. So, we conclude this chapter with a reflection on our findings and suggestions for curriculum development in science methods classes. This discussion focuses on the issues of teacher development, the conflict between the demands of the content and the use of cases, and programmatic concerns related to the placement and reinforcement of inclusive teaching strategies.

### Teacher Development

As mentioned previously, the adaptation plans included in our preservice teachers' lesson plans indicated movement toward a broadening conception of diverse student populations and specific instructional methods to attend to this diversity. However, this movement did not carry through to the unit plans, which often revealed less reflection than we had hoped for. This finding is consistent with other studies of teacher development (Dana & Dana, 1995; Feiman-Nemser & Buchmann, 1986; Paine, 1989). Although our preservice teachers voiced commitments to inclusive science education, perhaps they had maximized the movement they could make at this point in their development as teachers. In temporal portraits of learning to teach, Feiman-Nemser and Remillard (1996) argue that different forms of knowledge are valued at different phases of learning to teach. This is echoed by Hollingsworth (1989), who noted that preservice teachers are concerned primarily with issues of classroom management.

Only after achieving a level of comfort in this area can they begin to attend to general concerns of pedagogy and content. Using this line of reasoning, while preservice teachers may become aware of the differences in their students, they are not yet capable of fully attending to the specifics of how this diversity can be addressed, that is, how the quality of learning can be enhanced for everyone through the purposeful selection of the content and teaching strategies (Lacey, 1977; McDermott, Gormley, Rothenberg, & Hammer, 1995).

## Demands of Content and the Use of Cases

The curriculum we have described represents a substantial change from that which we used in the first year of field testing. Our initial attempts included a greater emphasis on the use of cases and case writing. This resulted in disappointment, as our preservice teachers perceived our focus to be on inclusion rather than on science teaching methods. As course instructors, we understood our focus to be on methods for inclusive science teaching. These differing perceptions were never fully resolved during the first year, potentially fostering a negative attitude toward inclusion by our preservice teachers (Southerland & Gess-Newsome, 1996). Based on our early efforts, we restructured the curriculum to use cases as just one of the many ways we talked about inclusion.

We feel the need to bring to light this curricular revision and its role in fostering positive student attitudes, and to note the tension between the demands of pedagogy and those of content that may occur in preservice science methods courses. As mentioned previously, most preservice teachers enter our classes with a positivistic, technical approach to teaching. This approach shapes their desire for content, including knowledge of teaching strategies for specific concepts. While our instructional goal may be to push our students toward reflective practice, their need for specific technical strategies must not be ignored. We suggest that the issue of inclusion, even when couched in the very situated world of teaching cases, must be taught within the context of science content and teaching methods if preservice teachers are to be moved toward an understanding of inclusive science teaching. We will elaborate on this point in the next section.

Unfortunately, there is a paucity of science-based cases that focus on any teaching issue, and far fewer that illuminate issues of inclusive science instruction. While the very local aspect of our students' cases proved to be pedagogically fruitful, better crafted cases are needed. Because issues of inclusion are inherently complex, and because teaching cases are ideally suited to address complex, situated, highly contextual issues, we suggest that there needs to be a concentrated effort to increase the number of inclusive, science-based teaching cases.

## Programmatic Concerns

Based on our efforts, we have a renewed appreciation of the complexity of both inclusive education and teacher education. Given what is known about teacher development, we believe that as science educators we can successfully introduce preservice teachers to the goals of inclusive teaching and encourage them to become reflective teachers; however, we must recognize that our preservice science methods courses represent only an introduction to these goals and skills. We suggest that issues of inclusion must be integrated across the whole of the elementary teacher education curriculum if recognizable impacts are to be realized. Inclusive education needs to be a cornerstone in what and how all prerequisite and content area methods courses are organized and taught. We feel it is important that issues of inclusion be given a programmatic rather than course-specific orientation.

Part of this programmatic goal should be to ensure that each of the content area methods courses reinforces and attends to issues of inclusion as they relate to a specific subject area. Science methods instructors, however, may encounter issues that other methods instructors may not face. Preservice teachers not only have limited backgrounds in science and a fear of the content, but few enter the field of elementary education with the assumption that they will be responsible for teaching science. This ambivalent-to-negative view of science and its role in the elementary classroom can be contrasted with preservice teacher's views toward reading and mathematics. Whether or not they are enthusiastic about teaching these subjects, preservice elementary teachers see reading and mathematics instruction as an integral part of their ongoing responsibilities. In content areas such as science, preservice teachers may need to overcome affective as well as content knowledge barriers as they prepare to become teachers. Confronting issues of inclusion on top of these other overwhelming and very real obstacles may place more demands on many preservice teachers than they are able to adequately address in the confines of one science methods course.

Based upon our observations, it is important that students become immersed in the content area they are to teach and become comfortable with writing and teaching lesson plans in this content area prior to the focus on issues of inclusion. We feel that students must personally recognize the need for adaptations related to inclusion before they can value the issues raised while attempting to teach science to all students. Our own efforts and past research demonstrate that such recognition of the needs of individual students comes only after more immediate concerns of management, content, and general pedagogical strategies are met. While all our goals for inclusive science education may not have been completely met in this elementary methods course, positive gains towards recognizing and meeting the needs for teaching science for all were achieved. We must recognize the challenges presented by inclusive education in our own teaching, as well as the teaching of our preservice teachers. As Fran reminds us in this chapter's opening quote: "[Science for all students:] It's a goal . . . [and] as a goal it means that we should actually be taking steps to go toward it." Hopefully, our experiences in helping our preservice teachers recognize and attend to the needs of their diverse student populations act as our initial step toward achieving the goal of inclusive science education for all.

# REFERENCES

American Association for the Advancement of Science (AAAS). (1989). *Science for all Americans: Project 2061*. New York: Oxford University Press.

Birrell, J. R. (1995). Learning how the game is played: An ethnically encapsulated beginning teacher's struggle to prepare black youth for a white world. *Teaching and Teacher Education, 11*, 137–47.

Dana, T. M., & Dana, N. F. (1995, April). *A look at cases in the development of reflective practice: A case study of prospective teachers of elementary school science*. Paper presented at the annual meeting of the National Association for Research in Science Teaching, San Francisco, CA.

Doyle, W. (1990). Case methods in the education of teachers. *Teacher Education Quarterly, 17(1)*, 7–15.

Feiman-Nemser, S., & Buchmann, M. (1986). *When is student teaching teacher education?* Research Series No. 178. East Lansing, MI: National Center for Research on Teacher Learning.

Feiman-Nemser, S., & Remillard, J. (1996). Perspectives on learning to teach. In F. B. Murray (Ed.), *The teacher educator's handbook* (pp. 63–92). San Francisco: Jossey-Bass.

Goldberg, M., & Harfey, J. (1983) A nation at risk: The report of the National Commission on Excellence in Education. *Phi Delta Kappan, 65(1)*, 14–18.

Grossman, P. (1992). Teaching and learning with cases. In J. Shulman (Ed.), *Case methods in teacher education* (pp. 227–239). New York: Teachers College Press.

Harrington, H. (1995). Fostering reasoned decisions: Case-based pedagogy and the professional development of teachers. *Teaching and Teacher Education, 11*, 203–214.

Hollingsworth, S. (1989). Prior belief and cognitive change in learning to teach. *American Education Research Journal, 26*, 160–189.

Kowalski, T. J., Weaver, R. A., & Henson, K. T. (1990). *Case studies on teaching*. New York: Longman.

Lacey, C. (1977). *The socialization of teachers*. London: Methuen.

Matthews, M. R. (Ed.) (1997). Philosophy and constructivism in science education [Special issue]. *Science and Education, 6(1/2)*.

McDermott, P., Gormley, K., Rothenberg, J., & Hammer, J. (1995). The influence of classroom practica experiences on student teachers' thoughts about teaching. *Journal of Teacher Education, 4,* 184–191.

Moje, E. B., Remillard, J. T., Southerland, S. A., & Wade, S. E. (1999). Researching case pedagogies to inform our teaching. In M. Lundeberg, B. Levin, & H. Harrington (Eds.), *Who learns what from cases and how? The research base for teaching with cases.* (pp. 73–94) Mahwah, NJ: Lawrence Erlbaum Associates.

National Research Council. (1996). *National science education standards.* Washington, DC: National Academy Press.

Nix, D., & Spiro, R. (Eds.). (1990). *Cognition, education, and multimedia.* Hillsdale, NJ: Lawrence Erlbaum Associates.

O'Loughlin, M. (1992). Rethinking science education: Beyond Piagetian constructivism toward a sociocultural model of teaching and learning. *Journal of Research in Science Teaching, 29,* 791–820.

Paine, L. (1988). *Prospective teachers' orientations toward diversity.* Paper presented at the Annual Meeting of the American Educational Research Association, New Orleans, LA.

Sibbett, J. (1997). *Reflection in practice: An exploratory study of student teacher reflection.* Unpublished doctoral dissertation, University of Utah, Salt Lake City, UT.

Shulman, L. S. (1992). Toward a pedagogy of cases. In J. Shulman (Ed.), *Case methods in teacher education* (pp. 1–30). New York: Teachers College Press.

Southerland, S. A., & Gess-Newsome, J. (1996, April). *Using cases of inclusion in an elementary science methods course.* Paper presented at the annual meeting of the American Educational Research Association, New York.

Swanson, H. L., O'Connor, J. E., & Cooney, J. B. (1990). An information processing analysis of expert and novice teachers' problem solving. *American Educational Research Journal, 27(3),* 533–556.

Sykes, G., & Bird, T. (1992). Teacher education and the case idea. In G. Grant (Ed.), *Review of research in education* (Vol. 18, pp. 457–521). Washington, DC: American Educational Research Association.

# 5

# Using Cases of Inclusion in a Content Literacy Methods Course

*Elizabeth B. Moje*

> I think it's good that you are using the type of case where it's a special education student in a regular classroom because there are few chances for special educators to interact with regular educators. So I think this was great as a special educator, and I'd like to thank you for that. (Chuck)

I had been struggling for several years to integrate discussions of students' diverse talents and needs into my secondary content literacy methods courses for preservice teachers, so this comment from Chuck, a special education major in my content literacy methods course, was especially important to me. How had we been able to achieve such a conversation between general and special educators in my class? It began with a project funded by the Joseph P. Kennedy, Jr. Foundation to develop, use, and study case-based curricula designed to prepare preservice teachers for inclusive education. I was interested in participating in the project because I had read a great deal about the case method and had wanted to try using a case-based curriculum for several years. Moreover, I had never been comfortable with my efforts to incorporate special needs and inclusion issues into my literacy courses. This seemed like the perfect opportunity to enhance my teaching and my students' learning.

## THE POTENTIAL OF CASE PEDAGOGY IN LITERACY TEACHER EDUCATION

In recent years, a variety of pedagogies have been advanced for the purpose of highlighting the complexity of classrooms and schools, while also capitalizing on the socially constructed understandings that teachers bring to and develop within teacher education courses. Because theorists and researchers are beginning to understand literacy as a complex sociocultural construction, it makes sense to use methods that highlight the situated nature of teaching and learning in literacy teacher education courses. Teaching cases can be used in a course on theories of literacy development, for example, to foster discussion about the many ways in which people can be considered literate and can learn to be literate. In elementary literacy methods courses, cases can reveal the complexity of teaching literacy processes to young children. Such cases would highlight the importance of various reading and writing processes, such as decoding, comprehension, and composing, while also revealing the critical nature of the classroom context and social interaction as conditions for optimal literacy learning (cf. Cambourne & Turbill, 1987). In secondary literacy course work, teaching cases can be helpful for examining how the context of secondary schools, with literacy learning tied to disciplines, shapes literacy teaching. In addition, secondary literacy cases can highlight how adolescents begin to use literacy to carve out social and academic spaces for themselves.

Few instances of the use of teaching cases in teacher education course work, especially in literacy courses, have been described in the literature. Although I have used teaching cases in both elementary or secondary literacy courses, in this chapter I focus on their use in a secondary content literacy course. Secondary preservice teachers' resistance to required literacy courses is well documented (Holt-Reynolds, 1992; O'Brien, 1988; Stewart, 1990), making an examination of innovative methods in such a course especially compelling. My specific objectives in writing this chapter are (a) to present a description of the development and use of teaching cases as a model for using cases, (b) to illustrate how cases can be used to integrate issues of inclusive education into the discussion of content literacy, and (c) to provide documentation and analysis of students' responses to cases and of their thinking about teaching.

The data upon which the chapter is constructed are drawn from a variety of sources. First, during each case discussion, I tape recorded the interaction among students as they discussed the case events and their analysis of the case. Second, at the end of each case discussion, I led a debriefing session with my students in which I asked them to reflect on what they felt was useful about the case and case discussion and to offer suggestions for improvement. Third, after the case discussion sessions, I met with a teaching peer (and the editor of this volume), Suzanne Wade, who had observed the class. During our discussions, we focused on what I thought went well and what I would like to change. She asked probing questions that stimulated my thinking and also offered suggestions or insights from her perspective on the discussion. Fourth, following these sessions, I listened to audiotapes of the case discussions as prompts of the class events, and I recorded my observations as field notes. Finally, I interviewed students after the completion of the course. These interviews took the form of (a) focus group interviews, in which groups of three to five individuals responded to my semi-structured interview protocol (cf. Patton, 1990); and (b) individual interviews, which I held with selected individuals after the focus group interviews were complete.

## CONTEXT OF THE COURSE

"Content Area Literacy" for secondary education majors is a course offered at the University of Utah, which is located in Salt Lake City, a large metropolitan area (population over 1,000,000). Utah is populated primarily by people of European American, American Indian, and Latino/a descent. Many Salt Lake City community members are also recent immigrants from Southeast Asia and the Pacific islands.

The 3-credit-hour, 10-week content literacy course is required for certification of secondary education students in all content areas, including special education. Most of the students who enroll in the course are preservice teachers who represent a mixture of undergraduate and master's degree students, although some are nontraditional students and teachers seeking a second certification. The student population of this class was comprised primarily of European Americans. However, the group included one African-American student, one Chinese student, and one Eastern-European (Azerbaijianian) student. Most of the 30 students were in their mid- to late twenties, with 11 students over the age of 30. One student already possessed a degree in elementary education, and the student from Azerbaijian was a 17-year teaching veteran in her home country who needed to take the class to obtain teaching certification in Utah. The students represented a variety of content areas, including art, biological and physical sciences, dance, English literature and composition, foreign languages, history, and mathematics.

I am a teacher with 16-dated years of teaching experience in diverse elementary, secondary, adult, and postsecondary settings. At the time of this course, I had taught the content literacy course, in various iterations, 10 times over the course of my postsecondary teaching career. The course I write about in this chapter represented my first experience with using formal teaching cases and structured case discussions. Since then, I have used teaching cases in other literacy courses. (Recommendations at the end of the chapter are based on the data gathered in this course and my experiences and reflections since then.)

I built the content literacy course around five case sessions, four of which were case discussions. In the fifth case experience, the preservice teachers in the course wrote their own case reports, based on their field experiences. In this chapter, I focus on how I used three cases on inclusion, which appear in *Inclusive Education*—"Reading in Biology Class" (case 7), "When She's Ready, She'll Catch Up" (case 8), and "Conflicts in Collaboration" (case 14)—to introduce important issues in the course. (Questions for discussion and activities I used are described in detail in the teaching notes section of this volume.) I also briefly discuss the preservice teachers' experiences with case writing. The chapter concludes with evaluation of and reflections on using cases in literacy classes.

## CASE DISCUSSIONS AND CASE WRITING

### "Reading in Biology Class"

I began the course with a discussion of "Reading in Biology Class." My purpose in using the case was to help students construct their own understandings of what literacy is and why it is important to content area teachers. In previous courses I had structured the first class period as an open discussion in which we tried to construct a definition of literacy. Along with our constructed definition, I usually tried to provide a rationale for why secondary content area teachers needed to concern themselves with literacy. Specifically, I wanted preservice teachers to know that, first, students need to learn the skills necessary for learning with texts. Second, many students have difficulty with reading and writing in content areas. For some, the difficulties stem from not having learned the skills for learning with texts. For others, the difficulties stem from a lack of background knowledge in the specific domain. And still other students struggle with making sense of new concepts that often seem isolated and disconnected from their current understandings of topics.

Because knowledge is domain specific, and teachers' and students' epistemological beliefs (Schommer, 1989) differ from one domain to another, content teachers are the appropriate individuals to help their students learn to extract information from texts or to construct meaningful texts that represent their thinking. The content teacher must provide opportunities for all students to interact with texts, whether in reading, writing, discussion, or critique. The content teacher must also have the skills to help students construct meaning as a result of their interactions with text. Content literacy strategies are designed to assist students who struggle to make sense of texts they are reading or writing, but content literacy strategies are also designed to encourage all students to move beyond the texts to construct meanings that connect with their own lives and experiences and to think critically about society and the world. Thus, a content literacy methods course is an appropriate site for conversations about inclusive education because one of its goals is to teach preservice (or inservice) teachers strategies that meet the needs of diverse readers, writers, and thinkers (Readence, Bean, & Baldwin, 1992).

By deciding to start the quarter with a teaching case instead of my usual discussion or presentation format, I was hoping that students would take control of a discussion about what literacy was and why it was important. Thus, my primary objective in using the case "Reading in Biology Class" was to stimulate a conversation about reading, writing, discussion, and critique as tools for students to use to learn content. Other objectives included (a) encouraging preservice teachers to examine their beliefs about appropriate or effective teaching by examining another teacher's beliefs, (b) stimulating discussion about whether students could and/or would read assigned texts or complete assigned writings, and (c) highlighting the diversity of students' needs and perspectives in secondary content area classrooms.

I introduced the case at the end of the first class period by asking students to read the case silently and then discuss in small groups the "Questions to Think About." To lead the case discussion during the next class meeting, I used a highly structured approach that requires students to understand the context of the case well by describing the setting, key players, and case events. This is especially helpful to students and instructors who are unfamiliar with case discussions.

Some of the students were more interested in analyzing events and motives than in describing the school, students, and teacher. Nevertheless, I believed that it was important to focus at this point on contextual information to help students think about differing interpretations of the case events. In some instances, students found that they had missed important information when reading the case; in other instances, they realized that they had all read the same words, but they had read from different perspectives and had constructed different interpretations of the same events. For example, in the excerpt that follows, students discussed what they thought the biology teacher in the case, Elizabeth, was thinking about her situation. Notice that each of the following students ("S"=student) focused on a different aspect of what the teacher was thinking as described in the case, and, as a result of the discussion, individual students may have become more aware of the different possibilities.

S1:   She was questioning.
S2:   Confused, and then questioning philosophy and methods.
S3:   She also justified to herself what she did, especially after she'd had observations [from principal and other teachers].
S4:   For the remainder of this teaching year she comes to the conclusion that she was right, her teaching method was fine, she doesn't need to change it. . . . In later years, in other subjects, these same questions come back to haunt her.
S5:   I think it may be important to mention that she justified herself because she used a lot of hands-on activities and experiences in the classroom.

The next portion of the case discussion ("Framing the Problem") was more open ended. I ("T" in the excerpt that follows) began with a question that asked students to evaluate the biology teacher's response to the student and parent in the case, and found that my subsequent questions could be interwoven in a more spontaneous way as the discussion progressed. Although some of the questions seemed redundant to me at times, new ideas emerged with each question I asked, resulting again in a variety of interpretations. In this excerpt, we see different interpretations regarding whether and why students read assigned texts in school—a basic issue in a secondary content literacy class.

T:     What do you think of the argument that students won't, can't, or don't read?

S1:    If they can get away with not reading, they will not read.

S2:    The teacher is totally responsible. The traditional method in teaching is that the student is supposed to sit there and receive instead of having the student be an active learner in the process . . . . There is no real motivation because the teacher is going to tell them what to read anyway.

S3:    I think everyone is being grossly stereotypical, because I had read my entire high school physics text by the end of the 2nd quarter of a 1-year class, and I cannot be the only student in the world who has ever read . . . . This is too all-encompassing. Not all students [will not read]; most, yes, but not all.

S4:    Even though we might be calling this an assumption, students don't read if they don't have to. This assumption is based in fact; the other teachers have observed that students don't read, that they just don't do it. So we can say that we are overgeneralizing, but that's what has happened in the past, so we are just going to keep going that way because of what has happened in the past?

Excerpts from the case discussion also illustrate how issues of inclusion were implicit in the discussion. We came back to these issues throughout the course. In the following excerpt, participants discuss how the teacher's perception of her students' abilities and interests shaped her pedagogy and how that pedagogy in turn shaped students' literacy practices.

T:     Why was the teacher resorting to what we call a pedagogy of telling, especially after she hears Larry saying, "Well, I've read the book"?

S1:    It kind of shows she was going on the assumption of this view of the lowest common denominator. In the classroom, Larry was bright and smart, and of course he read the book, but not all the other ones are as smart as Larry, so she is teaching to the lowest group.

S2:    The biggest thing is she comes back to the fact that the students have not shown her that they could learn from the book. Therefore, the material in the book was as low as they needed to know, because she had to just tell it to them. Some of them may have not gotten it because they didn't read. Some of them may have just not gotten it because they wouldn't have understood what they read.

As a conclusion to the case discussion, students participated in a role-playing activity designed to examine possible solutions to the problem in the case. Virtually all the groups offered a number of teaching and learning strategies, including teacher-modeled think-alouds, prediction activities, previewing the texts, and imaging.

## "When She's Ready, She'll Catch Up"

For the next class session after our discussion of "Reading in Biology Class," I asked students to read the case "When She's Ready, She'll Catch Up." I had several goals for using this case. First, I wanted to present a contrast between Larry, the student in the first case, who had read the assigned text chapters and wanted class activities to expand beyond the book, and Sue, a student who struggled to complete and make sense of assigned readings. I hoped that the contrast between the two cases would make my students more aware of the range of needs, talents, and experiences their students would bring to the classroom. Second, I wanted the class to analyze the solutions they had proposed for the biology teaching case in light of the needs of different students. What pedagogical strategies might they adopt to capitalize on students' needs and interests? Could these same strategies be used to meet the needs of all students? If so, how might they need to modify the strategies? How might they also modify their curricula or texts?

Third, I wanted to develop an awareness of the many different experiences people have as secondary school students. In the past, I had found that students in content literacy classes were good readers and had been successful in secondary school without being taught explicit strategies. As a consequence, they often viewed the strategies as burdensome. Many of them could not imagine that they might someday teach students who struggled with reading and writing. In addition, many content literacy students tended to focus on the content of their discipline, rather than on pedagogy designed to focus on students' needs, interests, and questions. This case, which illustrates a highly conscientious student who struggled with reading and writing, presented a new perspective on interacting with students in secondary school classrooms.

Finally, I wanted to encourage my students to think about issues of communication among students, parents, specialists, and colleagues. The many players in this case represented a range of perspectives; consequently, the case was an excellent way to teach my students to think about different perspectives and to communicate among many different groups.

The content literacy students read the case together with related text readings during the week between class meetings and came to class prepared to discuss it. As a class, we reconstructed the context of the case as students addressed questions about key players and about the teacher's philosophy and methods. As in the biology teaching case, this portion of the discussion was critical because students had many different interpretations of each character's perspective. For example, when responding to the question of what they knew about the history teacher from their reading of the case, the group offered these diverse perspectives:

S1:   From a special education point of view, I just see a teacher who is set in his ways . . . when one of his students is having difficulty. I think that the teacher should make a little bit more of an effort.

S2:   I wonder how aware the teachers really are of the extent of the problem because they all report that [Sue] is a very hard worker, participates fully. It's like almost that they are in denial. It sounds like they say, "Well, on the surface she seems to be performing pretty well."

Bringing out these many perspectives on the context of the case created a starting point for the discussion that followed. To initiate the discussion, I asked these questions:

1. What do you think are the important problems or key issues in the case?
2. Do you think Sue would see the problem the same way?

Students identified the main problem of the case in terms of Sue's struggles, but disagreed on who should be held responsible for them—the student, her mother, or her history teacher. Our discussion revolved around this question of responsibility, with the majority of preservice teachers assigning blame, or at least responsibility, to the teacher. The teacher was criticized as "traditional," "not interested in helping Sue beyond class time," and "lacking in knowledge of how to help Sue." For example, James stated:

My opinion is the real main problem with this case is that she's [Sue's] getting Cs on her work, the teacher knows there is a problem. He knows that she is not learning the material at the level she should be. So it's not a matter of him not realizing that she doesn't get it. He knows she's not getting it. He's just not willing to accommodate her learning disability by changing his teaching.

Although Sue's mother was discussed briefly—some students felt that she had perhaps exerted too much pressure on Sue or had done Sue a disservice by withdrawing her from the resource room—the primary focus of the discussion revolved around Sue and her history teacher.

Following the discussion, I presented students with five different scenarios for role playing. The scenarios presented questions for discussion based on the perspectives of one or two of the case characters. These scenarios encouraged the preservice teachers to take the perspective of a particular player in the case and to try to communicate with others represented in the case. After discussing the scenarios in small groups, volunteers from each group participated in one of two role plays: (a) Sue and her mother sharing their concerns with a new teacher Sue would have in another content area, and (b) two teachers consulting with the special education resource teacher for ideas about how they could meet all of their students' needs and interests. These role plays required the preservice teachers to think through various perspectives, to interact with people taking different perspectives, to discuss the application of literacy strategies in an inclusive setting, and to articulate their new understandings of literacy learning and teaching.[1]

## "Conflicts in Collaboration"

Throughout the quarter I felt like I was in a special education methods course; this class blended so well with my other classes, sometimes I'd forget that it wasn't a special education course. Everything came together and it was really nice. (Sharla, special education major)

Sharla made the comment just quoted after the discussion of the case "Conflicts in Collaboration." The case describes the challenges faced by a reading specialist as she attempted to collaborate with content area teach-

---

[1]In subsequent content literacy courses, my colleague Suzanne Wade has also used this case and has tried several variations on this role-playing arrangement. One particularly effective variation is a role play of a case management meeting involving Sue, Sue's mother, the history teacher, a speech and debate teacher, and the special education teacher, who serves as a facilitator of the meeting (see p. 182, this volume).

ers to teach literacy strategies in their classrooms. To set the stage for this case discussion, I asked four class members to take on the four characters in the case and to present a reader's theater, which I thought would be a novel way to present the case and to model the reader's theater strategy. The "actors" presented the reader's theater at the end of one class period; the rest of the students in the class read the formal case in its entirety during the next week.[2]

In our next class meeting we began with a discussion of the case, focusing first on the context. As in the previous case discussions, this discussion yielded many disagreements as students engaged in interpretation, evaluation, and critique of what they had read in the case. For example, in discussing one of the teachers in the case (John), the students had this conversation, which was initiated by James, a physics major:

S1: He doesn't follow one type of method or ideas that I've been approached with the entire time I've been learning about education. He just throws something out there. He doesn't seem to have a philosophy.

S2: Well, his philosophy is that the kids learn by hands-on approaches, so that's what they have to do to learn. The other stuff is just filler.

S3: He's a constructivist . . .

S1: Well, he isn't very good at it!

Because the character's teaching method did not fit with what James had learned about philosophies and methods in science teaching, James was ready to dismiss the character as having no teaching philosophy. The conversation may not have convinced James, as indicated by his final statement, "Well, he's not very good at [being a constructivist]"; nevertheless, the conversation brought multiple interpretations of the case teachers' philosophies and methods to light.

I then asked students to identify and explain what they saw as the main issue or problem in the case. One student immediately identified the central issue as one of inclusion versus noninclusion by stating, "None of the teachers wants these lower readers in their classes." Lisa, a general education English major and reading education minor, built on that statement by saying:

There seems to be an issue of to have or not to have inclusive education—whether to put those kids in the class or have them taken out

---

[2]For a variety of other activities, see the teaching notes for this case by David Dynak in Part II of this volume.

by the resource specialist. And then going back to the conflict of her ideal [taking certain kids out of class for resource] and the teachers wanting her ideal, but the school saying that they need to stay in.

One preservice teacher, Shalise (a general education art major), argued that this was a case of teacher resistance. She said that "the teachers aren't willing to share their ground with her. It's their ground and that's the way they are going to be. "Shalise did not think there was any way that the consulting teacher would ever be able to collaborate with teachers who were resistant to change. Vytas, a physical education and biology major, disagreed with Shalise. He believed that the consulting resource teacher portrayed in the case had not been open about her approach to collaboration:

> It seems to me that what Joan really has in mind to accomplish is to educate the teachers, and maybe she should just be doing that. If she feels that she can't accomplish her task by going one on one with the students, then I'm not exactly clear why she's going into this class for one day or for a week and then into another class. What is she going to accomplish doing that?

Staci, a special education preservice teacher, offered a political interpretation. She believed that the case was about the problems that occur when reforms are imposed on teachers as top-down mandates. Staci argued that because the principal had forced two of the teachers to participate, collaboration would be unlikely.

Although multiple interpretations were raised by several students, many did not seem to change their interpretation or make room for multiple factors to explain the case. Staci, for example, repeated her assertion about the case being "political" and about "the problem with top-down reform" three times throughout the course of the discussion. Similarly, Vytas and Shalise repeated their arguments multiple times. In fact, during the debriefing of the case discussion, Shalise complained that the case discussion was somewhat "tedious" because "we spent all this time discussing just so we could come to the conclusion that what I thought was the problem—teacher resistance—was the problem." This reveals a potential problem with the case discussions: It was sometimes a struggle to encourage the kind of dialogue that challenged students' deeply held beliefs. Shalise, for example, apparently failed to hear the different ideas raised by others in the class and felt that the discussion was simply time consuming and frustrating.

Following their discussion, I asked students to work in small groups to discuss their responses to an accompanying reading guide I had distributed the previous week. Afterward, we came back together in a whole-class discussion in which we talked about possible solutions to the problems highlighted in the case. In this final discussion, Chuck, a special education major, made a comment that indicates some of what this complex case discussion accomplished:

> I think the main problem is the way they collaborate. Collaboration doesn't mean the special educator going into the classroom and fixing it. It means as the special educator, you collaborate with the regular educator [to figure out] what both of you can do with the situation. . . . In terms of inclusion, inclusion basically is not a required law. If special educators take their students and throw them into a classroom and leave them there and then leave the classroom, the kids are going to fail. So they have to collaborate. They have to be in that classroom with the regular education teacher so they can provide services in the classroom to those kids.

## Case Writing

The final case experience in the content literacy class required that students write their own case reports based on their field teaching experience. I provided them with a case report format and some questions for reflection and analysis. Their assignment was to plan and teach at least one lesson and write a teaching case, using the teaching cases we had read throughout the quarter as models. In addition, I invited preservice teachers who had been content literacy students the previous quarter to visit our class and lead discussions on cases they had written about their teaching. Based on students' comments, this modeling appears to have been important to the students as they thought about the cases they were to write and about their teaching.

The case report writing proved to be a popular and valuable experience for the students. In both formal focus group interviews and in informal interviews, all students commented that the case writing was an important aspect of their teaching experience. The students I talked with asserted that the act of reflecting on the experience in writing taught them more about teaching than the experience of teaching did alone. One student, Kathy, reported in a postcourse interview that after she had taught the first of two sections of an English class, she asked herself, "What will I write in my teaching case about this lesson?" and "If I led a case discussion over this lesson, what would people say about my teaching?" As a result of her thinking about the case she would later write, Kathy changed her teaching for the next section.

Many of the students suggested that the case writing experience would have been more valuable had they been able to present their case reports to their peers in small-group discussions. In fact, I had planned to hold small-group discussions during the final exam period, but decided against such an activity at the end of the quarter, thinking that the students were emotionally and physically exhausted at that point. Several of them expressed disappointment during the last class when I explained that I had decided to end the class session after they finished their portfolio evaluations. They wanted to talk about the cases they had written, and several have volunteered to present their cases for discussion in my future sections of this course.

## EVALUATING THE USE OF INCLUSION CASES IN CONTENT LITERACY

### Positive Outcomes of Using Inclusion Cases

The teaching cases provided a rich context that promoted discussion of content literacy and inclusion issues. The context of each case helped preservice teachers think about how the contexts of classrooms and schools are complex and how strategies and methods for effective teaching are complicated by the contexts in which they are used. Moreover, each case provided a thread that could be woven throughout the quarter. For example, when modeling the use of particular strategies, I could refer back to the biology case or the struggling student case to give students ideas about how these strategies could be used to benefit all students. In addition, the consulting teacher case provided a reference point for talking about collaboration, inclusion, teacher resistance, and the politics of schools and classrooms. It is especially beneficial that these points for discussion came from the preservice teachers themselves. Their concerns, interests, and issues were raised through case discussions, and as a result, I was able to gear my teaching about strategies toward concerns and issues they had raised and were interested in.

During the debriefing at the conclusion of each case discussion, I asked students to comment on the cases and on the structure of the case discussions. In general, the students valued the cases because they described real teaching events. Ted, an English major, shared this comment:

> I think it's a really good way to talk about theories, philosophies, some of these terms that we have in real-life settings so that they have practicality. . . . For example, it's sometimes difficult to envision metacognition when you read about it, but when you think about it in terms of a real biology class, it makes a little bit more sense.

Many of the students agreed that reading the cases helped them make sense of the course text. Several of them claimed that they could see the reason for a class on literacy in the content areas after having read the first two cases and the first two chapters of the course text. One student commented that the case "helped us think about different strategies that we could use." Other students linked their reading of the case to their reading of the course textbook: "[The case] helped me read the chapters in the course text because I had a context for thinking about the ideas and strategies." A student who was new to the field expanded on this idea by asserting that, "I couldn't have understood the course text without the cases." Kathy, another English major, stated:

> I don't know if the other cases that we might be covering are going to be discussing problems, but I think it's very helpful to be able to watch something explode and backfire without having to suffer the consequences. We can see a problem and really get in and analyze it and realize, "Oh, that's why it happened." I think it's valuable to be able to do those kind of non-contact things.

Perhaps because the cases provided a rich context for thinking about teaching and learning literacy, students were highly engaged during the case discussion. According to my records, every student in the class made at least one comment in one of the four case discussions, and many students made several contributions during each discussion. In addition, the nature of the case discussion called for extensive small-group work, which allowed for even greater participation on the part of all students. Although attendance and engagement in class cannot be explained solely by the use of cases, it is important to note that each class session was well attended, and the majority of the students were prepared in regard to reading the cases and preparing case notes when assigned. As one student commented, "Reading the cases is interesting because they're real. The text is dense and difficult to read, but the case is the real thing." The discussions in this class, whether case discussions or discussions about strategies or methods, were among the best I had participated in during the 10 times I had taught this course.

The following comment from Staci, a philosophy major, emphasizes the value of these excellent and engaged discussions by highlighting the diverse perspectives the students brought to their reading of the cases:

> In what we've done up here on the board [she gestured to the board, where the "Understanding the Context" case notes were written], I can look at that, and I can really see a construction of knowledge there, because there is much that is up there that flat was not in the reading. I think that's a very good thing because if we critically look at that we'll see there are our assumptions and stereotypes that we have, and we'll have an opportunity to critically examine those if we want to by putting stuff up on the board and letting our constructive models show.

Students also liked using role play and reader's theater activities because, as Wendy stated, "That way we got different perspectives, and it made more sense watching somebody than just writing it on the board." During an in-class debriefing, one student suggested that the reader's theater was helpful because it "created a sort of picture in my mind as I went back through and re-read the text. It was much easier reading because I could kind of visualize it." Students also suggested that it might be useful to extend the reader's theater by having participants work in groups to take on the different perspectives:

> I think if we would extend the reader's theater to a role play, what we might see is how people communicate or just the basis of the problem, and I think that exposes a lot of things. . . . I had to play the part of the special educator [in the "When She's Ready" role play], and it was very difficult. I had no idea, and I was scared, but when I did it, it was basic communication, and it seemed like it was successful because of that, and I think we need to remember that, before all of these strategies and things, we are people, and that without being a successful communicator, you won't be able to do anything.

The cases of inclusion also helped me integrate issues of special education into my content literacy methods class in ways that I had not been able to do previously. In the past, my treatment of issues in special education consisted mainly of an assignment to read the chapter in the course text on students with special needs, combined with a lecture and discussion on aspects of collaboration. As illustrated by both Chuck's comment (which opened this chapter) and Sharla's comment during the discussion of "On Becoming a Consulting Teacher," our discussion of students' needs was woven throughout the quarter. Furthermore, the cases provided a site for conversation between the general and special educators in the class. Although the special education teachers were the most vocal in expressing their interest in such conversations, the general education teachers echoed their comments. Specifically, they raised questions about how to go about meeting the needs of all of their students, and they shared their fears that they would not be able to reach many of their students because of the increasing diversity of public school classrooms. It could be argued that using a case like this developed "intersubjectivity," or shared understandings (Rogoff, 1990), among the preservice teachers.

Finally, the teaching cases provided a model of reflection that students rarely witness but are often asked to replicate. In recent years, researchers and theorists in teacher education have suggested that prospective and practicing teachers should be taught to reflect on their practice (cf. Grimmett & MacKinnon, 1992; Schon, 1987). Reflective thinking, however, is difficult to learn; preservice and practicing teachers need models to help them think about practice. To my surprise, when asked during the focus group and individual interviews which case had made the most impact on their learning about teaching, all but one preservice teacher responded that the cases they had written themselves had influenced their learning the most. They only regretted that we did not have more time for them to share their cases with one another. Based on the students' responses to case writing, I suggest that the cases stimulated ways of thinking about teaching that other kinds of course work experiences do not stimulate.

Although these student comments indicate that students were enthusiastic about the case pedagogy, a subsequent analysis of data collected during and after the course revealed that, though the case pedagogy was successful in many ways, students also maintained several assumptions about teaching, learning, ability, and knowledge that are troubling and that need to be considered as teacher educators develop case pedagogies. In the next section, I highlight the concerns I had about my case pedagogy based on what we learned about the preservice teachers' thinking about teaching and learning (cf. Moje & Wade, 1997).

## Concerns About Case Pedagogy
## and Teacher Thinking

My colleague, Suzanne Wade, and I conducted a study of the use of cases in this class (Moje & Wade, 1977). The study, which was guided by sociocultural theory, examined students' talk to reveal their thinking about teaching. We asked three research questions, drawn from questions suggested by Sykes and Bird (1992):

1. What mediational tools and processes of reasoning do pre- and inservice teachers employ in dealing with cases?
2. What range of issues do cases raise for them?
3. What images of teaching do they derive from various case materials and case discussions?

Our findings indicate that these students, who were, with two exceptions, preservice teachers, used a number of different tools to make sense of the cases. In particular, they used (a) their experiences as students, (b) theories and texts from their university education, and (c) assigned role-playing activities that encouraged them to take other perspectives. In addition, the cases themselves served as tools for helping the preservice teaching students think about teaching.

We also found that the students constructed images and issues of teaching that reflected a technical approach to teaching. When we use the phrase "teaching as technical," we mean that students saw teaching as a matter of applying strategies to student problems, rather than as viewing students' needs and interests in relation to the context of schools and classrooms. This technical approach suggests an understanding of teaching that was devoid of an awareness of social and contextual constraints on teachers' work. Despite our intention to use cases to illustrate the complicated and complex nature of teaching and classrooms, and despite the students' talk about constructivist theory and diversity, we found that they wanted simply to find and apply solutions to the issues raised in the cases.

We also found that these students talked about the knowledge represented in the curriculum and texts as fixed, rather than relative, fluid, or changeable, a finding consistent with other studies of teacher thinking (cf. Lortie, 1975; Richardson, 1995), and one that we believe is related to the technical image of teaching that these students held. They did not question the knowledge upon which their curricula were based, nor did they seek to restructure that knowledge. In fact, even though many of them argued for a constructivist theory of learning, little in their talk suggested that they saw knowledge as a construction, either social or individual. Specifically, when arguing for more active approaches to learning, the students' talk betrayed beliefs about knowledge that signified transmission. Their arguments for involving students in more active inquiry experiences often appeared to stem more from the purpose of motivating students—and thus solving management concerns—than from the idea that knowledge is socially constructed and that learning is an act of constructing knowledge.

Similarly, the students in both groups also talked about their students' abilities and needs as innate and fixed, rather than malleable and learned. Our findings indicate that these students viewed ability as an individual construct that is psychologically or physiologically determined and unresponsive to attempts to change or develop it. This view of ability seemed to be related to the students' images of literacy strategies as technical solutions for dealing with their students' diverse abilities.

A last finding relates to issues of diversity and inclusion. Although these students highlighted the diverse nature of classrooms, the diversity revolved around ability, rather than sociocultural differences. The teachers raised no questions about possible connections between assumptions about students' abilities and needs and assumptions about ethnicity, class, or gender, even though many of the students had previously taken courses that focused on these issues.

Although a number of these findings are supported by the findings of others who have studied teacher thinking (Grossman, 1992; Kagan, 1992; Lortie, 1975; Richardson, 1995), Suzanne and I were troubled by the extent to which these students appeared to view teaching as a technical act; their students as mainstream, White, middle-class beings; and literacy strategies as "props" to help students achieve success within the limitations of their fixed abilities and the curriculum. These findings suggest that teaching cases and case pedagogies do not represent cure-alls for difficult issues in teacher preparation. Because the assumptions that students expressed about knowledge, ability, and literacy learning reflect assumptions embedded in the university and the schools—as well as in the larger, meritocratic institutions of schooling and society—we must ask how teacher educators might use cases differently to challenge such assumptions. Specifically, what aspects of case pedagogy could help bring to the fore conceptions of knowledge and ability as relative and changing, and how might teacher educators encourage teachers to examine assumptions about relationships between knowledge or ability and ethnicity, class, or gender? In the next section, I address these questions as I offer suggestions for using teaching cases in different ways based on my experience with this and other courses.

## Changes in My Case Pedagogy

Based on students' feedback, subsequent experience with case pedagogies, and our research findings,[3] I have made several changes to the case curriculum in the content literacy methods course. First, I now model and deconstruct literacy strategies directly after case discussions when motivation is high and direct connections can be made. Modeling various strategies gives the students experience with the strategies and provides a further context (beyond the case) for thinking about the complexities of classrooms and schools that make teaching more than a technical act of applying a strategy to a problem. This thinking about complexities will not occur without guidance, however. It is important to deconstruct the strategy, asking students to talk about how the strategy met their needs for a particular situation, but also how it may have overlooked or even masked some of their interests, questions, or struggles. Such a change in the pedagogy helps to move students beyond the thinking that literacy strategies can serve as props to help secondary school students keep up in school. Instead, preservice teachers are challenged to realize that their job may not be to change the students, but rather to change the strategies they use to meet different students' needs.

Similarly, I now also focus on how teachers might assess and modify their *curricula* and *texts* in addition to adding pedagogical strategies to their repertoires. Although I did not realize it during the actual case discussion, our analysis illustrates that when discussing "When She's Ready, She'll Catch Up," my students seemed to think that the solution to Sue's struggles was to provide props to help her meet an unchangeable curriculum (cf. Moje & Wade, 1997). The findings suggest that I should have asked my students to consider whether what Sue was being asked to learn was important. In addition, I should have encouraged them to think about whether the strategies they suggested (e.g., having Larry read the chapter

---

[3]It is worth noting that most of the suggestions for change in this section stem from the findings of my research on the uses of cases in this class. Although I do not recommend that all teacher educators conduct systematic research of all classes they teach, I do urge teacher educators to, whenever possible, conduct debriefings with classes, tape and transcribe class discussions, and conduct informal focus-group interviews at the completion of a course.

to Sue) would really help to develop independence and critical thinking in Sue. A focus on what changes might be necessary in the curriculum or in the texts being used moves the emphasis away from changing students or from supplying strategies.

To facilitate the discussion of these critical issues about knowledge, ability, curricula, and texts, it is important to vary the approach one takes to structuring and facilitating case discussions. Because my students and I were new to the art of case discussion, we started with the structured approach described in this chapter. As I have become more comfortable with case discussions, I have moved toward less structured approaches, beginning with the question, "What is this a case of?" or "What do you see as the central issues or problems in this case?" Rather than maintaining one format for all discussions, I now decide what approach to use on a case-by-case basis. I assess which approach fits the content and form of the case I'm using and which approach meets my teaching objectives most appropriately. I think carefully about my purpose and what I hope to achieve with each case, both as I select cases and as I plan the case discussions or activities.

More important, based on my experience that students often did not listen carefully to the ideas of others, I now include a discussion of what it means to engage in a dialogue, and I ask students to analyze their own dialogues. The advantage of engaging in an explicit discussion about dialogue goes beyond improving dialogue among students in a content literacy methods course; these explicit discussions of dialogue also have the potential to help students think about how they can have productive and dialogic discussions with their future secondary students.

I also suggest using videotaped cases (cf. Sykes & Bird, 1992) as a way of drawing students' attention to diversity. As noted previously, our students tended to assume White, middle-class teachers and students as they read and discussed the cases (Moje & Wade, 1997). They also made assumptions about gender. Thus, I believe that our preservice student teachers may need to be visually confronted with the diversity in classrooms (cf. Eisner, 1994) if we hope to push them to think about how teachers' assumptions about ethnicity, class, or gender may shape teachers' thinking about students' abilities or literacy practices. In addition, actually watching adolescents experimenting with different kinds of social practices—that is, seeing the nature and depth of student underlife in classrooms—may enrich case discussions.

A final recommendation that I would make for a case-based curriculum stems from the case writing aspect of the class. To strengthen the benefits of the case writing activities, I provide more guidance for writing cases—while also modeling a modified writer's workshop approach—and I build in more opportunities for class members to debrief cases with one another while they are writing and after they have completed their case writing. To highlight issues of inclusion, I ask case writers to pay special attention to the context section of their cases, highlighting the different experiences, interests, needs, and talents their students bring to the classroom. Similarly, case writers should be asked to weave that diversity into their treatment of case events and reflections on the case. Asking students to focus on the many forms of diversity in their own field settings may stimulate discussions about how literacy practices are related to students' race, class, and gender, while also emphasizing how assumptions about ability may be confounded by assumptions about race, class, and gender.

In summary, I found teaching cases and case discussions to be powerful pedagogy. The discussion of cases highlighted the complex sociocultural situation of teaching and learning. Cases encouraged my secondary content literacy students to think about how literacy can take many different forms, how literacy is a part of all learning settings, regardless of discipline, and why we need to help secondary students negotiate texts. Moreover, teaching cases can be used productively in both literacy methods courses and literacy theory courses, as well as in elementary or secondary level courses. Like Levin (1995), I have found that good case discussions are critical components of case pedagogy, and I strongly suggest incorporating case writing as a way to help students reflect on their teaching and begin to engage in dialogue with their teaching peers.

# REFERENCES

Cambourne, B., & Turbill, J. (1987). *Coping with chaos.* Portsmouth, NH: Heinemann.

Eisner, E. (1994). *Cognition and curriculum reconsidered* (2nd ed.). New York: Teachers College Press.

Grimmett, P. P., & MacKinnon, A. M. (1992). Craft knowledge and the education of teachers. In G. Grant (Ed.), *Review of research in education* (pp. 385–453). Washington, DC: American Educational Research Association.

Grossman, P. (1992). Why models matter: An alternate view on professional growth in teaching. *Review of Educational Research, 62,* 171–179.

Holt-Reynolds, D. M. (1992). Personal history-based beliefs as relevant prior knowledge in course work. *American Educational Research Journal, 29,* 325–349.

Kagan, D. M. (1992). Professional growth among preservice and beginning teachers. *Review of Educational Research, 62,* 129–169.

Levin, B. B. (1995). Using the case method in teacher education: The role of discussion and experience in teachers' thinking about cases. *Teaching and Teacher Education, 11,* 63–79.

Lortie, D. (1975). *Schoolteacher: A sociological study.* Chicago: University of Chicago Press.

Moje, E. B., & Wade, S. E. (1997). What case discussions reveal about teacher thinking. *Teaching and Teacher Education, 13,* 691–712.

O'Brien, D. G. (1988). Secondary preservice teachers' resistance to content reading instruction: A proposal for a broader rationale. In J. E. Readence & R. S. Baldwin (Eds.), *Dialogues in literacy research* (pp. 237–243). Chicago: National Reading Conference.

Patton, M. Q. (1990). *Qualitative evaluation and research methods.* Newbury Park, CA: Sage.

Readence, J. R., Bean, T. W., & Baldwin, R. S. (1992). *Content area reading: An integrated approach* (4th ed.). Dubuque, IA: Kendall/Hunt.

Richardson, V. (1995, April). *Teacher education: Research and policy.* Keynote address presented at the annual meeting of the National Reading Conference, New Orleans, LA.

Rogoff, B. (1990). *Apprenticeship in thinking: Cognitive development in social context.* New York: Oxford.

Schommer, M. (1989). *Students' beliefs about the nature of knowledge: What are they and how do they affect comprehension?* (Tech. Rep. No. 484). Urbana, IL: Center for the Study of Reading.

Schon, D. (1987). *Educating the reflective practitioner.* San Francisco: Jossey-Bass.

Shor, I., & Freire, P. (1987). What is the "dialogical" method of teaching? *Journal of Education 169*(3), 11–31.

Stewart, R. A. (1990). Factors influencing preservice teachers' resistance to content reading instruction. *Reading Research and Instruction, 29,* 55–63.

Sykes, G. & Bird, T. (1992) Teacher education and the case idea. In G. Grant (Ed.), *Review of research in education* (Vol. 18, pp. 457–521). Washington, DC: American Educational Research Association.

# II

# TEACHING NOTES
# FOR THE CASES IN
# *INCLUSIVE EDUCATION:*

# *A Casebook and Readings
for Prospective
and Practicing Teachers*

# Case 1

# One Parent's Struggle
# for Inclusion

## *Staff*

## SYNOPSIS OF THE CASE

Written from a parent's perspective, this case chronicles a mother's efforts
to secure an inclusive program for her adopted son Reed, who has Down
syndrome. It describes Reed's early childhood educational experiences,
his experiences at a neighborhood school where inclusion is attempted,
and his involvement in his community. The focus is on the parental role in
promoting, shaping, and coping with the attitudes and expectations of
those who work with children with disabilities in different contexts.
Specifically, the case describes the mother's search for an appropriate
inclusive setting for her son, the instructional issues that arise once Reed
is placed in a neighborhood school, some of the social issues that Reed
and his parents have faced, and how being part of a neighborhood school
has helped Reed learn to be part of the community.

# ISSUES IN THE CASE

*1. The Advantages of Inclusive Education from a Parent's Perspective.*
As participants in making placement decisions, many parents of children
with severe disabilities feel strongly that their children should be placed in
inclusive settings. This case examines some of the reasons such parents
are advocates of inclusion and the goals they may have for their children.
It also examines the role of parents as advocates for their children and
their roles in their children's IEP.

*2. Why Some Administrators and Teachers Might Be Resistant to
Inclusive Education.* In this case, we see some examples of administrators and teachers who were resistant to inclusive education because
of low or negative expectations, fears, and beliefs. Two common
beliefs illustrated in the case are that students with disabilities have to
"earn" their way into general education classrooms and that some
teachers and schools are not ready to include such students. The case
also describes some of the effects of different teachers' attitudes and
behaviors on children with disabilities, and how attitudes can change
with experience.

*3. What It Takes to Make Inclusion Work.* This case suggests some
of the things that are needed for inclusive education to be successful,
such as flexibility and specific adaptations in curriculum and assessment of students, as well as the view that parents and special educators
can be important resources, providing background information and
support.

*4. Other Issues:*

# QUESTIONS TO THINK ABOUT

*(These questions can be given to students prior to reading the case or to
small groups for review in class before the whole-class discussion.)*

1. What is this case about?
2. Why did Reed's mother want her son to be in an inclusive
   setting?

3. Why were some teachers and administrators opposed to the idea of having Reed in general education classes?

4. How did Reed's teachers adapt the curriculum and instruction to meet his needs?

## THE DISCUSSION OUTLINE

This discussion outline consists of three parts: understanding the context and key players in the case, framing the problem, and developing plans of action. These three headings can serve as main headings on the chalkboard for the purpose of recording students' comments during the discussion. Under each heading on the board, you might also have subheadings (e.g., under the heading, "Understanding the Context and Key Players," you might list "Reed," "Karen Hahne," "teachers and administrators"). In this section, we present one way to open the discussion, followed by questions you might ask during each segment of the discussion:

> The case you have just read chronicles a mother's efforts to secure an inclusive program for Reed, her adopted son with Down syndrome. Let's begin our discussion by talking about the context and the key players in the case.

### A. Understanding the Context and Key Players

- What does Karen, Reed's mother and the narrator of the case, tell us about Reed?
- What does she tell us about herself?
- Imagine that you are Reed's mother or father. What would be your goals for Reed? What kind of educational placement and support services would you want for Reed, and why? How do they compare with what Karen wanted?
- Think of the teachers, special educators, and administrators in this case who were opposed to the idea of placing Reed in inclusive classes. What were their reasons? Do you think their reasons were justified?
- Why did some of the teachers who were initially opposed to having Reed in their class change their minds?

## B.   Framing the Problem

- Do you think Karen has reasonable expectations for her son?
- How would you describe the conflicts in the case?

## C.   Developing Plans of Action

You might have students engage in role playing activities centered around decision making as to the least restrictive placement for Reed and the support services he should be given. In preparation for the role play, students should review the most current regulations for the implementation of the Individuals with Disabilities Education Act (IDEA) (PL 101-476) in their state, which can be obtained from their state office of education or office of special education. In small groups before the role play, students could discuss the following questions:

1. Imagine that you are a teacher sitting on Reed's IEP committee. What would you recommend as the best placement for Reed as he enters sixth grade? How would you state your position to others on the committee who might disagree with you?
2. Now decide what it would take to make inclusion work for Reed. Set up a program for Reed that will help him reach his potential in a general education classroom. Think of possible approaches to adapting the curriculum, instruction, and assessment, as well as the necessary supports for both Reed and his classroom teacher (see chapter 3 of *Inclusive Education*).
3. Do you think that Reed can be taught successfully in inclusive classrooms when he enters junior high school? What are some difficulties to be overcome at the secondary level that may be less of a problem at the elementary level?

After students have discussed these questions in small groups, ask for volunteers to role play an IEP meeting for Reed. The goal of this meeting is to determine the most appropriate placement for Reed as well as the necessary support services and accommodations. Volunteers can be assigned to different roles, including his parents, a special education teacher, his sixth grade teacher, and the school principal. Another group of students could then role play an IEP meeting for Reed when he is in junior high school. Roles for this scene might include various content area teachers who differ in their attitudes toward inclusive education, as well as

Reed's parents, a special educator, and the principal. After the role playing is concluded, you might ask the audience to evaluate the outcomes of the meeting.

## FOLLOW-UP ACTIVITIES

*Library Research.*   Have students gather information about IDEA and its amendments, then contrast differing views held by individuals and groups regarding the least restrictive environment, the continuum of educational placements, and inclusive education. For a starter list of references, see chapter 1 of *Inclusive Education* and chapter 2 of this volume.

*Interview and Observational Research.*   Students might interview parents of students with different kinds of disabilities to find out what goals they have for their children, what they see as ideal placements, and what their children's schooling experiences have been like. These could be written as narrative cases, case studies, or research reports. In addition, or as an alternative, students could interview and observe how general education teachers adapt instruction, curriculum materials, and assessment to accommodate children with disabilities in their classrooms. Or, they could shadow special education teachers who are working with general education teachers to provide services to students with disabilities in inclusive settings. Findings could be supplemented with research on the services, resources, and supports that the literature suggests are needed for successful inclusion.

# Case 2

# The Dialogue That Might Be Silencing

*Janine T. Remillard*

## SYNOPSIS OF THE CASE

"The Dialogue That Might be Silencing" examines current debates about the relevance of mathematics education reform for minority and under-served populations. In the case, Janine, a teacher and mathematics educa-tion graduate student (and the case author), questions whether her approach to teaching math is inaccessible to her three African-American students. The case describes Janine's efforts to foster discussions about mathematical ideas in her first grade class. Her aim was for students to learn to think through problems for themselves and be able to decide whether a particular answer made sense. She also wanted them to commu-nicate about their ideas to others and to learn from listening to each other. While most of the students in Janine's class were from White, working-class families, three were African-American students bused to the school from the inner city. Several weeks into the school year, she noticed that these three students were not participating in class discussions like the others.

Janine's concerns for these three students were further heightened when she read "The Silenced Dialogue" (Delpit, 1988) for one of her graduate classes. In the article, Delpit criticized progressive teaching approaches associated with constructivism because they assume middle-class patterns of interaction, which tend to avoid direct instruction. She argued that direct instruction is particularly important for African-American students who are not familiar with these cultural codes. As a result, Janine began to question the appropriateness of her instructional goals and approaches for these students.

## ISSUES IN THE CASE

*1. Cultural Assumptions Implicit in Reforms.* In this case, the teacher is forced to examine the cultural assumptions implicit in her goals and pedagogy, such as the belief that children will discover the discourse patterns of mathematics and problem-solving skills through structured experiences rather than explicit instruction. As a result, the case raises questions about whether educational goals, particularly those associated with current reforms, are influenced by cultural or class-based ideals. It also examines the question of cultural bias in educational research and theory generation.

*2. The Challenge of Providing All Students Access to Learning Opportunities.* Because the teacher in the case is struggling with how to engage three African-American students, the case invites readers to consider how to make learning accessible to all students. The case suggests that one pedagogical approach will not meet all students' needs.

*3. Cultural Congruity of Curricular Goals and Educational Practices.* The case also raises questions about the need for cultural congruity in educational practices and goals. The teacher's questioning of the appropriateness of her educational goals for the African-American students in her class invites readers to engage in this debate. Rather than locate the problem in the students who are not succeeding, Janine critically examines how her curriculum may be the problem.

*4. How Teachers Might Bridge Gaps Between Cultures.* The case provides an opportunity for readers to consider specific actions a teacher might take to bridge the gaps between cultures in the classroom. It also asks students to explore the consequences that their decisions may have on students, both personally and academically, and on schools and society.

  *5. Other Issues:*

## QUESTIONS TO THINK ABOUT

*(The question can be a handout for students that is given prior to reading the case or to small groups for review in class before the whole-class discussion.)*

1. What have you learned about Janine's students?
2. How would you characterize Janine's teaching goals?
3. In what ways might her goals or approach be culturally biased?
4. What questions would you like to ask Janine about her math teaching or about her class?

## DISCUSSION OUTLINE

To open the discussion, you might say, "The case you have read describes a situation that arose with three students in Janine's first grade class. Let's begin by describing the class and the context of the case.

### A.  Understanding the Context and Key Players

- What does the case tell you about Janine's students? About Janine? About Janine's teaching?
- What happened that caused Janine to be concerned?
- What was Janine's assessment of the problem?

### B.  Framing the Problem

Once the students have clarified what they know about the context, key players, and events from reading the case and have described Janine's assessment of the problem, ask them:

- Do you believe Janine's assessment of the problem is accurate?
- This question is intended to stimulate the heart of the case discussion. In facilitating the discussion, provide opportunities for students to respond to and question one another's reasons. It might be productive to have them discuss this question with a partner before reporting to the whole class. Their reasons can be listed on the board in "yes" and "no" columns. (See "Board Work, discussed later.) If students' comments imply larger issues or questions related to the case, list these under a separate column on the board. Before leaving this portion of the discussion, refer to the board work and ask students to summarize the main issues raised by the discussion.

## C.  Developing Plans of Action

- What should Janine do?

When asking students to suggest plans of actions that Janine might take, be sure that they connect them to the issues and reasons previously raised. Students should be pushed to take actions that are responsive to their analyses. Responses to this question might include actual approaches for making instruction culturally relevant as well as further information the teacher would need to gather.

## D.  Individual Reflection

- What questions or concerns do you have about the problem in this case?

It is often helpful to give students a few minutes to reflect individually on the issues raised during the case discussion. At the end of the discussion, give the students time to respond to this question in writing. These might be used in a follow-up activity.

## BOARD WORK

Below is a possible way to record key aspects of the discussion on the board. It is important before the discussion takes place that you anticipate the connections you would like students to make in your structuring of the board work.

| Context and Key Players Issues | Is Janine's Assessment of the Problem Accurate? | | Issues |
|---|---|---|---|
| Janine's students? | _yes_ | _no_ | |
| Janine? | | | **What Should Janine Do?** |
| Janine's teaching? | | | |
| What happened that caused Janine to be concerned? | | | |
| Janine's assessment of the problem accurate? | | | |

## FOLLOW-UP ACTIVITIES

*Read and Discuss Delpit's Article.*    Students can be assigned Delpit's (1988) article or a related piece on culturally relevant instruction. A follow-up class discussion can focus on the arguments made by the author and Janine's interpretations.

*Develop Plans for Field Sites.*    If students are placed in field classrooms, they can be asked to analyze the cultural concerns in their classrooms and develop plans for addressing them.

*Critically Analyze Curricula for Cultural Sensitivity.*    Many new curriculum materials claim to be culturally sensitive. Students can work in small groups to critique these materials for cultural sensitivity.

## REFERENCES

Delpit, L. (1988). The silenced dialogue: Power and pedagogy in educating other people's children. *Harvard Educational Review, 58,* 280–298.

# Case 3

# Teachers' Attitudes Toward ESL Students and Programs

*Ruth Trinidad*
*Sofia Villenas*

## SYNOPSIS OF THE CASE

This case revolves around teachers' attitudes about second-language learners and the efforts of an English as a Second Language (ESL) teacher, Sarah Townsend, to provide services for these students and have them fully included in mainstream classrooms. Hawthorne Junior High is described as a diverse school situated in a very diverse and working-class neighborhood. About 20% of the school's population is not fluent in, or does not speak, English. In this case, Sarah describes a year in which all of her students were Spanish speaking, and a majority were recent immigrants from Mexico. Sarah's efforts take place in the midst of a monolingual school environment, which had not made room for students who speak a language other than English. The ESL students were marginalized in the school through inequitable facilities and resources and lack of acceptance in the school as a whole. The school is set up so that ESL students are grouped together for part of the day to receive instruction in English from Sarah. For the remainder of the day, these students are in mainstream classrooms. Unfortunately, the other teachers in the school are not trained to teach second-language learners, and some are resistant. Moreover, there are no general education classes where the subject areas are taught in a manner that facilitates learning for second-language learners of English (called sheltered content classes), nor are there classes where content is taught in the students' native language.

This case deals with the dilemmas Sarah faces with respect to her fellow teachers' often negative views about second-language learners. Since there is no structure in place to help these students thrive academically in mainstream classes, Hawthorne teachers hold differing opinions about what to do with this "problem," which some of them frame in deficit and racist terms, placing blame on the ESL students themselves, their families, and their cultures. Sarah describes three different ways in which teachers in her school reacted to the education of second-language learners in the school. One group of teachers believed that ESL students should not receive special treatment and should be mainstreamed without any services or support; thus, ESL classes would be unwarranted. At the other end of the continuum, a group of teachers believed that ESL students should be segregated in self-contained classrooms for the entire school day until they are proficient in English. Although these two groups of teachers have made life hard for Sarah, a third group of teachers has been more receptive to the idea of inclusion and has sought advice and help from Sarah as to how they can meet the needs of ESL students in their classes. It is obvious from this case that until second-language learners are reframed as intelligent, "linguistically enriched peers"[1] rather than as "limited English proficient" (LEP, a term often used to label students based on their performance on English language tests), and until bilingualism is considered an asset all students should strive for, schools and classrooms will not move to provide these students with high-quality education in a multilingual and multicultural society.

## ISSUES IN THE CASE

*1. What Vocabulary Is Best to Use When Referring to "ESL" Students?* When choosing vocabulary with which to refer to students who speak a language other than English, it should be made a priority to avoid connotations of deficiency. The common label LEP emphasizes what the children do not have—that is, English—and suggests that second-language

---

[1]We have heard this phrase used by Dr. Steve Sternfeld from the Department of Languages and the Linguistics Program at the University of Utah.

learners are "limited" and thus deficient in language. In contrast, terms such as emerging bilinguals, second-language learners, and linguistically diverse students connote enrichment rather than deficiency and emphasize what children do have—that is, an intact native language and the potential for bilingualism. Reframing students in positive ways promotes respect for their native languages and the language skills of bilingualism.

*2. What Are the Origins and the Effects of Teachers' Attitudes Toward Linguistically Diverse Students?*  Teachers' attitudes toward bilingual students cannot be divorced from the larger discourses about difference in society and the global history of unequal power relations between the so-called first worlds and third worlds. Attitudes of superiority on the part of the former are a reflection of this historical relationship of colonization and neocolonialism and form the basis for attacks on people who are immigrants and speak a language other than English. These beliefs circulate in schools with minority populations such as Hawthorne Junior High, as exemplified by the following remark by a teacher, who made a distinction between a Polish-speaking (white) student and immigrant children (of color): "Teachers don't mind this kind of ESL student. It's the ones that don't try to learn that we object to."

Other beliefs equate the ability to speak English with intelligence, Americanization, success, and human worthiness (McKay & Wong, 1996). The consequences of negative attitudes from the school community toward students' native language and culture prove to be more detrimental than the language barriers themselves (Nieto, 1996). When students' native languages are viewed negatively or as a hindrance to learning, the knowledge base that students bring through their language is ignored. This knowledge base may or may not be school knowledge, but certainly it is rich and sophisticated cultural, family, and community knowledge. Indeed, well-meaning teachers often speak of second-language learners as "not knowing anything," when in fact they mean "not knowing" in English. Educators of multicultural, bilingual, and critical education argue that learning must start from the children's experiences and knowledge base so that students become creators and transformers of knowledge. Moreover, when students' native languages are viewed as a hindrance, teachers lower their expectations and "dumb down" the curriculum rather than change the way they teach the same cognitively demanding content. In the same manner, when their language is not respected, linguistically diverse parents are also likely to be framed in a negative, deficit way. The beliefs that children cannot learn anything until they learn English, or that they are "dumb" until they and their parents learn English, translate into a schooling experience that denies linguistically diverse children access to high-quality education.

*3. What Happens When Second-Language Students Are Mainstreamed in English-Only Classrooms Without Native-Language Support or Specially Designed Instruction?* Linguistically diverse students cannot function to the best of their abilities in an all-English classroom without receiving ample support in their native language or through specially designed, sheltered content instruction that is tailored to their language proficiencies. The level of English competency that is expected of students in content area instruction is especially high. Thus, to expect second-language learners to enter mainstream classes and function at grade level or to compete with native English speakers is unrealistic. While nonnative English speakers may learn everyday English language skills, or *Basic Interpersonal Communication Skills* (BICS), in a short period of time, it takes them a minimum of five to seven years to learn the more sophisticated academic aspects of language, or *Cognitive Academic Language Proficiency* (CALP). In the classroom, BICS is often mistaken for full English proficiency, when in actuality these language skills are not sufficient for the full comprehension of content material (e.g., science, social studies, and mathematical word problems). Indeed, if it takes five to seven years to learn CALP, then without an emphasis on content learning through native-language instruction or sheltered content instruction, there is much academic content that will be missed in those years. Many second-language learners, therefore, may lag behind their English-speaking peers and feel distressed and unmotivated at the possibility of ever catching up. In order to maintain dignity in the face of cultural and linguistic assault, many second-language learners strive to maintain collective group identities. This group solidarity offers an alternative to the ways in which they are demeaned as ESL students, who are relegated to second-class status in the school. Languages and cultures that are not respected in the schools then become markers for resistance on the part of linguistically diverse students to school systems that refuse to acknowledge and respond to their cultural and linguistic needs.

*4. Can Bilingualism Be a Goal for Students? How Can Native-Language Instruction Through Bilingual Education Enable Students to Become Fluent in Both Their Native Language and in English?* Bilingualism is not only an asset in itself, but also an affirmation of the students' cultural identities. Bilingual education constitutes the best method of providing non-native English-speaking students with the necessary tools to succeed. It concentrates on the knowledge students bring to the classroom and views students' native language and culture as assets to be recognized and incorporated in the school curriculum. Bilingual education's primary goal is to create bilingual/biliterate students by developing literacy in the native language. During the beginning years, students receive content instruction in their primary language, while simultaneously acquiring the English language. Students, therefore, do not miss out on content instruction during the years they are acquiring the English language. Further, the acquisition of the English language is as essential as maintaining the students' native language. Neither language is seen as less or more powerful than the other, but rather, both are seen as possessing equal value.

*5. In the Absence of Native-Language Instruction, How Can Mainstream Classrooms Be Organized to Effectively Teach Content Knowledge to Second Language Learners?* Although the most effective method of ensuring bilingualism and biliteracy is through the use of bilingual education, many times this is not possible due to political or economic reasons. In the absence of native-language instruction, specially designed (sheltered) instruction in mainstream classes that is tailored to the second-language abilities of ESL students can provide them with content instruction in a comprehensible manner. For example, teachers can alter their presentation of material (e.g., decrease the speed of their speech), focus on language goals as well as content goals, and employ innovative teaching methods such as role playing, cooperative groups, diagramming and charting, and using an array of manipulatives and pictures (cf. Ovando & Collier, 1997; Peregoy & Boyle, 1997). However, specially designed instruction alone does not guarantee student success. Cultural and linguistic affirmation needs to exist so that students feel empowered by the learning that takes place in the classroom. The acknowledgment of student experiences, knowledge, and learning strengths is an important aspect of a successful learning environment (Nieto,1996).

# DISCUSSION OUTLINE

We have organized the case discussion around a role play designed to contrast the various views of the ESL program and its students that are portrayed in the case as well as the view of advocates of native-language instruction and bilingual education. In preparation, we recommend that a good deal of time be spent reading and discussing some of the articles and books listed in the "References and Suggested Readings" at the end of this set of teaching notes. In particular, we suggest Cummins (1996), Delpit (1995), McDermott and Varenne (1995), McKay and Wong (1996), and Nieto (1996). Or, you might have students conduct library research on topics related to bilingual education (see "Follow-Up Activities"), thus using this case at the end of a course or unit of study. You might introduce the role-playing activity to the class in the following way:

> The discussion of this case will revolve around a role play of teachers in the case at a faculty meeting. The purpose of the faculty meeting is to develop a policy for Hawthorne Junior High that will best educate students who are linguistically diverse. To prepare for the role play, you'll be divided into five small groups, each of which will be assigned to one of these roles:
>
> 1. Teachers who want to mainstream ESL students without providing special services or support.
> 2. Teachers who want second-language learners out of the classrooms and isolated in self contained ESL classrooms until they are proficient in English.
> 3. Teachers who are receptive to working with ESL students in their own classrooms.
> 4. ESL teachers like Sarah, who are responsible for providing instruction to students in the school.
> 5. Teachers who are proponents of native-language instruction and bilingual education.
>
> Once you are in your small groups, please choose a volunteer to play the assigned role in the faculty meeting when we reconvene for the role play. You will have 20 minutes to work in your small groups to discuss the case and help your delegate prepare. Please structure your discussions around the questions on the handout titled "Questions to Think About."

# QUESTIONS TO THINK ABOUT

*(This is a handout that is given to students in their small groups for review in class in preparation for the role play.)*

For the group of teachers that you have been assigned to role play:

1. What were their underlying assumptions regarding their linguistically diverse students' academic skills?
2. Give examples from the teachers' comments of how lowered teacher expectations affect second-language students' achievement.
3. How do they view their role and responsibilities as teachers?
4. What are their views about cultural and language differences as they relate to schooling? Would you characterize their views as most similar to the deprivation approach, the difference approach, or the culture-as-disability approach (McDermott & Varenne, 1995)?
5. What are their views of inclusion?
6. Sum up your understanding of why you think these teachers responded to the idea of mainstreaming the way they did (or, in the case of bilingual teachers, how they might).

## The Role Play

As the instructor, you might play the role of the facilitator at the faculty meeting, opening it by describing the purpose of the meeting (see the foregoing discussion). One way to promote discussion is to ask each participant to propose a policy and a rationale for educating linguistically diverse students at Hawthorne, which you could record on the chalkboard. As they do so, have participants include their views on inclusion and on their responsibilities as teachers as well as other issues pertinent to the roles they are playing that were discussed in the small groups. The ensuing discussion could then focus on deciding which of the policies should be implemented. Participants should feel free during the debate to consult with their small groups, and "time outs" could be called to discuss issues or address concerns and questions as they arise with the whole class.

## Whole-Group Reflective Activity and Discussion

After the role play, you could open the discussion with a call for reflection on what took place during the faculty meeting. We see two parts to this whole-class discussion. Part 1 asks participants to compare and analyze the positions taken by the five teachers in the small groups and subsequent role play. You might begin by dividing the chalkboard or butcher paper into three sections: (a) ESL students, (b) attitudes about bilingualism, and (c) beliefs about language and learning. Ask the class to compare and chart the underlying assumptions and points of views as expressed by each of the five groups, referring to the "Questions to Think About" as necessary. In part 2, the class could discuss ways to restructure Hawthorne so that linguistic diversity is embraced in the school, using the following questions:

- What needs to happen at the school structural level?
- How can parent involvement be inclusive of the different languages and cultures?
- How can bilingualism be promoted?
- How can teaching and learning build on students' native languages and cultures?
- How can all classrooms value the contributions of emerging bilingual students?

Below are additional questions and issues to explore:

- From the point of view of the students, explain motivation, resistance, and group solidarity.
- What was Sarah's role as an ESL teacher, and how effective was it in terms of reorganizing Hawthorne to promote quality education for emerging bilinguals? Can her role be re-visioned?
- Name some of the ways in which the "receptive" teachers attempted to alter their teaching and curriculum in order to include second-language students as actively engaged learners. What were some of the questions and needs of these teachers?
- How can mainstream teachers best accommodate and integrate their second-language students?
- What kind of training should all teachers receive in order to effectively teach emerging bilingual students?

## FOLLOW-UP ACTIVITIES

*Research of Linguistic Resources in the Community.*   Students can gather information about the variety of languages spoken in particular communities. This research should include immersion in another language and culture through visiting homes, stores, churches, social events, and other gathering places. What knowledge and information does the language in these communities unlock for children who are speakers of that language? What possibilities are there for bringing speakers of the language into the schools?

*School and Library Research.*    One way for teachers to start re-visioning a multilingual school is to visit schools that are affirming linguistic diversity in a variety of ways, including with bilingual education. Even within a district, there are differing beliefs and attitudes about ESL students in the various schools. Library research will also provide information on innovative schools across the country and the different language experiments being conducted. Some of the literature is provided in the "References and Suggested Readings" section.

*Convince a Peer About the Benefits of Bilingualism.*    There are two decades of study about language and the education of linguistically diverse students. However, much of this information does not circulate among the general public, where anti-bilingualism sentiment is common. Students should arm themselves with the information necessary to advocate on behalf of all students who speak a language other than English. Addressing misconceptions is a crucial step in opening up the conversation. Krashen's book *Under Attack: The Case Against Bilingual Education* (1996) provides ways to respond to the common misconceptions, attitudes, and beliefs circulating among our peers.

## REFERENCES AND SUGGESTED READINGS

Carger, C. L. (1996). *Of borders and dreams: A Mexican-American experience of urban education.* New York: Teachers College Press.

Crawford, J. (1995). *Bilingual education: History, politics, theory and practice* (3rd ed.). Los Angeles: Bilingual Educational Services.

Cummins, J. (1996). *Negotiating identities: Education for empowerment in a diverse society.* Ontario: California Association for Bilingual Education.

Delpit, L. (1995). Language diversity and learning. *Other people's children: Cultural conflict in the classroom.* (pp.48–69). New York: The New Press.

Diaz-Soto, L. (1997). *Language, culture and power: Bilingual families and the struggle for quality education.* Albany: State University of New York Press.

Faltis, C., & Hudelson, S. (1998). *Bilingual education in elementary and secondary communities.* Boston: Allyn and Bacon.

Genesee, F. (Ed.). (1994). *Educating second language children*. Cambridge, England: Cambridge University Press.

Krashen, S. (1996). *Under attack: The case against bilingual education*. Culver City, CA: Language Education Associates.

McDermott, R., & Varenne, H. (1995). Culture *as* disability. *Anthropology and Education Quarterly, 26*, 324–348.

McKay, S., & Wong, S. (1996). Multiple discourses, multiple identities: Investment and agency in second-language learning among Chinese adolescent immigrant students. *Harvard Educational Review, 66*, 577–608.

Moraes, M. (1996). *Bilingual education: A dialogue with the Bakhtin Circle*. Albany: State University of New York Press.

Nieto, S. (1996). *Affirming diversity: The sociopolitical context of multicultural education*. White Plains, NY: Longman.

Ovando, C., & Collier, V. (1997). *Bilingual and ESL classrooms: Teaching in multicultural contexts* (2nd ed.). New York: McGraw Hill.

Peregoy, S., & Boyle, O. (1997). *Reading, writing and learning in ESL: A resource book for K-12 teachers* (2nd ed.). White Plains, NY: Longman.

Thomas, L. (1996). Language as power: A linguistic critique of U.S. English. *The Modern Language Journal, 80*, 129–140.

Vasquez, O., Pease-Alvarez, L., & Shannon, S. (1994). *Pushing boundaries: Language and culture in a Mexicano community*. Cambridge, England: Cambridge University Press.

# Case 4

# Overcoming Cultural Misunderstandings

*Donna Deyhle*

## SYNOPSIS OF THE CASE

In this case a Pacific Islander, Sione Ika, describes his life experiences through the lens of both a student and a teacher as he navigated through the educational system in the United States. Moving to the United States to attend a university, his story speaks loudly of the struggles a culturally different student faces in a new cultural context. Reflecting back on those first few years, he acknowledges that his cultural behaviors and beliefs were often at odds with those of the dominant culture surrounding him. However, with the support of university professors sensitive to his cultural identity, he successfully completed his university degree and started a teaching career.

As a teacher in a small rural community, Sione's cultural difference did not "blend away." He vividly describes both cultural clashes and institutional racism in his interactions with the school administration. When asked how much he wanted to be paid for teaching in the summer, he gave a reply imbued with his own cultural values: "You just give me whatever you want." In his Pacific Island culture, he had been taught to be humble,

149

to give of himself without a specified reward, to work cooperatively, and to avoid disagreement with authorities and peers. However, in the dominant European-American culture in which he now lived and taught, individual assertiveness, competition, work for pay, and challenging authority were values that were appropriate and guided his fellow teachers' lives. He later learned that the other teachers were paid three to four times what he was paid for the same teaching assignment. In this instance, his cultural differences were used by the administration to deny him equal pay. In effect, it could be argued that Sione faced not only cultural differences but institutional racism, in that these differences were used as an opportunity to take advantage of him.

As Sione reflected on his teaching in this community, his interactions with one student, an American Indian, painfully stood out in his mind. With this student he worried that he had failed. Using a competitive teaching strategy, which involved pitting student against student for valued band seats, he watched this American Indian student slip from first to second chair and finally drop out of the band. By creating a culturally conflictual situation for this student, Sione found himself replicating the cultural conflict he had experienced in school. Today, armed with the knowledge of the importance of cultural differences and power relations, he works to affirm and understand the cultures of his students as a means to enhance their educational success.

## ISSUES IN THE CASE

*1. What Were the Causes of the Conflict in This Case?*   This question might be answered differently, depending on whether the problem is viewed from the perspective of the teacher or the student. Sione used a competitive teaching strategy that conflicted with both his and the student's cultural norms and that may have been a reason why the student dropped out of the band. This case illustrates one way that different values and behaviors that were appropriate for a Pacific Islander conflicted with the values and behaviors exhibited by the European-American culture of the other teachers and students. From a European-American cultural perspective, the use of competition is thought to increase motivation.

*2. How Do Cultural Differences Influence Learning?*   Cross-cultural research demonstrates that the ways in which children have learned to learn prior to entering the formal educational environment are influenced by early socialization experiences. Different sociocultural environments result in behaviors that differ from culture to culture. The approach to learning and the demonstration of what one has learned is influenced by the values, norms, and socialization practices of the culture in which the individual has been enculturated. Differences between the home learning style (which includes verbal and nonverbal interactional patterns, and norms for behavior) and the school learning style are often manifested when an American Indian child goes to school. Specifically, there is evidence of the predisposition of American Indian children to participate more readily in group or team situations and to avoid individual competition, especially when one individual appears to be better than another.

*3. What Happens When Cultural Differences Are Viewed as a Deficit?* Sione views his own cultural values as responsible for creating a situation in which he did not receive equal pay for his work. From this perspective, he blames himself rather than the administrators who chose to pay him less than the other teachers. From another perspective, however, this may be seen as a result of institutional racism. In other words, his cultural differences are used against him as a justification to deny him equal pay. "Blaming the victim" too often occurs in schools and classrooms where the cultural differences of teachers, students, and their families are seen as problems or deficiencies. Cultural differences themselves do not necessarily lead to school failure; it is teachers and administrators misunderstanding or using these differences incorrectly that creates the possibility of a situation that leads to failure or discriminatory treatment.

*4. How Can Teachers Prevent and Resolve Cultural Conflict in the Classroom?* The pedagogies a teacher chooses can have a significant effect on whether students learn or fail. A teacher's misunderstanding of a student's cultural behavior—for example, viewing an American Indian student's reluctance to compete with peers as a lack of desire and motivation—can result in student withdrawal and failure. When teaching culturally different students, teachers should be as fully aware as possible of the language, customs, beliefs, and values of that culture so he or she can avoid classroom misunderstandings and, in turn, become an effective teacher.

*5. Other Issues:*

## Suggested Background Reading for Students
## Prior to Reading the Case

Deyhle, D. (1995). Navajo youth and Anglo racism: Cultural integrity and resistance. *Harvard Educational Review, 65,* 403–444.
Deyhle, D., & Swisher, K. G. (1997). Research in American Indian and Alaska Native Education: From assimilation to self-determination. *Review of Research in Education, 22,* 113–194.
Reyhner, J. (Ed.). (1992). *Teaching American Indian students.* Norman, OK: University of Oklahoma Press.

## QUESTIONS TO THINK ABOUT

*(These questions can be given to students prior to reading the case or to small groups for review in class before the whole-class discussion.)*

1. What were Sione's cultural beliefs and behaviors? Are they similar to or different from your own?
2. If you had been the teacher, would you have relied on competitive practices to increase motivation? What do you think are the underlying assumptions of this practice? Are they valid? What would you do if your students had different values?
3. Why is it important to understand cultural differences?
4. How can teachers avoid a deficit perspective that views cultural differences as a student's "problem?"
5. Why is it important to understand how cultural and racial relations in the classroom and in school can work against both equity and educational success?

## DISCUSSION OUTLINE

This discussion outline consists of three parts: understanding the context and key players, framing the problem, and developing plans of action. These three headings can serve as main headings on the chalkboard for the purpose of recording students' comments during the discussion. What follows is one way to open the discussion, which is followed by questions you might ask during each segment of the discussion:

The case you have just read is a vivid example of what can happen when cultural differences become barriers to educational success. By themselves, cultural differences are not the cause of student failure. Research shows that a strong cultural identity enhances the chance of school success for minority youth. What is important is how teachers react to cultural differences. With a multicultural approach, recognizing students' cultures can be used to build an effective educational environment. In some cases this means teachers will need to use a variety of instructional strategies, including group work, avoiding singling out or "spotlighting" individual students in front of the class, and the use of cooperative rather than competitive exercises. This case illustrates some of the dilemmas any educator may face in our increasingly multicultural classrooms.

## A. Understanding the Context and Key Players

- What does Sione tell us about his cultural background?
- What are we told about Sione's experiences in U.S. schools?
- What are we told about Sione's teaching style?
- What are we told about the reasons for Pacific Islander students' difficulties in school?
- What do we know about the American Indian student?

## B. Framing the Problem

- What went wrong between Sione and his American Indian student?
- How would the key players in the case answer this question? How would their answers differ from yours?

## C. Developing Plans of Action

Students can work in small groups to determine how Sione might have created a more culturally compatible or appropriate educational environment. As students think about how to create a multicultural classroom, they can refer back to the suggested readings on American Indians and education. Each group can then "report" their plans for a multicultural classroom by writing their key points on the board, followed by a whole-class discussion focusing on how the proposed plans will create a more equitable classroom for all students. Once all the plans are listed and discussed, you could bring the students' attention to any issues from the discussion that were not considered in their plans. Students can then develop additional plans or modify their existing plans to take these issues into account, or they can explain why these issues might not be relevant.

# FOLLOW-UP ACTIVITIES

*Community Research.*    Students can gather more information about the diverse cultures and ethnicities in their own community. Community organizations can be visited and interviews conducted with minority leaders. School board members, school administrators, and teachers can be interviewed for information about the minority populations in the school district or in particular schools. Students should be asking questions such as: Who are they? What can I learn about their cultures? What enhances minority students' school success? Why do they leave school? In a multicultural classroom, the more culturally aware teacher is a more effective teacher.

*Library Research and Curriculum Materials.*    A starting point for further knowledge about culturally diverse students would be to examine the research on culture and learning. Guiding questions for this inquiry could be: What is the role of competition in different cultures? What are some of the different interactional patterns in different cultures? What would a critical analysis of cross-cultural research tell us about cooperative learning? Research studies can be found in cross-cultural psychology, sociology, curriculum studies, and anthropology. Specific journals, such as the *Anthropology & Education Quarterly*, the *International Journal of Qualitative Studies in Education*, and the *Journal of American Indian Education,* provide information on how culturally different students learn, and on educational contexts that provide for successful educational experiences. In the field of education, students could examine specific texts on multicultural education such as *Making Choices for Multicultural Education* (1988), by Christine Sleeter and Carl Grant; *Affirming Diversity: The Sociopolitical Context of Multicultural Education* (1996), by Sonia Nieto; and *Multicultural Education, Critical Pedagogy, and the Politics of Difference* (1995), by Christine Sleeter and Peter McLaren. Using curriculum centers in school districts, students could also review the multicultural curriculum for materials that would create a more culturally inclusive learning environment, both in how and what to teach.

# Case 5

# Tragedies and Turnarounds

## *Staff*

## SYNOPSIS OF THE CASE

In this case, written from the perspective of an elementary classroom teacher, Linda Nesi describes the experiences of one of her students, Tommy, who had been considered a behavioral problem and a low-achieving student throughout his schooling. With one exception, none of his previous teachers had wanted him in their classrooms, and school officials had tried to have him placed in a program for students with behavioral disorders. All of this changed when Tommy entered Linda's fifth grade classroom. Rather than describing the specific behavioral management interventions that Linda tried, the case focuses on the importance of classroom structures and curricular approaches that made it possible for Tommy and other students who were low achieving to succeed. Before entering Linda's classroom, Tommy's main experience of school involved round-robin reading and individual seatwork assignments consisting of worksheets. In contrast, Linda's curricular approach involved a great deal of cooperative learning, hands-on activities, and student choice. Although Tommy's adjustment to the class was not without incident, he eventually became a successful student and an important member of the classroom community. He wrote and illustrated the best stories she had ever seen and he became an effective peer tutor. Modeling himself after Linda, he helped explain concepts and guided his peers to figure out problems themselves. Eventually, he was accepted into a pull-out program for the "gifted and talented," where he also excelled. The tragedy in this case occurred the following year, when Tommy entered sixth grade and Linda was transferred to another school. One day, when Linda ran into a teacher from her previous school and inquired about Tommy, the teacher told her that Tommy had entered a classroom in which students spent most of the day doing individual seatwork, with no discussion or cooperative learning. She concluded by saying that "it was the worst year he had ever had."

## ISSUES IN THE CASE

*1. How to Handle Students Who Are Disruptive.*   This issue raises questions that are of concern to every teacher: What does a teacher do with students who are disruptive? Should they be placed in regular classrooms? Is this fair to other students? If disruptive students are placed in mainstream settings, what classroom management approaches might teachers take? What supports and resources should be provided to teachers?

*2. How to Meet the Diverse Needs of Students in a Classroom: Classroom Structures and Curricular Approaches That Facilitate Inclusion.* Although this case takes place in a school that had many different kinds of pull-out programs and was not inclusive, we see what a teacher can do to create an inclusive classroom. We also see the effects of the classroom structure and curricular approach—namely, cooperative learning, student choice, and hands-on activities—on student behavior and achievement. Thus, an important issue in the case is how and why students who are labeled as gifted, behaviorally disruptive, low achieving, or at risk can all succeed to their fullest potential in such an environment.

*3. How to Successfully Implement Cooperative Learning and Other Curricular Approaches That Facilitate Inclusion.*   It is not enough to know that certain curricular and instructional approaches may facilitate inclusion. They also have to be implemented successfully. This may be especially difficult when these approaches run counter to the prevailing norms in a school. Discussion of this issue can lead to a discussion of what teachers should do to plan and prepare students for cooperative groups, peer tutoring, and hands-on activities. Follow-up research activities on this topic would be especially valuable for students.

*4. How to Bring About Institutional Change as a Teacher.* The tragedy in this case occurs when Tommy returns to the kind of classroom in which he had failed throughout his earlier schooling. The curricular and instructional approach of this sixth grade classroom was one of individual seatwork with little peer interaction. Unfortunately, this was the prevailing norm of the school. How is instruction in one's classroom affected by the larger institutional context? What can and should a teacher do to implement innovative teaching practices?

*5. Other Issues:*

## QUESTIONS TO THINK ABOUT

*(These questions can be given to students prior to reading the case or to small groups for review in class before the whole-class discussion.)*

1. What is this a case of? (Think of three issues that are involved in this case.)
2. In this case, Linda Nesi says: "I like to think that the way I teach fits with inclusion." What teaching practices does she use to create an inclusive classroom? Do you think these are effective inclusion strategies? Why or why not?
3. What do you think are the central problems or dilemmas in this case?
4. Why did Tommy do so well in Linda's class but then have "the worst year he had ever had" when he entered sixth grade?
5. If you were a teacher at West End Elementary, what could you do to change the overall curriculum and methods of instruction to facilitate inclusion?

## THE DISCUSSION OUTLINE

The discussion outline consists of three parts: understanding the context and key players, framing the problem, and developing plans of action. These three headings can serve as main headings on the chalkboard for the purpose of recording students' comments during the discussion. Under each heading on the board, you might have subheadings (e.g., under the heading, "Context and Key Players," subheadings could include "West End Elementary," "Linda," and "Tommy"). Here is one way to open the discussion, followed by questions you might ask during each segment of the discussion:

> The case you have just read opens with a description of an inner-city school where students struggle with a host of problems. Nevertheless, Linda Nesi, the fifth grade teacher who tells the story, wants an inclusive classroom within that school. Let's begin by describing the context and the key players in the case.

## A.   Understanding the Context and Key Players

- What are we told about West End Elementary?
- What are we told about Linda's class in particular?
- What are we told about Linda? Why is Linda in favor of inclusion?
- What are we told about Tommy when he first enters Linda's class?
- What is Linda's attitude toward Tommy?

## B.   Framing the Problem

- What do you see as the major problem in the case?

This question can be answered in two parts. When Tommy first enters her classroom, Linda is faced with the problem of how to manage Tommy's disruptive behavior and help him to succeed. The more complex problem occurs at the end of the case, when Linda is told that sixth grade was the worst year Tommy had ever had. In such situations, teachers face the problem of sending students to traditional classrooms (e.g., individual seatwork, lectures, etc.) in which little or nothing is done to meet the students' needs. This problem raises the question of what a teacher does to bring about change in an educational institution. If this problem is not raised, you might ask: "If Linda had stayed at West End, is there anything she could have done to help her students continue to be successful after they left her classroom?"

## C.   Developing Plans of Action

To develop solutions to managing Tommy's disruptive behavior, you might have students list what Linda did. Her solution included not only dealing with Tommy's behavior directly but also creating a learning environment that made him a valued member of the classroom and gave him some choice over how he would spend his time. After her actions and pedagogical practices have been listed on the board, students might then evaluate them, drawing on theory and experience as tools. Finally, you could have students think of some additional strategies that could be tried; list these on the board and have students evaluate them.

To address the issue of educational change that could facilitate inclusion throughout a school building, you might have students meet in small groups, with an appointed scribe and spokesperson, to come up with plans of action. After about 20 minutes of discussion, each spokesperson then describes the group's plan of action, which you could record on the board to enable students to see the range of solutions that have been proposed. After each group has given its report, you could have the class compare and evaluate the solutions.

## FOLLOW-UP ACTIVITIES

This case introduces students to several curricular and instructional approaches that facilitate inclusion, namely, cooperative learning, peer-mediated assistance, and project learning. If appropriate to your teaching objectives, students could engage in library research to learn more about specific strategies for facilitating inclusion. Besides cooperative learning and peer-mediated instruction, these include strategy instruction, multilevel teaching, and alternative assessment practices. You might advise students to critically examine the research literature on one of these topics as well as the problems and difficulties associated with implementation.

# Case 6

# Small Victories:
# Pedro's Story

*Tamara L. Jetton*

## SYNOPSIS OF THE CASE

In "Small Victories: Pedro's Story," a prospective teacher and tutor, Carminda Ranches, describes some of the obstacles that confront Pedro, a Chicano adolescent who is struggling academically in his middle school. In the past, Pedro was involved in gang activity. As Carminda notes, Pedro's appearance, behavior, and chosen written discourse all reflect the influence of the gang culture. However, Pedro has demonstrated a desire to avoid the gang scene because he is concerned that his brother will also involve himself in the gang.

Pedro has been in resource classes since the second grade, and he remains in them, except for his science class. In the past, the school attempted to integrate the resource students into the regular content classes, but the teachers, who had received no training in inclusion, protested, and the practice of integration was discarded. Pedro's teachers do very little to motivate Pedro to learn. Their tasks include worksheets, vocabulary exercises, and other activities that do not allow students to have much control over content. The teachers are satisfied if Pedro merely completes the assignments and uses good handwriting.

His teachers would describe Pedro as a withdrawn student. According to Carminda, he only socializes with other resource students, and he feels at odds with most of the White students in the school. He is unwilling to participate in class activities, because he is also bored with school in general and does not find many of the topics in his resource classes interesting. However, as Carminda notes, he is driven by individual interests and will work much harder if his interests are tapped. In addition, Pedro finds science, the only class in which he is not in resource, very difficult because of his absences and the homework required. To date, Pedro has not been doing well academically.

Carminda's assessment of Pedro's reading difficulties reveals many problems commonly associated with struggling readers. For example, rather than carefully attending to the text, he often relies on his background knowledge to guess at words and meaning. He is also unfamiliar with the nature and structure of textbooks or how to distinguish important from unimportant information and, therefore, has difficulty understanding what he reads. However, Carminda has made some successful attempts at helping Pedro figure out unknown words through decoding by analogy and facilitating Pedro's understanding of text through motivational activities.

## ISSUES IN THE CASE

*1. Biased Perceptions Leading to Low Expectations.*   One of the impediments to Pedro's success as a student in Van Buren Middle School is the biased lens through which others view him. Even Carminda's views of Pedro are initially influenced by his gang-related appearance, behavior, and written discourse, which she admits caused her to be skeptical of Pedro's sensitivity about his academic difficulties. Therefore, her expectations of his behavior lead her to doubt that Pedro could cry over the shame and humiliation that he feels about his science class. In addition, Pedro's teachers see him as a gang member and struggling resource student; thus, they set very low expectations for his performance. As long as he copies out of an encyclopedia or uses good handwriting, the teachers are satisfied with his work.

*2. School Culture Versus Home and Community Culture.*   Perhaps one of the greatest obstacles facing Pedro is that he does not feel a part of the school culture. He and other resource students, especially those from minority groups, are isolated from the dominant White, middle-class culture of the school. This is clearly evident in their social isolation from the White students in the school as they huddle near the resource classrooms. This isolation is also evident in the reported reluctance that Pedro has in interacting with other students and the teacher in class. He is viewed as a withdrawn student, unwilling to participate. Possibly Pedro's reluctance to communicate is due to his limited access to the kind of discourse that exists in a predominantly White culture. That is, the transition from the kind of oral discourse spoken in his home and community to the academic discourse spoken in the school might be very difficult for Pedro. In addition, Pedro is unfamiliar with the discourse found in the textbooks that he must read in school. As Carminda points out, he knows very little about the structure of the expository texts that he reads in science and history. Furthering this problem, the history teacher, who must photocopy text material for the students, does not provide him with either aids found in texts such as the glossary, which he could use to make sense of the material, or with strategies for learning with text.

*3. Failure of the School Curriculum to Engage His Interests and Increase His Motivation.*    Another barrier for Pedro is his lack of motivation and interest in assigned school tasks. This is particularly disconcerting since, as Carminda points out, Pedro is highly motivated when he is able to work with computers or read texts on topics of high personal interest such as the Bermuda Triangle. Some of his teachers were reluctant to allow any sort of student control over the content and others provided monotonous tasks such as filling in workbook pages and writing definitions from the dictionary. Little, if any, instruction was focused on building students' interest to increase motivation, such as allowing students to get personally involved in interesting topics.

*4. The Mismatch Between Pedro's Needs and Instruction.*    Carminda's assessment of Pedro's reading difficulties reveal problems commonly associated with readers who struggle, such as overrelying on background knowledge to guess at words and meanings. Until his tutoring sessions with Carminda, Pedro had received no instruction in strategies for reading his content area texts such as decoding multisyllabic words, summarizing information, or analyzing the structure of the text. Without the explicit instruction in these strategies that Carminda provided, Pedro's chances of overcoming his reading difficulties would have been insurmountable.

*5. Other Issues:*

# QUESTIONS TO THINK ABOUT

*(Theses questions can be given to students prior to reading the case or to small groups for review in class before the whole-class discussion.)*

Before reading the case:

1. What are some factors that lead teachers to set low expectations for the academic performance of their students?
2. How might students from minority groups feel isolated from a school culture that is predominantly White?
3. What are the factors that motivate you to learn? How might teachers motivate and interest students in learning?

Reviewing the case:

4. If you were Pedro, how would you feel about your tutor, your teachers, and your school in general?
5. In your opinion, what are the most important issues or problems raised in the case? Of these, which issue are you the most concerned about? Why?

# THE DISCUSSION OUTLINE

This discussion outline (intended for whole-class discussion) consists of three parts: understanding the context and key players, framing the problem, and developing plans of action that include a role-playing activity. These three headings can serve as main headings on the chalkboard for the purpose of recording students' comments during the discussion. What follows is one way to open the discussion, followed by questions you might ask during each segment of the discussion:

The case you have just read involves a preservice teacher, Carminda, who tutors an eighth grade student, Pedro. The case reveals the challenges facing Carminda as she attempts to instruct Pedro and the barriers that Pedro faces as an isolated Chicano student who spends most of his school time in resource classes that he finds boring and unmotivating. Let's begin the discussion by describing the context and the key players in the case.

## A. Understanding the Context and Key Players

- How does Carminda depict Van Buren Middle School? Relate the history of how the school community has dealt with students with special needs.
- What is Carminda's role as Pedro' tutor? What are her goals as a tutor in general, and what are her goals for Pedro in particular?
- How does Carminda describe Pedro?
- How does Pedro view the school?
- What are Pedro's general strengths and difficulties in school? What are his specific reading and writing strengths and difficulties?
- What role does each of Pedro's teachers serve in his education? What are their goals for Pedro's education?

## B. Framing the Problem

- What would Carminda identify as the most significant problem in this case?
- What other problems does Carminda note in this case?
- What do you see as the most important issues in this case?

## C. Developing Plans of Action

To develop plans of action, students form small groups for a role-playing activity. Each group should be assigned to the role of one key player in the case:

Carminda, Pedro's tutor
Pedro's mother
Pedro
The resource English teacher
The resource reading teacher
The resource history teacher
The science teacher
The principal or special education administrator who will
    facilitate the meeting

Give students approximately 10 minutes in small groups to prepare for the role play. Then reconvene the class and introduce the role play. One way to begin is as follows:

A case management or Individualized Educational Program meeting has been scheduled to determine a plan of action for improving Pedro's school performance. The purpose of the meeting is first to determine the problems Pedro is experiencing both personally and academically, and second to brainstorm possible ways that all participants can better meet Pedro's needs. As an outcome to this meeting, you will need to develop a list of recommendations that will accommodate Pedro's needs and increase his academic success.

After the small groups have completed the role-playing simulation, you could have students convene as a large group to discuss the role play and additional issues that arose during it. One way to begin is to ask students who participated in the role play to describe what the experience was like for them. Then ask the class to elaborate more extensively on the issues of this case.

## FOLLOW-UP ACTIVITIES

*Observation.*    Visit a local school in your area and observe various cultural groups that exist in the school. These cultures may include groups of students who associate by age, race, ethnicity, gender, socioeconomic class, and academic interests, to name a few. Note the way these groups communicate and act toward one another and toward other groups. Consider the knowledge, rules, traditions, attitudes, and values that guide behavior in these particular groups. Describe how these groups might be advantaged and/or disadvantaged both socially and academically within the school context.

*Library Research.*    Through the books and articles that you find in the library, explore issues related to motivation. These issues might include various theories of motivation, goals and motivation, needs and motivation, attributions, beliefs and motivation, and strategies for increasing motivation.

*Interviewing.*    Interview three or more content area teachers in secondary schools. Describe Pedro's reading difficulties to these teachers, asking them questions such as:

- Have you ever taught students with reading difficulties similar to Pedro's?
- What teaching strategies would you use with students like Pedro to improve their academic success?
- Have you taught students who had reading difficulties that differed from Pedro's?
- What were those difficulties and what kinds of teaching strategies did you design to help these students become more successful?

After you have completed the interviews, construct profiles of struggling readers and describe the teaching strategies you would use to improve their success in learning and literary.

# Case 7

# Reading in Biology Class

*Elizabeth B. Moje*

## SYNOPSIS OF THE CASE

This case was written to encourage prospective and practicing teachers to reflect on common questions that they and teacher educators often struggle to answer: (a) Why do secondary school teachers often resort to a pedagogy of telling,[1] instead of encouraging their students to read content textbooks and other print materials as one means of constructing knowledge? (b) How can we encourage students to read course textbooks and other print materials? and (c) How can we help students learn to use print materials to aid their own learning in and outside of our content classes?

Although written in the third person, this case is built around my own experiences as a first-year biology teacher. Early in the school year, I encountered resistance from students to reading the textbook and to my

---

[1]O'Brien, Stewart, and Moje (1995) discuss the "pedagogy of telling" as part of a call to reconceptualize secondary content literacy teaching. Sizer (1985) introduced the concept in *Horace's Compromise*. The pedagogy of telling refers to teachers' reliance on lecture and recitation as a means of covering content material. As a result, students see little need to read assigned texts (Wade & Moje, in press).

pedagogy of telling. During class one day, a student named Larry (a pseudonym) asked me why I bothered to assign textbook reading when I was just going to tell them what the textbook said during my lecture. Larry's question, and a subsequent challenge by Larry's father a few weeks later, rocked the foundations of my beliefs about teaching, learning, and learners. I had resorted to the pedagogy of telling because, based on my own school experiences, what other teachers had told me about the students, and my student teaching experience, I believed that students would not read the assigned textbook chapters. I believed that some of the students would not read because they felt that the readings were boring or unimportant, whereas others students were unable to understand what they had read. As a result, I thought that I needed to tell students what the text said so they would have a basic understanding of the concepts they would be discussing or exploring in laboratory activities. However, because of Larry's challenge to my methods, I was forced to question these assumptions and methods, although my soul searching remained ambivalent for a time, as I took comfort in the support for my methods I received from my colleagues, the other students, and parents. The case closes with my confusion as to whether my methods were helpful to students or whether I needed to change, and, if so, what I could do differently. This case can be a good starting point for discussing different curricular and pedagogical approaches and what each contributes to helping students construct subject matter knowledge (for an overview, see Wade & Moje, in press).

## ISSUES IN THE CASE

*1. Alternative Curricula and Assessments.*    An important issue in this case is how to use reading, writing, speaking, drawing, and other forms of representation to capitalize on the diverse interests and needs that students and teachers bring to classrooms. In this case, we see that Elizabeth had adopted a pedagogy of telling as a way to reach the most students. Although her approach was based on her beliefs about her students' needs and abilities, Elizabeth did not stop to consider whether her textbook or curriculum were important, interesting, or accessible to students. This opens the discussion to issues of students' reading abilities and interests, but should also provide a forum for discussing whether the readings (and other literacy activities) are useful and engaging to students. Discussion of this issue can focus both on what the students bring to a secondary school classroom and on what the teacher, texts, and curriculum might (or should) contribute. In addition, although the case is not explicitly about alternative assessments, this issue follows naturally from a discussion of alternative curricula. In other words, Elizabeth judged her success by means of multiple-choice, short-answer, and fill-in-the-blank tests, which are consistent with her emphasis on lecture and recitation. If she were to use texts in ways more consistent with participatory, socioconstructivist pedagogies, she would be likely to want and need to change her assessment practices.

*2. Developing Critical Literacy Skills and Processes.* An alternative to the pedagogy of telling, content area literacy instruction involves more than merely assigning texts to students and asking them to extract information from the text. Equally important is the goal of helping students to become critical readers. This case provides an opportunity for a discussion of how teachers can help their students become thoughtful, careful, and critical readers and writers who ask questions about what they read and who challenge ideas in writing.

*3. Teacher Beliefs, Self-Assessment, and Change.* A less obvious, but equally important, issue in this case is that of teacher beliefs about pedagogy, about the nature of biology and other subject areas as disciplines, about knowledge, and about students and their abilities. How do teachers decide what methods to use in their classrooms, and how are these decisions different for different subject areas? For example, why did Elizabeth become more concerned about her students' reading when she began teaching history? How can teachers assess their practice using students' comments and performance on assessments? How can they use that information to change or refine their practice? How should teachers respond to students' challenges?

*4. Other Issues:*

## QUESTIONS TO THINK ABOUT

*(These questions can be given to students prior to reading the case or to small groups for review in class before the whole-class discussion.)*

1. What is this a case of? (Think of the different issues involved in the case.)

2. What do you think are the central problems in this case?

3. Why was Larry frustrated with Elizabeth? Was his frustration justified?

4. What advice would you give Elizabeth to help her resolving her confusion over Larry's and his father's questioning of her teaching practice, on the one hand, and the positive feedback she had received from her mentors, peers, the other students, and parents, on the other?

## THE DISCUSSION OUTLINE

This discussion outline consists of three parts: understanding the context of the case, framing the problem, and developing plans of action. These three headings can serve as main headings on the chalkboard. Under each heading on the board, you might have subheadings (e.g., "Light High School," "the biology classes," "Elizabeth," etc.) for the purpose of recording students' comments during the discussion. Below is one way to open the discussion, which is followed by questions you might ask during each segment of the discussion:

The case you have just read opens with a description of a first-year teacher's background and experience, together with a description of her first teaching assignment. Let's begin our discussion by talking about the context and the key players in the case.

## A.   Understanding the Context and Key Players

- What do we know about Light High School and its students?
- What do we know about the biology classes that Elizabeth was assigned to teach?
- What do we know about Elizabeth: her education, her background, her feelings about teaching?
- What were Elizabeth's teaching methods and philosophy?
- What happened that floored her? Why was she floored?
- What happened next?
- What was she thinking at the end of the case?

## B.   Framing the Problem

- What do you think of Elizabeth's response to Larry's and Mr. Hall's questions?
- Why did Elizabeth resort to the pedagogy of telling?
- What do you think of the argument that students don't, won't, or can't read their textbooks and other assigned readings?
- What do you think of the pedagogy of telling as a solution?
- What do you think of just relying on hands-on activities such as observations, demonstrations, and experiments as a solution?

## C.   Developing Plans of Action

To develop plans of action, you might have students engage in an informal role play in small groups, in which students take on the role of a school literacy consultant whom Elizabeth has approached for advice. Specifically, Elizabeth wants ideas about how to work with Larry while also meeting the needs of students who don't read, aren't interested in science, or who struggle to understand the reading. Role playing the reading consultant, the groups should draw on prior class discussions, their own experiences, and the course readings to come up with a list of strategies, pedagogical approaches, or curriculum and textbook revisions to suggest. Below is an outline of how you might structure the role play, which you could provide in a handout to the small groups:

Assume that you are the reading consultant in Elizabeth's school. For several years now, Elizabeth has been haunted by Larry's questioning of her teaching methods, despite her rationalizations that she has been doing the right thing. She's been thinking more about this issue lately because she's found that most of her classes are filled with students who have different literacy needs and interests. She finally comes to you to talk over this dilemma and seek advice. In your small groups, decide on what advice you would give Elizabeth to help all of her students become more independent and motivated to read and to rely less on lecturing and explaining the content of the texts she assigns. As you do so, think about what you read for today, and consider the following questions:

1. What literacy strategies might she teach her students?
2. What should she do about texts that are too difficult for some of her students?
3. What changes might she make in her curriculum? Her pedagogy? Her assessment practices?
4. What teaching philosophy and underlying assumptions does your advice reflect?

After each small group shares their ideas with the whole group, the rest of the class could be asked to respond to the proposed solutions by answering the questions below:

1. What do you like about this/these approach(es)?
2. What difficulties do you foresee in trying to implement it/them?

## FOLLOW-UP ACTIVITIES

One particularly useful follow-up activity is to tie this case to the next case you use. For example, you may wish to use a case of a student who struggles to read or write texts in a content area class (cf. "When She's Ready, She'll Catch Up," case 8 in *Inclusive Education*). A helpful role-play or discussion question would be to ask your students how they would change their texts, curricula, or pedagogy to work with a student who struggles, while also working with a student like Larry, who reads and writes texts with ease. You might also consider asking students to keep the cases and their case notes in literacy portfolios. Throughout the term or as an assessment and reflection activity at the end of the term, it might be useful to revisit several of the cases, asking students how their perspectives on the problems and solutions in each might be different as a result of their increasing experience and growing familiarity with new theoretical and research perspectives. In addition, students might conduct library or action research on the many issues this case addresses such as critical reading, the use of texts in content learning, participatory curricula and pedagogical approaches, alternative assessment, and teacher beliefs about the nature of knowledge and ability.

# REFERENCES

O'Brien, D. G., Stewart, R. A., & Moje, E. B. (1995). Why content literacy is difficult to infuse into the secondary school: Complexities of curriculum, pedagogy, and school culture. *Reading Research Quarterly, 30,* 442–463.

Sizer, T. R. (1985). *Horace's compromise: The dilemma of the American high school.* Boston: Houghton Mifflin.

Wade, S. E., & Moje, E. B. (In press). The role of text in classroom learning. In *Handbook of Reading Research Vol III.* Mahwah, NJ: Lawrence Erlbaum Associates.

# Case 8

# When She's Ready, She'll Catch Up

*Tamara L. Jetton*

## SYNOPSIS OF THE CASE

In "When She's Ready, She'll Catch Up," Wendy Besel Hahn describes the reading and writing difficulties of Sue, a high school student with a learning disability who attends regular education classes. The case details Sue's experiences with reading and writing during the first years of her schooling as well as her continuing struggle in high school content area classes.

During Sue's first few years of schooling, Sue's mother, concerned with her daughter's progress in reading, began requesting that Sue receive special services such as extra help in reading and testing to determine any learning difficulties. At first, the teacher did not consider Sue to have any particular problems. Rather, she thought that Sue was not ready to learn, and she would "catch up" when she was ready. When Sue was found to have learning disabilities through testing, Sue's mother and the school personnel were at odds regarding how to meet Sue's needs. The school's solution was to hold Sue back in first grade and place her in resource. Sue's mother requested that Sue be fully included in the regular curriculum with extra help in reading. Throughout Sue's life, her mother has taken an active role in Sue's education to ensure that Sue's needs are met.

Sue is well aware of her own learning difficulties, which include problems with short-term memory, letter reversal during decoding and spelling, reading comprehension, and mechanical errors in writing. She has particular difficulty in history because she has problems understanding the textbook, and the teacher does little to help her comprehend the text. Despite the seemingly insurmountable difficulties Sue faces in high school, she has used her strengths to help her earn a C average. She is highly motivated to learn. This is evidenced by the amazing amounts of time and effort she expends to complete her assignments both in and out of school. She is also able to avoid failure in school because of her perseverance and the strategies that she employs to learn the subject matter. However, Sue is unhappy with her performance, and she suffers from stress-related headaches.

## ISSUES IN THE CASE

*1. Sue's Mother as Advocate.* Throughout Sue's life, her mother has acted as an advocate to ensure that Sue received the appropriate accommodations for her learning disability. From the beginning of Sue's school life, her mother attended closely to Sue's reading difficulties and communicated her concerns to Sue's teachers. Sue's mother also made sure that Sue was tested to understand where any specific difficulties might lie, and she involved herself in the selection of Sue's teachers in order to ensure a good match between instruction and Sue's needs. Part of determining the best match, as her mother saw it, was to ensure that Sue be fully included in the regular school curriculum rather than attend a pull-out resource program. Since elementary school, her mother has continued to play an active role in Sue's education by having her tested by a neurologist and by requesting special assistance in reading. Despite her efforts, Sue's mother does not feel that Sue is receiving enough help.

*2. Motivation to Learn.* Perhaps one of the greatest strengths that has enabled Sue to succeed in school has been her motivation to learn. Sue expends an incredible amount of time and effort to complete her school subjects. Her motivation is evidenced by her willingness to study and write for many hours and to reread assigned texts. She also expresses a sense of accomplishment in reading difficult novels that are at her frustrational level. Sue's motivation is also evident in the high achievement goals that she sets for herself. She wants to earn better than C average grades, and she desires to earn a college degree. However, her achievement motivation might possibly be the reason that Sue suffers physically from stress and anxiety.

*3. Sue's Metacognitive Ability.*    Sue is highly aware of her own reading and writing processes. She recognizes strategies that increase her ability to read and write. She is also aware of the time and effort it takes her to complete her academic work. She is able to identify weaknesses that she has with her reading and writing, and she knows her strengths on which she can rely. Her awareness of when something is going wrong as she is reading or writing, and her understanding of the strategies that she can employ to fix such reading or writing problems are certainly assets for Sue.

*4. Sue's Strategies for Reading and Writing.*    Sue employs particular strategies that help her overcome her reading and writing difficulties. In order to increase her understanding of information she reads, Sue uses letter –sound correspondences to figure out unknown words, reads aloud, rereads the text, and draws illustrations to glean the meaning of text. She also revises and edits her writing in an attempt to eliminate the difficulty she has with spelling and punctuation errors. Most likely, Sue's use of these varied strategies has enabled her to avoid failure in her content area classes. However, Sue still has difficulty with her history text, which is dense with information and technical vocabulary.

*5. Limited Scaffolded Instruction in Reading and Writing Strategies.* Sue's greatest struggle with reading and writing is in her history class. Her teacher provides little scaffolded instruction as to particular reading and writing strategies that students might use to be successful with the assignments. Rather, her instruction comes after the assignments have been completed. Possibly her teacher has received little training as to the reading and writing strategies that students could employ to increase their comprehension. As is the case in many secondary teacher-preparation programs, content area teachers attend, at the most, one course devoted to reading comprehension. Often, the course does not make sense to these teachers because they believe that students should already know how to read by the time they attend high school; thus they take the content of the course less seriously. Whatever the case, the instruction that Sue received from her history teacher came too late to help Sue because all instruction occurred after she had read or written the assignments.

*6. Other Issues:*

## QUESTIONS TO THINK ABOUT

*(These questions can be given to students prior to reading the case or to small groups for review in class before the whole-class discussion.)*

Before reading the case:

1. What are some ways in which schools have or could accommodate students with learning disabilities?
2. How can parents act as advocates for their children who have learning disabilities?
3. How can motivation improve the school performance of someone who faces difficulties in reading and writing?
4. What is metacognition? How does the ability to be metacognitively aware of reading and writing processes help students comprehend and learn?
5. What are effective reading and writing strategies that secondary students can use?

Reviewing the case:

6. If you were Sue's mother, how would you feel about Sue's school experiences?
7. How does Sue motivate herself to learn in her content area classes?
8. What are the reading and writing strengths and difficulties of which Sue is aware? What strategies does she employ to overcome these difficulties?
9. What are some of the reasons you think Sue wants so badly to succeed in general education classes?

## THE DISCUSSION OUTLINE

This discussion outline (intended for whole-class discussion) consists of three parts: understanding the context and key players, framing the problem, and developing plans of action. These three headings can serve as main headings on the chalkboard for the purpose of recording students' comments during the discussion. What follows is one way to open the discussion, followed by questions you might ask during each segment of the discussion:

> The case you have just read concerns Sue, a high school student with a learning disability who struggles to read and write in her content area classes. Let's begin the discussion by describing the context and the key players in the case.

## A. Understanding the Context and Key Players

- How does the case author depict Sue's experiences as a student with a learning disability?
- What has been Sue's mother's role throughout Sue's education?
- How did Sue's elementary school accommodate her learning disability?
- At Forest Hills High School, what is the special education teacher's role in Sue's education?
- What is Sue's current school situation? How are things working out for her in high school?
- What do we know about Sue's reading strengths and difficulties? What about her strengths and difficulties in writing?
- What do you think of Sue's belief that her grades on writing assignments are based on her problems with the mechanics of writing?
- How would Sue's history teacher describe Sue's academic performance?

## B. Framing the Problem

- How does Sue view the problem?
- How do others, such as Sue's mother, her special education teacher, and her history teacher view the problem?
- Is your interpretation of the problem similar to these views?
- What are the key issues in the case?

## C.  Developing Plans of Action

To develop plans of action, assign students in small groups to one of the roles outlined in what follows. Have small groups discuss their role for about 15 minutes, to prepare for the role-playing activity that follows.

- Put yourself in Sue's place. What would you tell the history teacher about yourself as a student and about your goals for high school and adult life? What would you want the history teacher to do differently? How would you go about asking him?
- Take the role of Sue's mother. What questions would you ask the history teacher? What would you tell this teacher about Sue's strengths and struggles? What other members of the school faculty might you contact for help? What would you say to them? What would you try to do to help Sue at home?
- Take the role of the history teacher. What are your beliefs and assumptions about both teaching and learning? How would you assess Sue's difficulties in your course? What do you see as some possible solutions?
- Take the role of the speech and debate teacher. How would you assess Sue's strengths and needs or sources of difficulty in your course? What would you recommend for her?
- Take the role of the special educator who serves as a resource teacher and case manager for the school. How would you act as an advocate for Sue? How would you approach her teachers, and what recommendations would you make to them? What kinds of recommendations would you make to Sue and her mother?

After groups have had time to discuss the questions related to these roles, ask for one volunteer from each group to engage in an improvisational role-playing activity based on the discussion in their groups. The setting is a consultation meeting to decide on a plan to help Sue become more successful in her history class. In this role-playing activity, the special education teacher might act as the facilitator, first asking Sue, her mother, and the history teacher for their assessments of Sue's strengths and difficulties. After this issue has been adequately discussed, then the group could begin discussing strategies that would be beneficial to Sue. After the role-playing activity is concluded, you might ask participants to describe what the role playing was like for them. Then you could wrap up the discussion by asking the rest of the class to evaluate the success of the consultation meeting and the solutions that have been proposed.

## FOLLOW-UP ACTIVITIES

*Library Research.*    Through library research, find possible explanations for Sue's difficulties with reading and/or writing. Compose an annotated bibliography that includes secondary sources teachers would find useful in helping their students with similar problems.

*Interviewing.*    Interview a content area teacher at the secondary level who has a student struggling with reading and/or writing. Some interview questions might include: What specific difficulties in reading and/or writing is this student experiencing? How were they first brought to your attention? What strategies have you used to help this student learn the content material in your course? How effective were the strategies? Do you think this student should be in your class? What additional help and resources do you think this student needs? After you have completed your interview, write a two- to three-page discussion of what you found.

*Developing Teaching Strategies.*    Try out one of the teaching strategies that has been recommended in your readings or library research. One option is to try this strategy with a student who is having difficulty with reading and writing. You could also try developing a key word diagram or other graphic representation of the content in a textbook to understand how Sue composes illustrations of her history textbook. Then, write a one-page description of what you learned and include ideas on how you think illustrating or graphically organizing a chapter helps Sue and perhaps other students.

# Case 9

# "We Are Chauvinists": Sexual Entitlement and Sexual Harassment in a High School

## *Audrey Thompson*

### SYNOPSIS OF THE CASE

When a large number of lower-income students, many of them students of color, enrolled in an overwhelmingly White, upper-middle-class high school, administrators and teachers anticipated racial tensions among the students. Instead, the school erupted in gender conflict. In Part A of this disturbing case, Karen Jones, a teacher at the school, traces the escalation of sexual harassment that, by mid-year, had paralyzed the school. Outraged by a number of highly public incidents, Karen and several other teachers confronted the principal, who told them to "lighten up." Under the tolerant gaze of administrators, sexism at the high school became so pervasive that during school assemblies students were allowed to perform sexually suggestive skits and show videos derogatory toward women. Despite increasing pressure from Karen and other faculty members, school administrators refused to address the issue. When student elections were held in March and the hallways were covered by posters that showed men brutalizing women, Karen and some of the other teachers decided to act outside of regular channels.

Part B describes the actions Karen and some of her colleagues took to pressure the principal to put a stop to the incidents of sexual harassment, after it became clear that neither the principal nor members of the School Improvement Council were prepared to take action on their own. Rebuffed by those with the power to set a new course within the school, Karen sent the ACLU a letter signed by almost half the faculty. Together with a colleague, she also encouraged a local television reporter to run a story on the issue. The day after the television broadcast, Karen was publicly humiliated by her principal and subjected to taunts and ridicule by a number of the students. Although some changes eventually were implemented at the school, several years later there are still no school guidelines prohibiting discriminatory or degrading content based on gender or ethnicity.

## BACKGROUND INFORMATION

Making unwelcome, sexually suggestive remarks and overtures is part of the definition of sexual harassment; also included in that definition is fostering a hostile *climate* in which people feel intimidated or threatened on the basis of sexual identity. While sexual harassment is perhaps most often equated with intrusive sexual attentions of a personal nature, such as making lewd comments or groping, at Roosevelt High School sexual harassment took on a more pervasive character, creating a climate of sexual attention in which women in general were targeted as sexual objects. The many forms of sexual harassment tolerated by the administration included displaying sexually derogatory posters, advertising males-only clubs explicitly committed to "chauvinism," performing skits demeaning to women, and calling women by insulting names associated with their sexuality. Thus, the concerns regarding sexual harassment at Roosevelt had to do less with any personal actions directed at individuals (although these also occurred) than with the creation of a threatening climate in which women teachers and students were treated with marked disrespect and in which even the curriculum (as in the case of women novelists, for example) was sexualized and treated dismissively.

## ISSUES IN THE CASE

*1. The Tension Between the Freedom of Speech Claimed by Members of the "We Are Chauvinists" Club and the Right of Women Teachers and Students at the School to be Treated with Respect.*   The rights claimed by one group of students, the "We Are Chauvinists," were framed specifically to override the right of women to be treated with respect. Thus, an exclusionary situation was fostered in the name of the Chauvinists' *right* to treat women as inferior, as sexual objects, and even as slaves. The perceived *entitlement* of the popular boys was set against the perceived humorlessness of the teachers who raised objections.

It is worth asking whether administrators and community members would have rallied to the boys' cause if the boys in question had been outsiders or misfits. Lefkowitz's (1997) analysis suggests that the "boys will be boys" defense is most likely to be invoked on behalf of privileged boys. Had the members of "We Are Chauvinists" (WAC) been unpopular, or had they been working-class and/or Black, for example, administrators might well have been less tolerant. Certainly, the parental and media outrage directed against black rap artists who use sexist epithets suggests that the appeal to free speech is reserved for some men, but not all (hooks, 1994).

*2. The Question of Whether Hostile or Disrespectful Language, Imagery, and Performances Constitute Harmful Behavior.* The old elementary school saying has it that "sticks and stones may break my bones but words can never hurt me." For many students, however, sexual slurs, racial hate speech, homophobic taunts, and otherwise demeaning and disrespectful treatment create a hostile climate that makes it difficult for them to concentrate on their studies, let alone grow and flourish. For teachers, obviously, lack of respect makes it difficult to teach, yet Walkerdine (1990) reports that even small boys may enjoy the power to taunt teachers with comments like "Miss Baxter, show your bum off" (p. 4).

*3. The Role of Social Power and the Perceptions of the Dominant Social Group in Identifying What Is Appropriate Behavior Toward Those With Less Power.* Sexist discrimination takes a variety of forms. The difficulty in appealing to a standard of *appropriate* behavior toward others is that, in a sexist (and/or racist, homophobic, etc.) society, sexist (racist, homophobic, etc.) behavior will commonly be seen as unproblematic by those in a position of relative privilege, including some "privileged" victims of sexist behavior. In a culture such as our own, in which sexuality is glamorized, individual women who believe they may benefit from a "celebration" of female sexuality will sometimes accept their treatment as sex objects as a legitimate way to gain access to power. And because some women do accept this treatment, and enjoy a resulting popularity with those in power, those who object to being treated as sexual objects will often be given outsider labels such as "humorless," "ugly," "Nazi," "man-hating," or "politically correct," as a way of reinforcing the perceived legitimacy of the prevailing structures of power and the illegitimacy of any objections to existing power relations.

*4. Racial and Ethnic Tensions Are Sometimes Displaced Onto Gender Tensions, Which May Be Seen as a More Natural, More Legitimate Form of Exclusion or Discrimination.* In consolidating their position at the top of Roosevelt's student hierarchy, the popular boys chose an approach that allowed their parents and the administrators to support them. Had the White, privileged boys at Roosevelt explicitly targeted race or ethnicity in their campaign of exclusion, it might have been far more difficult for any administration or community that wished to appear open-minded to take the line that "boys will be boys." Because the boys targeted girls and women, however, they were protected by the administration.

A question worth asking is whether the boys' tactics served to marginalize lower-income women and women of color in particular. As Bodroghkozy (1992) observes, White hostilities toward people of color are sometimes channeled into discriminatory treatment of Black women, which may be considered an acceptable, supposedly natural, form of discrimination. If Black men or boys express sexist attitudes, on the other hand, White parents and school authorities are liable to be far less tolerant than they are of White boys' or men's sexism. As indicated earlier, White authorities are often outspoken in their view that Black rap music is insulting to women, and their objections to that music tend to fuel racist stereotypes of Black men. Ironically, however, neither the White teenage boys who are the primary audience for rap music nor the (usually White) owners of the corporations that profit from the sales of rap music are held accountable for their own participation in rap's sexism (hooks, 1994). In considering how and when sexual harassment gains legitimacy, then, the intersections between racial and sexual bigotry, along with class and other factors, must be examined.

*5. Other Issues:*

## QUESTIONS TO THINK ABOUT

*(These questions can be given to students prior to reading the case or to small groups for review in class before the whole-class discussion.)*

1. How do the issues connected with sexual harassment as a question of school climate compare and contrast with the issue of sexual

harassment as objectionable behavior directed toward individual students or teachers? How might the interventions taken in each case differ?

2. What is the school's responsibility to create and protect a particular learning environment? Is the issue of climate especially salient for schools, or are the issues of freedom of speech and sexual harassment the same for schools as they are for businesses, communities, government offices, and other public settings?

3. Why is the principle of freedom of speech important? How is it related to the flourishing of individuals in a democracy? How is it related to notions of truth, inquiry, and communication? How important is the issue of freedom of speech in the Roosevelt High School case?

4. Why is the principle of respect for all individuals important? How is it related to the flourishing of individuals in a democracy? How is it related to beliefs about ethics, inquiry, and education? How important is the issue of respect in the Roosevelt High School case?

5. If individual girls claim not to mind being treated with disrespect, is the issue of sexual harassment in schools moot? Do schools have an obligation to insure inclusiveness, so that all students are treated with respect regardless of their stated preferences, or should sexual harassment be judged on a case-by-case basis, depending on how students and teachers feel about how they are treated?

6. How should input from parents be weighed? If some parents are more outspoken than others, if some parents have better access to the media or are more influential with administrators, or if a particular group of parents is more involved on boards and councils, for example, what weight should administrators give to their views?

7. If schools adopt clear sexual harassment guidelines and enforce them themselves, how might the results of intervention differ from cases in which sexual harassment is monitored by parents, the public, and the press, and enforced through litigation? How might the climate of inclusion be affected, for example?

## DISCUSSION QUESTIONS

The discussion outline consists of three parts: understanding the context and key players, framing the problem, and developing plans of action. These three headings can serve as main headings on the chalkboard.

Under each heading on the board, you might have subheadings for the purpose of recording students' comments during the discussion. What follows is one way to open the discussion, followed by questions you might ask during each segment of the discussion:

> The sexual harassment case you have read concerns the role that sexually demeaning characterizations of women play in creating an exclusionary social and educational climate. To understand how teachers, students, parents, and administrators negotiated questions of appropriateness and legitimacy, and how their decisions affected both the school climate and the curriculum, let us begin by considering the context and the key players described in the case.

## A.  Understanding the Context and Key Players

- What are we told about Roosevelt High School and its students?
    - What is the socioeconomic make-up of the school?
    - Who are the popular students?
    - What role do the popular students play in the organization and daily life of the school (e.g., assemblies, clubs, parental pressure on administration, etc.)?
    - Which female students do you think would have been most likely to lend their support to clubs and activities that were demeaning to students, and why?
- What are we told about the administrators?
    - How did the principal's position on sexual harassment shift?
    - Is there evidence as to why he altered his position at various times?
- What are we told about the School Improvement Council?
    - Whose interests were most represented by council members?
    - How might the make-up of the School Improvement Council have led the principal to believe that Karen's and the other teachers' concerns could be handled in-house, with no damage to his reputation?
- What are we told about the parents who are vocal with regard to the issue of sexual harassment in the school?
    - Which parents became involved at which points in the developing situation?
    - Why might some parents claim an entitlement to affect school issues while others do not?

How did parents differ in their responses to the situation at the school and how did they differ in what they regarded as the salient issue?

- What are we told about Karen and the other teachers?

   Why did Karen and some of the other teachers object to the instances of sexual harassment that they observed? What did they see as the problem?

   Why did some teachers believe that there was no problem and that Karen and her supporters were overreacting? What did these teachers assume or believe?

   For what reasons might still other teachers avoid taking a position? Karen speaks of having broken an "unspoken bond" among teachers to not go public with the school's problems. Does such a bond exist among teachers in the school where you work? If so, why do you think it exists? Whose interests does it serve?

- What role did the media play in addressing the issue of sexual harassment?

   Why did Karen and her supporters decide to contact outside agencies?

   To what extent was this decision helpful, harmful, or ineffective, and why?

## B. Framing the Problem

- Why do some students, parents, and teachers believe that a problem exists while other students, parents, teachers, and administrators insist that there is no problem?

   Which values are considered relevant by each group?

   What assumptions do the two groups make?

   How do members of each group attempt to influence one another's perception of or response to the situation?

   How does the degree of power that each group has to affect the situation shape the action that members of the group take to consolidate or alter the situation?

- What perspectives need to be taken into account to fully understand the problem?

- To what extent is the problem amenable to common sense and to what extent does understanding and resolving the issue require studying sexual harassment as a more general problem?

- What would count as a climate of trust in resolving this situation?
- Which communication forums might best help to address the problems at stake, and which approaches to communication might prove unsatisfactory?
- For those who believe that the primary issue is the protection of students' rights to freedom of expression, what is implied with regard to their more general beliefs about schooling and education?

    Are those who take this stand more likely to see education in transmission terms, for example, or in terms of student growth and flourishing?

    Is the focus of those taking this stand on all students or on a particular few?

- For those who believe that the primary issue is fostering an educational climate in which all students and teachers feel respected, what is implied with regard to their more general beliefs about schooling and education?

    Are those who take this stand more likely to see education in transmission terms, for example, or in terms of student growth and flourishing?

    Is the focus of those taking this stand on all students or on a par ticular few?

## C.   Developing Plans of Action

Students can work in small groups to develop and defend plans of action for addressing sexual harassment in the schools. Plans of action may take at least two forms: plans intended to prevent such situations in other schools; and plans intended to resolve the existing situation at Roosevelt High School. In addition to developing policy guidelines, groups working on plans to resolve the situation at Roosevelt may wish to consider curricular approaches such as Karen herself used.

Informed by their answers to the "Questions to Think About" discussion sheet and the large-group discussion about "Framing the Problem," students should work together in small groups to decide what they see as the key points to be understood and addressed before developing a plan of action; they should be prepared to explain their analyses to the rest of the class. Students working specifically on plans of action for Roosevelt will also need to consult their answers to the questions concerning the "Context and Key Players." While students preparing a plan of action for Roosevelt High School must take account of the specific social and political dynamics as well as other factors described in the case, students preparing plans of action for other schools may decide whether other settings might lead to other plans of action. For example, students may choose to consider such questions as whether age and grade level make a difference to the plans they develop; how courses of action would differ if a particular group (for example, parents or a principal) were adamantly opposed to the implementation of sexual harassment guidelines; which other settings and research materials they might study; and how or whether they would involve particular groups in the decision making process.

Recording the small groups' key points and their arguments as to what is relevant on the board will enable the instructor to focus a large-group discussion on the question of how various solutions foreground, frame, or ignore particular issues. The large-group discussion should allow students to revisit the plans of action they recommend, informed by alternative readings of what is relevant and how the issues are best framed in order to secure the most inclusive educational environment.

## FOLLOW-UP ACTIVITIES

*Using Different Communication Formats to Address the Issues.* Stage at least four different mock forums for publicizing and working through the issues raised by this case. The object is for students to investigate the ways in which particular communications settings foster or inhibit inquiry and change. Among the examples students might choose from are the following:

1. A reader's theater featuring parents', teachers', students', administrators', religious leaders', community members', and activists' letters to the editor of the local newspaper.
2. A television talk show in which "both sides" are invited to share their opinions and the audience is invited to deliver the final verdict.
3. A courtroom in which attorneys for the "accused" and "accusers" argue their different cases before a jury, drawing upon the testimony of the "accused" and the "accusers" for supporting evidence.
4. A therapists' support group in which victims of sexual harassment gather together to work through their understanding of the issues.
5. A group of the students accused of sexual harassment together with their parents, in which they attempt to work their way through an understanding of the issues.

6. An on-line newsgroup in which commentators worldwide are invited to air their opinions.
7. A workshop devoted to designing sexual harassment policies, facilitated by leaders with experience and expertise in the area.
8. A fictional narrative, such as a television "movie of the week," devoted to highlighting and dramatizing the costs and consequences connected with sexual harassment.

*Interviewing.* Students may be asked to interview one another, fellow students in other courses, or students and/or faculty and administrators at a local school to discover whether sexual harassment is recognized as a serious issue and whether students, staff, and faculty are prepared to identify sexual harassment when they encounter it. An important aspect of this project would be for students to determine together what would count as a productive set of interview questions. Simply asking, "Have you seen any evidence of sexual harassment at your school?" for example, would yield limited information if the interviewees were unable or unwilling to recognize sexual harassment in the first place. Coupled with other questions that allowed for a more complete picture of the school environment, however, this question might yield valuable information about students', teachers', and administrators' attitudes.

*Focusing on Media.* Students may be asked to collect examples of media treatments that glamorize sexual harassment, that contribute to a climate that is intimidating to some people but not others on the basis of sexual identity (in some cases, for example, women or gay men will be targeted, but not heterosexual men), and/or that objectify certain people as sexual objects. While sexual harassment does not apply only to the treatment of marginalized groups, it does refer to sexualized treatment in a situation in which there is an unequal balance of power and in which sexual attention is unwelcome, even when tolerated. In particular cases, this may include how some heterosexual men treat other heterosexual men (for example, in fraternity hazing rites). Students looking for examples of media treatments that contribute to a climate in which sexual harassment is seen as legitimate, therefore, should not confine their inquiry to examples of women being treated as sex objects, but should look for intersections of power and sexual objectification more generally.

Because the use of sexual objectification in advertisements and television shows is widespread, it may be most valuable to ask students for one obvious example of how media contribute to a climate of sexual harassment and one subtle example. Students should be prepared to explain the subtle example. They should also be prepared to suggest why the media in question have chosen to use sexual objectification as a framework or device—that is, how it serves their purposes.

*Research Activities.*   Given that the issues in sexual harassment cases may require stepping back from a so-called common sense perspective before students can fully appreciate what is at stake, it is recommended that students pursue at least some outside reading. While a complete list of references would be extensive indeed, students should find the articles, reports, and books listed below quite helpful.

## REFERENCES AND SUGGESTED READINGS

American Association of University Women. (1993). *Hostile hallways: The AAUW survey on sexual harassment in America's schools.* Washington, DC: The American Association of University Women Educational Foundation and Harris/Scholastic Research.

Best, R. (1983). *We've all got scars: What boys and girls learn in elementary schools.* Bloomington: Indiana University Press.

Bodroghkozy, A. (1992). "Is this what you mean by color TV?": Race, gender, and contested meanings in NBC's *Julia.* In L. Spigel & D. Mann (Eds.), *Private screenings: Television and the female consumer* (pp. 143–167). Minneapolis: University of Minnesota Press.

hooks, b. (1994). Gangsta culture, sexism and misogyny: Who will take the rap? In *Outlaw culture: Resisting representations* (pp. 115–123). New York: Routledge.

Lefkowitz, B. (1997). *Our guys: The Glen Ridge rape and the secret life of the perfect suburb.* Berkeley, CA: University of California Press.

MacKinnon, C. A. (1979). *Sexual harassment of working women: A case of sex discrimination.* New Haven, CT: Yale University Press.

MacKinnon, C. A. (1993). *Only words.* Cambridge, MA: Harvard University Press.

Regan, A. (1994). "Type normal like the rest of us": Writing, power, and homophobia in the networked composition classroom. In L. Garner (Ed.), *Tilting the tower: Lesbians teaching queer subjects* (pp. 117–27). New York: Routledge.

Rice, S. (1996). The "discovery" and evolution of sexual harassment as an educational issue. *Initiatives, 57*(2), 1–14.

Stein, N. D. (1993). Sexual harassment in schools: Administrators must break the casual approach to objectionable behavior. *The School Administrator, 50*(1), 14–21.

Toobin, J. (1998, February 9). The trouble with sex. *The New Yorker, 73(6),* 48–55.

Walkerdine, V. (1990). Sex, power and pedagogy. In *Schoolgirl fictions* (pp. 3–15). London: Verso.

# Case 10

# Help, With Strings
# Attached

*Janine T. Remillard*


## SYNOPSIS OF THE CASE

In "Help, With Strings Attached," a first-year teacher, Emma Magleby, describes the unanticipated struggles she had accommodating a Chapter I aide in her fifth grade classroom. As a new teacher, she knew little about the Chapter I program, but was pleased about the prospect of having an aide for 30 minutes a day to help students during her math class. In teaching math, she was trying to engage her students in problem solving and reasoning. Most of the tasks she gave her students involved working in small groups, often with concrete materials. Although she used the topics in the math textbook to guide her curriculum, the students rarely used the text during the lessons. Since this type of activity was novel for her students, Emma thought an extra adult during part of each lesson could facilitate students' work on the mathematical activities. Even though the aide would be responsible for assisting specific students who were struggling in math, Emma believed that the most natural way to do this would be to assist any and all who were having difficulty, whether specifically identified or not, while they were engaged in the tasks she had assigned.

As it turned out, the Chapter I coordinator and the aide did not agree. Because the aide had to document how much time she spent with each child, she preferred to work with each student at the back of the room in order to give him or her as much individual attention as possible. Emma was uneasy with this approach because it pulled students away from the group work and labeled them as less capable than the others. It also required Emma to come up with tasks to give the aide to work on with the students. Because she was not following the textbook page by page, it was not possible to merely tell the aide which page the students were on.

As a new teacher, Emma was unprepared to manage this sort of philosophical conflict in her classroom. She wanted her students to receive the extra help available to them. At the same time, she worried about the impact that the Chapter I program was having on her students and her mathematics teaching.

## BACKGROUND INFORMATION

Chapter I is a federally funded program established to provide academic assistance in reading and math to students from low-income families who are achieving significantly below grade level. Guidelines for the administration of the program are periodically changed by the federal administration. At the time that this case was written, schools received Chapter I funding if more than 65% of the students qualified for free or reduced lunch. Schools and districts have some latitude in the way they deliver Chapter I assistance; thus, the programs tend to vary from school to school. Nevertheless, all schools are required to document the services they provide.

## ISSUES IN THE CASE

*1. Potential Benefits and Drawbacks of Using Resource Assistance to Support Struggling Students.* This case illustrates how resource assistance designed to support students academically without removing them from their regular classrooms might continue to exclude them from learning opportunities. The Chapter I program at Carlton Elementary was designed to be inclusive, serving students in their regular classroom. However, it was exclusive in its own way. In order to receive assistance, students were pulled away from their class work. Furthermore, those students who received in-class tutoring were labeled as less able by the others in the class. The case raises questions about how to design a resource assistance program that is genuinely inclusive, and how requirements for documentation of appropriate use of funds might be translated into a more flexible set of procedures.

*2. Dealing With Conflicts Between Teacher and Program Goals.* This case also illustrates that teaching is not an insulated endeavor. Choices that one teacher makes often affect the choices of others. In this case, we see a new teacher whose attempts to create an inclusive classroom seem to be thwarted by the format of the Chapter I program. At the same time, the intent of the Chapter I program is to provide direct assistance to those students who traditionally have not succeeded in schools. The case provides opportunities for teachers to consider how such conflicts affect students' learning opportunities and to consider alternative approaches.

*3. The Effects of Testing on Decision Making and Instruction.* The case provides an example of how tests can influence instructional decisions. The Chapter I supervisor insisted on documentation of students' deficiencies, considering Emma's observations of her students to be insufficient. Thus, Emma felt obligated to arbitrarily select a test from the textbook. The selection of this test had a powerful impact on students, as it determined whether they qualified for Chapter I assistance. Thus, this case illustrates the authority that tests are given in instructional decision making. It is worth noting that most of the students who did not fare well on Emma's pretest were from low-income families. These students were not necessarily the ones that Emma had placed on her mental list. This point raises a number of questions about how class and ability are often intertwined in educational classifications.

*4. Other Issues:*

## QUESTIONS TO THINK ABOUT

*(These questions can be given to students prior to reading the case or to small groups for review in class before the whole-class discussion.)*

1. What do you think of Emma's philosophy and goals for teaching mathematics? Are they similar to or different from your own?

2. In your opinion, what are the most important issues or problems raised in the case? Of these, can you identify one that is most important? Why do you think it is important?
3. If Emma came to you for advice, what might you tell her?

## DISCUSSION QUESTIONS

The discussion outline consists of three parts: understanding the context and key players, framing the problem, and developing plans of action. These three headings can serve as main headings on the chalkboard. Under each heading on the board, you might have subheadings for the purpose of recording students' comments during the discussion (e.g., "Context and Key Players: Carlton Elementary School," "Emma's class," "Emma," "Sandy Green," and "Jennifer Land"). What follows is one way to open the discussion, followed by questions you might ask during each segment of the discussion:

The case you have read opens with a description of Carlton Elementary School, where Emma teaches. Let's begin by describing the context and the key players in the case.

### A.  Understanding the Context and Key Players

- What are we told about Carlton Elementary School?
    The community Carlton is located in?
    The demographics of the students?
    The Chapter I program?
- What are we told about Emma's class?
- What are we told about Emma?
    What are Emma's views about teaching math?
    What does her curriculum and pedagogy look like?
- What are we told about Sandy Green, the Chapter I supervisor?
- What are we told about Jennifer Land, the Chapter I aide?

### B.  Framing the Problem

- What do you see as the major problem in the case?

This question can be answered in several ways. The case focuses on the conflicts that Emma felt about the way the Chapter I program is implemented in her classroom. From her perspective, the aide disrupted her regular activities, interfering with her goals and reinforcing social class divisions among her students. Nevertheless, from a broader perspective, the problem is one of conflicting philosophies or approaches. Both Emma and the Chapter I aide had their own responsibilities and agendas, which tended to interfere with one another. Further exacerbating the problem was the fact that both had little familiarity with the other's goals.

• In addition to what we've just discussed, what other issues are raised by the case?

Once the students have framed the problem, it is often helpful to ask them to list other issues raised by the case. This question gives students an opportunity to suggest related or unrelated issues or concerns that they see in the case that may not be directly identified by the descriptions of the central problem. (See the section "Issues in the Case" for a list of possible issues.) Keep in mind that preservice teachers are more likely to identify specific events than to frame broad, generalized issues. For example, a student might point out the discrepancy between Emma's mental list of students needing help and those identified by the test. As facilitator, you might suggest framing the issue broadly, for example, the effects of testing on instructional decisions.

## C.   Developing Plans of Action

Students can work in small groups to determine how Emma might accommodate or respond to the Chapter I aide in her classroom, which they later share with the class. When discussing them with the entire class, it is helpful to ask the students which issues raised during the earlier discussion figured most significantly in their decisions. Record students' plans on the board and identify the influential issues with colored chalk or connecting lines so the class can assess the extent to which their solutions addressed the issues raised. Once all the plans are listed and discussed, bring the students' attention to any issues from the discussion that were not considered in their plans. Students can then discuss why these issues did not seem relevant. They can also develop additional plans or modify their existing plans to take these issues into account. An underlying aim of this activity is to examine how the issues and problems that are identified and the way they are framed affect what plans of action are chosen.

## FOLLOW-UP ACTIVITIES

*Library and School-Based Research*    Students can gather more information about Chapter I programs and issues related to providing assistance for students in need of academic support. In addition to researching the Chapter I program, students can interview those involved with Chapter I in a school or district office. They can also interview classroom teachers who have worked with such programs in order to gain insights into the issues raised in the case discussion.

*Role Play.*    To draw on what they learned from their research on Chapter I programs, students can role play a meeting over the summer between Emma, Sandy Green, and Jennifer Land to resolve the problems that occurred around the Chapter I tutoring. Select three students to perform the role play and then allow them time to prepare with small groups consisting of the other students in the class. Other characters can be added to the role play if needed such as the school principal, a colleague of Emma's, the district math specialist, or a district or state representative for the Chapter I program. Any one of these individuals could serve as the facilitator of the meeting. If students engaged in the role play reach an impasse, they could "come out of character" and ask students in the audience for advice.

After the role play, you may want to have students who performed the role play talk about what the experience was like for them. Following this discussion, ask students to evaluate the plan of action that was proposed in the role play and suggest alternative possibilities.

# Case 11

# In the Best Interests
# of the Child

*Beth L. Tulbert*

## SYNOPSIS OF THE CASE

This case is presented in two parts. Part A describes the efforts of Heather
and Bill Bonn to find inclusive classroom placements for their son, Scott,
who was identified at birth as having Down syndrome. After a variety of
preschool placements, mostly in segregated special education settings and
in Head Start, Scott attended kindergarten in a cluster school, Hillview,
where he spent most of each day in a self-contained classroom with students who ranged in age from 5 to 12. This was not really what the Bonns
wanted for Scott; they wanted him to attend his neighborhood school,
Coleridge. Thus, prior to Scott's next IEP meeting, the Bonns requested
that Scott be allowed to attend Coleridge. In making this request, the
Bonns met with numerous administrators and teachers, without success.
Part A concludes with a disastrous IEP meeting for Scott, in which the
Bonns make a formal request that Scott attend his neighborhood school.
This request was denied because administrators did not feel that the
school was prepared to accept students with disabilities. Feeling frus-
trated, the Bonns walked out of the meeting, ready to file for due process.

Part B, which appears in the appendix to this set of teaching notes (see pages 209–211), begins with the compromise that was reached over the summer, in which Scott would be placed at Coleridge for a 30-day trial period beginning in the fall of the following year. When the Bonns met with the new incoming principal at Coleridge in April, they found that she was an advocate of neighborhood schools. Surprised that Scott did not already attend Coleridge, the principal recruited other students with disabilities in the neighborhood and arranged for a special education class to be placed at Coleridge; Scott has now been at Coleridge for the last four years, where he has slowly made the transition into general education classrooms. Although the transition was difficult for Scott and his teachers, it has been successful because of teacher inservice, adaptations of the curriculum, the Circle of Friends program that assigns a buddy to Scott each day, and the school's emphasis on ownership, that is, responsibility for all its students in the neighborhood. The Bonns now worry about what will happen in junior high school, where they believe their only option is a self-contained class.

## ISSUES IN THE CASE

*1. Determining the Least Restrictive Environment and Educational Placement.* An important issue in this case is determining the appropriate placement for Scott. The Individuals with Disabilities Act (IDEA) (Public Law 101–476) requires that placement decisions be made on the basis of each child's needs and must be in the least restrictive educational environment (with nondisabled peers) to the maximum extent appropriate. However, parents, administrators, and teachers may not agree as to what kind of placements would be most appropriate for individual students and would meet IDEA requirements. Thus, questions raised by this case include the following: How are educational placement decisions supposed to be made? How much input should parents have in making placement decisions for their children? What criteria should administrators use in making placement decisions and in determining support services? How can conflicts between parents and school personnel be avoided in IEP meetings?

*2. The Impact of Administrators' Attitudes Towards Students With Disabilities.* Administrators set the instructional tone within a school or district and can either facilitate or prevent reform in their school programs. In this case, we saw a variety of attitudes towards inclusion on the part of administrators when they met with the Bonns, which had an enormous effect on the placement decisions for Scott and on the support provided to Scott in his classes.

*3. Teachers' Beliefs About Children With Disabilities and the Need for Teacher Support.*   General education teachers often feel unprepared or unsupported in teaching students with disabilities. This case includes issues related to the concerns and attitudes of teachers toward students with disabilities, their concerns about meeting students' needs, and the kinds of support for teachers and for students that must be provided for inclusion to be successful.

*4. Other Issues:*

## QUESTIONS TO THINK ABOUT

*(These questions can be given to students prior to reading the case or to small groups for review in class before the whole-class discussion. To complete question 3, students will need to review the legal requirements for placement decisions specified in their state regulations for the implementation of IDEA.)*

1.  What is the central problem or dilemma in this case?
2.  If you were the Bonns, how would you have responded to the different school administrators they encountered over the years? Why were the Bonns so frustrated at the IEP meeting that took place at the end of Part A of the case?
3.  Why did the administrators and teachers want Scott to attend Hillview, the cluster school, instead of his neighborhood school, as his parents had requested? Is their position justified? (You should answer this question by reviewing current state regulations for determining placement based on IDEA, and evaluate the administrators responses' to the Bonns based on these requirements.)
4.  If you were facilitating the IEP meeting, what approach could you have followed to prevent the meeting from reaching a stalemate?

## THE DISCUSSION OUTLINE

The discussion outline presented below consists of three parts: understanding the context of the case, framing the problem, and developing plans of action. These three headings can serve as main headings on the chalkboard. Under each heading on the board, you might have subheadings for recording students' comments during the discussion. For example, under the heading, "Understanding the Context and Key Players," you might have the following subheadings: "Scott," "the Bonns," "teachers," "administrators," etc. What follows is one way to open the discussion, which is followed by questions you might ask during each segment of the discussion:

> The case you have just read, written from the Bonns' perspective, describes their attempts to have their son, Scott, placed in an inclusive general education setting. As you know from reading the case, the Bonns have had many frustrating experiences in their quest to have Scott placed in inclusive settings. Let's begin our discussion by reviewing what the case tells us about the context and key players. Then we will focus on the disastrous IEP meeting that concludes this part of the case.

## A.  Understanding the Context of the Case

- What are we told about Scott?
- What are we told about his parents, the Bonns? Why did they want him in inclusive settings and in his neighborhood school?
- What are we told about Scott's educational history and the schools that he has been in? Why had Scott changed schools and districts so frequently?
- What are we told about the attitudes of the teachers, principals, and district level administrators in the case?
- What organizational factors influenced the administrators' decisions about placements for Scott?

## B.  Framing the Problem

- To understand the problem from different perspectives, let's begin with the Bonns. Try to imagine yourself in their place. If you were Scott's mother or father, how would you describe the central problem in the case?

- How do you think the different administrators and teachers involved in Scott's first grade IEP meeting might perceive the problem?
- Why did the IEP meeting end so disastrously?
- In your review of IDEA and your state's regulations, did the administrators follow the intent of IDEA related to educational placement?
- What do you see as the central problem in this case?


## C.  Developing Plans of Action

This part of the case discussion can focus on decision making at the IEP meeting regarding placement and support services for Scott as he enters first grade. Now that students are familiar with IDEA, and after they have reviewed chapter 4 in *Inclusive Education* ("Collaboration as a Tool for Inclusion," by Marshall Welch) they can reenact the IEP meeting. To prepare for this role play, you can organize students in small groups, with each group assigned a role such as the Bonns, the Bonns' legal representative, the meeting facilitator, and any other roles you deem appropriate (these may include those listed in the case as having attended the meeting and/or others not listed). While representing the various perspectives suggested by the roles, students in the role play need to focus on what would meet the requirements of the law and be in the best interests of Scott in terms of both placement and necessary support services.

As an alternative, students who are prospective or practicing teachers at the secondary level can develop a plan of action for Scott's transition to junior high school by preparing a plan listing what classes Scott can be integrated into, and identifying the content and skills that Scott should be taught in the special education class. This could also be enacted as an IEP meeting.

Separately, or as part of the IEP meeting, students can assume the roles of different general education teachers and develop plans of action for including students like Scott in their classrooms. They might address the following questions: What support services might they need? How would they adapt their curriculum, instructional strategies, student groupings, etc.? How would they involve this student's parents in planning and evaluating their child's education at more informal meetings such as parent–teacher conferences? Chapters from *Inclusive Education* would be helpful to students in making planning decisions. At any point you can also distribute photocopies of Part B of the case, which appears in the appendix to this set of teaching notes.

## FOLLOW-UP ACTIVITIES

Although readings have been included in various parts of this case discussion, further research on IDEA and adaptative instruction would be particularly relevant as follow-up activities to the case discussion. Students could assume the role of a principal and develop a plan for integrating Scott into the general education class at Coleridge, which should include ways to fund their plan. For your information, in Part B of this case, the principal at Coleridge identified 10 students with disabilities in the school's boundaries, moved those students to Coleridge, and hired a special education teacher. Hiring the additional teacher could have been funded in one of several ways. First, the principal could have shuffled her current staff to open a funding line for a new special education teacher (e.g., consolidated four third grade classes into three classes because of low student enrollment in the third grade). Second, the principal could have reduced the number of third grade teachers and moved a third grade teacher with the appropriate special education credentials into the special education position. Third, the school district could have approved funds for an additional teacher if the increase in numbers of students with disabilities warranted such an allocation.

Students could relate this case to "Building an Inclusive School: Vision, Leadership, and Community" (case 12). In doing so, you could tell students that Scott is about to enter second grade in this school. Students could then assume the roles of the general education and special education teacher in this case and role play their collaborative efforts in accommodating methods, curriculum, and materials for Scott. They could also role play conversations between the administrators in this second case and the Bonns.

# APPENDIX

## PART B OF THE CASE "IN THE BEST INTERESTS OF THE CHILD"

### As told by Heather and Bill Bonn

After we left the meeting, our representatives from the legal center remained and negotiated a compromise. The agreement stipulated that next year Scott would transfer to Coleridge, but only on a 30-day trial basis. If, by the end of that time, Scott had not made sufficient progress, he would be sent back to Hillview, the cluster school. The compromise also stated that a new IEP would be written in April and would include a transition plan for the month of May. We accepted their offer. We felt that at least it was progress. We also knew that under state rules, if at the end of the 30 days they told us that it was not working, we could file for due process and automatically have an extension on our existing placement. So Scott would attend Coleridge, but for how long was still very much up in the air.

Coleridge was scheduled to change principals at the end of the school year. When we met in April with the incoming principal, she asked us, "Why do you want to do this on a trial basis? Why a transition period? Why not have Scott start second grade just like all the other students?"

We told her that the agreement was the best deal we had been able to get for Scott. She was appalled, saying that she believed all students with disabilities within her school boundaries should attend Coleridge. She said, "It's not a special privilege that he's here. He lives within the geographical boundaries, he is a member of this community school." This was the first person in the district who we felt was on our side. Over the years the district had been telling us that they couldn't have a special education classroom at Coleridge because they didn't have enough students to warrant a teacher. When we mentioned this, the new principal said, "Let me do some investigating."

Although the director of special education for the district was unhappy that someone else was taking the lead, the principal managed to find 10 students with disabilities within the school's boundaries. She called all the parents and asked them if they would like their child to attend their neighborhood school. They all said, "Yes!" The principal then hired a special education teacher. Scott's now been at Coleridge for four years. It took much anguish and five placements before we finally got what we wanted for our son.

Although his placement at the neighborhood school was finally resolved, his IEP was not. None of the authorities were willing to commit needed services. For example, just to maintain the same level of occupational therapy as he had had at Hillview took 90 days and 39 contacts with professionals in the district, including the special education teacher, the principal, the related services coordinator, and the director of special education. Only when we reached the superintendent of the district was Scott provided with this needed service.

The transition to Coleridge wasn't easy for either Scott or his teachers. To help him adjust to the new school, Scott spent most of the day working on academics in the special education classroom; he was integrated in the regular classroom only for short periods for art, music, lunch, and show-and-tell. At first, he did not like going into the regular classroom, but before long it was the reverse: He didn't want to leave. He would just sit down and not budge. When they tried to pull him up, he'd say, "I'm not going." By then he was enjoying the regular classroom—this was his room. As the year progressed, his teacher adjusted too, and said, "Yeah, this is a good thing, you know. He's listening to me more and he's found his first friend." She was referring to a boy in the class who was very good with him and who Scott always liked to sit next to and play with. The two of them even went to some hockey games together outside of school. We were thrilled that he finally had a friend in the neighborhood! He was jumping up and down and putting his arm around his pal—really excited to have a friend.

To make inclusion work, the school emphasized the idea of ownership: that all students in the neighborhood belong there. Some consultants came to do some inservice with the teachers, and the special education teacher showed students how the "Circle of Friends" works.

By third grade, the teachers began to adapt some of the curriculum for him, letting him use a calculator in math, answer fewer questions on timed tests, and dictate stories which he would then copy. During partner reading, students would read to Scott until they came to a word they thought he knew; then they would let Scott read it. Scott's teacher also set up a calendar on the wall and invited the students to sign up to be Scott's buddy for the day. There was never a lack of students to work with Scott. When it came time for group activities, students would say, "Can Scott be in our group?" They'd sit with him at lunch, play with him at recess, and make sure he had come in. At Hillview it had been the little girls who had watched out for Scott—he was their pet. Now, at his neighborhood school, it's the boys—they're the ones he plays baseball with in the summer and basketball with out on the playground. It's the boys now who sit next to him in the classroom and give him help if he needs it. If Scott gets hurt, those boys are right there to help him. And if he's doing something he shouldn't, they'll say, "Scott, stop that," or "Don't do that." And he responds to them.

Scott is now fully integrated. Lately, we've noticed that he is more verbal. For example, if you ask him, "Did you wash your hands before dinner?" he'll say, "Yes, I did." He's really trying to express himself more than he has in the past. His speech is still hard to understand, but he's attempting more and picking up some real phrases. He's less dependent on an assistant at school and has started to develop independent work skills and to stay on task.

We're worried about junior high, though, because when Scott goes there in a few years, it will be another cluster school, where he will be in a self-contained classroom most of the day. We're afraid his integration will decrease dramatically. Perhaps that's when he'll realize he's different. Right now he thinks he's just like everybody else. We hope to meet with the special education teacher before Scott goes into sixth grade to find out what skills he'll need for junior high. We'd like to see him continue with academics, but we realize that at some point he'll need to focus more on daily living skills. We want Scott to shoot for the stars, and if he trips over the moon, that's okay. There's nothing wrong with that. We hope his teachers will challenge him and expect something from him, and treat him as part of the student body. Yes, he's a little different, but then, in subtle ways, aren't we all?

# Case 12

# Building an Inclusive School: Vision, Leadership, and Community

*Beth L. Tulbert*

## SYNOPSIS OF THE CASE

This case is written from the perspectives of a first grade teacher (Bonnie), a special education teacher (Lisa), and an elementary school principal (Sue) as they describe the evolution of their school from a traditional pull-out resource room model to that of an inclusive school with no special education classrooms. Without realizing it, faculty at their school took their first steps toward inclusion when they began to use cooperative learning in their classrooms. Having students pulled out for resource during cooperative learning activities became problematic for the teachers and the principal. They were concerned that students going to resource were left out and that it was difficult to include them when they returned. Teachers were also concerned that students in resource were negatively labeled by their peers and considered someone else's responsibility. Finally, students who were not eligible for resource were not able to benefit from the additional help and support that special educators could have provided.

After these concerns were voiced and teachers began to talk about keeping students in their classes, Sue began to investigate the possibilities of inclusive education and teachers' attitudes regarding inclusion. After visiting another school that had become inclusive, Bonnie and the other first grade teachers were so impressed that they began to plan a pilot project for the next year, which was approved by the whole school faculty. As a result, Bonnie agreed to teach an "at-risk" class containing all students in the first grade who were deemed likely to fall behind. This class would follow the regular first grade curriculum, but unlike the other classrooms, it would have an aide and a smaller number of students. At the end of the first year, student progress was impressive and the faculty decided to develop a plan for making the whole school inclusive. The faculty decided to gradually implement the plan by adding grade levels each year.

As they reflect back on several years of implementation, the case authors suggest several factors that made inclusion successful. These included time for weekly teacher meetings, parent and community involvement, related innovations such as narrative report cards, and district support. The case concludes with the dilemma of how to sustain a successful inclusion program if they were to lose the necessary funding or if the principal were to leave for another position, which in fact did happen.

## ISSUES IN THE CASE

*1. How Services Are Delivered to Students in Special Education.* Legally, school districts are required to provide a continuum of service delivery options for students in special education. Additionally, students are to be placed in the least restrictive educational environment with their nondisabled peers to the maximum extent possible. How does inclusion fit into this continuum of service delivery options? How is the decision made as to what placement is best for each child? How is the least restrictive environment requirement determined? Who makes the placement decision, the school or the parents? Are all school staff responsible for all children? Do all neighborhood children belong to their neighborhood school? Why would a student be sent to a school other than his or her neighborhood school? What are the benefits of inclusion for students with disabilities and for general education students?

*2. How to Obtain and/or Allocate Resources to Provide Services for Students in Inclusive Settings.*   Federal funding for students with disabilities is provided using a funding formula based on level of special education support. The dilemma arises when special education support is provided to students in general classes, which keeps these students from ever needing to be labeled. In this situation, students are often provided services without any additional funding to support the teacher's time and resources used. If we prevent student referrals and placements in special education programs through proactive measures, how will funding levels be maintained to provide for the supports critical to effective inclusion efforts? Why do we label students? What are the advantages and disadvantages of labeling in a traditional versus an inclusion model? Can teaching assistants or aides take the place of special education teachers? How did the faculty and parents in this case find additional time to plan the conversion to an inclusive setting? What were the monetary, physical, human, and material resources required for the successful conversion to an inclusion school?

*3. How Administrators Support Faculty.*    Administrative support for faculty is critical, especially when faculty decide to engage in school reform efforts such as inclusion. What impact does the principal's attitude toward students with disabilities have on reform efforts such as these? How does a principal support faculty in making decisions about whether and how to move toward an inclusion model? In this case, was the decision to become an inclusive school a top-down or a bottom-up decision? Does this have an effect on the success of inclusion efforts? As they implement an inclusion model, how can faculty gain the support of the district administration?

*4. Roles of Teachers in Inclusive Classrooms.*    The roles of teachers, both general education and special education, and of related service providers and aides change as a result of becoming an inclusion school. Bonnie indicated that she was more than a teacher in the at-risk class; she was a coordinator. What did she coordinate? What are the implications for general education teachers if they teach in inclusive settings and need to coordinate various support staff? What types of support will a classroom teacher who has an inclusion class need? How can teachers support their colleagues who are teaching in inclusion classrooms? How might a special education teacher's role change as a result of inclusion?

*5. The Process of School Reform or Schoolwide Change.*    The process of school reform is complex and takes time. This case examines factors that facilitated the schoolwide change at Spring Lake Elementary such as faculty initiatives, parental involvement and education, and teacher inservice. What would have happened if any of those factors had been absent? What happened before any real change took place? How long did it take to change the service delivery for all students in all grades? What do you think would have happened if Sue, the principal, had left during this period of school reform? At the end of the case, new problems occur: There is the possibility of reduced funding , and Sue does leave. What will it take for the inclusion program to be maintained under these circumstances?

*6. Other Issues:*

## QUESTIONS TO THINK ABOUT

*(These questions can be given to students prior to reading the case or to small groups for review in class before the whole-class discussion.)*

1. How did Max's parents feel about placing their son in the resource program? How would you feel if the teachers for your child wanted to place him or her in a special education resource program?
2. What were the general education teachers' reservations about inclusion? Were they valid?
3. What were the special education teacher's reservations about inclusion? Were they valid?
4. Why was inclusion successful in this case? List all the things that the teachers and administrators did to assure its success. What outside factors also contributed?

## THE DISCUSSION OUTLINE

This discussion outline consists of three parts: understanding the context of the case and its key players, framing the problem and evaluating the solution, and developing plans of action. These three headings can serve as main headings on the chalkboard. Under each heading on the board, you might have subheadings for the purpose of recording students' comments during the discussion (e.g., under the heading "Understanding the Context and Key Players," you might list as subheadings: "Spring Lake," "Bonnie," "Lisa," "Sue," etc.). What follows is one way to open the discussion, which is followed by questions you might ask during each segment of the discussion:

The case you have just read is written from the perspectives of a first grade teacher, a special education teacher, and an elementary school principal as they describe the evolution of their school from a traditional pull-out resource room model to that of an inclusive school with no special education classrooms. Let's begin our discussion by reviewing what the case authors tell us about the context and key players.

## A.  Understanding the Context and Key Players

- What are we told about Spring Lake Elementary at the beginning of the case? What was the role of special education? Is it considered a place or a service? What were the problems with the pull-out program?
- What are we told about Bonnie? About Lisa? How did they feel about inclusive education in the beginning? Why do their attitudes change? Why does Bonnie agree to take the at-risk class?
- What are we told about Sue, the principal?

## B.  Framing the Problem and Evaluating the Solution that Was Tried

- In the beginning of the case, how do most of the educators at Spring Lake view the problem? Are there different viewpoints?
- What do you see as the central problem?

Initially, the problem is how to provide the additional special education support services to the students with disabilities without pulling them away from the instruction in the general education classrooms. The teachers decided to begin by keeping students with disabilities together in a smaller, at-risk first grade classroom, using the regular curriculum and bringing the special education support to them in the general education setting.

- Was the school's move toward inclusion successful? Why? Why not?
- To generalize from this case and others you have read, what conditions are necessary for a school to be successful in moving to an inclusion model?

- What other possible solutions might the faculty have tried? What are the advantages and disadvantages of each of your alternative solutions?
- What do you see as the problem presented at the end of the case?

## C.  Developing Plans of Action for Sustaining the Inclusion Model

Now that students have evaluated Spring Lake's move toward inclusion and explored alternative plans, you might have them focus on the problem raised at the end of the case: how to maintain funding and support for the plan the faculty has put in place. Students might begin by brainstorming ways to maintain current funding levels and identify new avenues of funding or volunteer help. For example, to develop solutions to maintaining the inclusion program in the face of reduced federal funding, Lisa can make sure that all students eligible for special education are identified, even if they are remaining in the general education classroom. Sue can negotiate with the school district and the state-level administration for a funding waiver that will allow the school to continue to receive the same level of funding that they received prior to their inclusion efforts. The school can work with the PTA and other service organizations in the community to solicit additional funding and volunteer support.

As part of the analysis or as a way to bring closure to the discussion, you may want to use this case to discuss the advantages and disadvantages of inclusion using a table similar to the one that follows:

|  | Advantages | Disadvantages |
| --- | --- | --- |
| Special Education Teacher |  |  |
| General Education Teacher |  |  |
| Students With Disabilities |  |  |
| General Education Students |  |  |
| Administrators |  |  |
| School Districts |  |  |
| Parents and Families |  |  |

## FOLLOW-UP ACTIVITIES

This case discusses a school's successful change to an inclusion model. You might ask students to compare and contrast the events and outcomes in this case with those provided in "Inclusion for All? The Dilemma of a School's Move Toward Inclusion" (case 13 in *Inclusive Education*), in which inclusion was less successful. Or, contrast it with some of the cases presented by R. F. Elmore, P. L. Peterson, & S. J. McCarthey in *Restructuring in the classroom: Teaching, learning, and school organization.* (Jossey-Bass, San Francisco, 1996). Additionally, students could interview teachers and students in schools that have become inclusive and schools using a traditional service delivery model to examine issues related to the planning process, how inclusion was implemented in these schools, their attitudes about inclusion, benefits and disadvantages of inclusion, etc. In addition, you might have students examine the research literature on the efficacy of traditional service delivery models and inclusion. Students may also want to list the legal requirements for determining placement based on IDEA and describe what inclusion would look like when it meets the legal requirements for determining placement. Students can research the steps required for effective change (school reform) and evaluate this case based on their findings.

# Case 13

## Inclusion for All?
## Dilemmas of a School's
## Move Toward Inclusion

*Beth L. Tulbert*

### SYNOPSIS OF THE CASE

This case describes one school's experience with inclusion, narrated by a
veteran kindergarten teacher. Broadview was once a prestigious suburban
school, but because of population shifts, has become an inner-city school.
In an attempt to provide a better, less fragmented education to the students
at Broadview, the faculty has implemented an inclusion service delivery
model in place of the traditional pull-out program model. These reform
efforts coincided with curriculum reform efforts, including cooperative
grouping and a whole language, literacy-based approach to teaching reading and language. Faculty who previously provided services to students in
a pull-out setting are now part of grade level teams and provide services
within the general education classes. Inclusion and team-teaching are
working well in some grade levels, but not so well in others. Additionally,
some grade levels have abandoned cooperative learning and gone back to
more traditional approaches. Concerns have been raised about teachers'
knowledge and skill levels regarding inclusion, working and teaching in
teams, and teaching students who bring diverse learning and behavior
needs into the classroom. Additionally, the lack of time for planning and

collaboration has been an issue. Teachers also complain about students
with severe behavior problems, who they see as taking an inordinate
amount of teacher time and attention. Identifying these students as eligible
for special education services is a lengthy process and has been made
lengthier because the special education staff have other responsibilities as
parts of grade level teams.

## ISSUES IN THE CASE

*1. Placement Options for Children With Disabilities.*   IDEA requires
that a continuum of placement options be provided for children with disabilities. The decision of which placement along that continuum is best for
a particular child is an individual decision based on the child's specific
strengths and weaknesses and the supports needed for that child. How
many placement options are available at Broadview? (Not all options
must be available at Broadview, but must be available at the district level.)
How does this meet the legal requirement of providing a continuum of
placement options? How could the situation at Broadview be changed to
meet the legal requirements?

*2. Implementing School Reform Efforts.*   School reform efforts require
a great deal of up-front time and planning. Some of the most successful
efforts in the literature have included pilot projects involving one grade or
exceptionality. Training prior to the implementation of reform efforts such
as inclusion is critical. School faculty must also realize that change does
not happen at once, but rather it takes time—most reform efforts take five
years. Change is also uncomfortable. How might Broadview's first year
have been different if the school had implemented inclusion at only the
first and second grades? How could the school staff find additional time
for planning? Did training occur before making the changes described in
this case? Is it clear that all teachers and staff had an opportunity to voice
their concerns before this change took place? Have all potential problems
been brainstormed and possible solutions generated?

*3. Skills and Knowledge Required for Teaming and Inclusion.*   Several
of the problems described in this case reflect a lack of skills and knowledge for the new roles and activities that the school staff were expected to
assume. Additionally, there were many changes made at once, which
added to the teachers' difficulty in mastering several new skills and

knowledge bases at one time. What were some of the new skills that teachers were expected to demonstrate? When should they have received training in these new skills? How many new skills or how much new knowledge can one person be expected to master and demonstrate at once? How could the transition to new roles and activities have been made more manageable?

*4. Other Issues:*

## QUESTIONS TO THINK ABOUT

*(The questions can be given to students prior to reading the case or to small groups for review in class before the whole-class discussion.)*

1. What do you think are the main issues and problems in this case?
2. If you were a teacher at Broadview, what would have been your solution to the problem of fragmentation in the education of the students? Would you have elected to stay when given the choice to leave? What types of training would you have wanted before starting the inclusion program?
3. Do you have other suggestions for teaching and managing the behavior of the students with behavior problems?
4. Have you ever worked in a team or team-taught in school? Was it easier or more difficult than working or teaching on your own?

## THE DISCUSSION OUTLINE

This discussion outline consists of three parts: understanding the context and key players, framing the problem, and developing plans of action. These three headings can serve as main headings on the chalkboard. Under each heading on the board, you might have subheadings for the purpose of recording students' comments during the discussion. For example, under the heading of "Understanding the Context and Key Players," you might have subheadings such as "Broadview Elementary School," "the General Education Teachers," "the Students," and "Support Services for Students with Disabilities." What follows is one way to open the discussion, which is followed by questions you might ask during each segment of the discussion:

This case describes Broadview's first year using inclusion as a service delivery model for all children in their school, seen from a kindergarten teacher's perspective. Let's begin by describing the context and the key players in the case.

## A.  Understanding the Context and Key Players

- What do we know about Broadview?
- What do we know about the general education teachers at Broadview?
- What do we know about the students?
- Why did the faculty want to move toward an inclusion model?
- What do we know about the support services that exist for students with special needs at the conclusion of the case?

## B.  Framing the Problem

- How does the case narrator, Lou Chestnut, view the problem at the end of the case?
- What do you see as the main problem(s) at this point?
- What factors contributed to the problems described in this case?

## C.  Developing Plans of Action

Students could develop a plan for implementing the reform efforts proposed by the faculty at Broadview in a way that would have circumvented many of the problems they are currently experiencing. Further, they could devise a plan for addressing the current situation at Broadview, which would provide solutions for the problems they are currently experiencing.

## FOLLOW-UP ACTIVITIES

The issues of implementing an inclusion model can be further explored through court cases, case comparisons, role playing, and narrative writing. For example:

- Students could research court cases that have resolved disputes related to inclusion. What have the courts said relating to placing students in inclusive settings? What have courts said relating to only one placement option?

- Students could compare this case with "Building an Inclusive School: Vision, Leadership, and Community" (case 12 of *Inclusive Education*) to examine why inclusion was more successful in that case.
- Students could role play the team meeting for the fifth and sixth grade teams in an attempt to resolve some of the problems within the teams.
- Students could describe in narrative or expository form a typical class period before the reform efforts, where there were large numbers of students with diverse needs who left class for various pull-out programs. Students could then contrast it with a typical class period in the current model with team-teaching and multiple staff in the room and support being provided to students within the class.

# Case 14

# Conflicts in Collaboration

*David Dynak*

## SYNOPSIS OF THE CASE

This case begins and ends with the grievances of Joan, a reading specialist, who is frustrated in her attempts to collaborate with content area teachers in a junior high school. Despite the support given her by the well-respected principal, most of the teachers in the school have not volunteered to work with her. She feels that the three who did—Mary, Harold, and John—are not really cooperative, and she distrusts the motives of some of them. After Joan presents her side of the story, the three teachers each describe their goals and versions of events. As a result of analyzing this case, readers can learn a great deal about the conditions that facilitate or inhibit educational change in general, and implementation of the consulting teacher model in particular. First, it reveals the kinds of skills and knowledge a specialist will need before assuming the role of consulting teacher. Second, it should help readers understand how the culture of a school and teachers' concerns, needs, and beliefs affect teachers' possessive attitudes toward change. Third, it should help in developing realistic goals and plans of action, which a consulting teacher could use as a starting point to initiate and maintain collaborative relationships.

# ISSUES IN THE CASE

*1. What Were the Causes of the Conflict in This Case?*   To answer this question, you might begin by viewing the problem from the different perspectives of the case participants. In other words, how would each participant frame the problem? How are these framings similar and different? What led Joan to feel that Mary, Harold, and John were not cooperative? Were they resistant to change? What were their motives in working with Joan? In what ways did Joan contribute to the problem?

*2. What Are Prerequisites for Successful Collaboration?*   Huefner (1992) described a number of conditions that are necessary for successful implementation of the consulting teacher model, including willing participation, inservice training as a team, a focus on helping individual children rather than on teachers' effectiveness, organizational support, adequate planning time, effective communication skills, and realistic expectations.

*3. How Does Language Affect Images of Collaborative Teaching?* Dynak, Whitten, and Dynak (1997) built a case for using specific terms to describe discrete co-teaching models in order to help teachers design, communicate, and monitor collaborative classroom experiences. They identified five models in the literature: (a) *complementary teaching*, where one teacher takes the lead in presenting content while the coteacher complements instruction by modeling strategies in action (e.g., note-taking, concept mapping, summarizing, etc.); (b) *station teaching*, where coteachers design and monitor a variety of tasks that students, working in small groups, complete at various stations; (c) *parallel teaching*, where coteachers divide students into equal-sized groups to communicate and monitor instruction using the same content and the same strategies but with a smaller number of students; (d) *alternative teaching*, where coteachers design, communicate, and monitor atypical tasks and activities to re-teach and/or supplement key instructional content; and (e) *shared teaching*, where coteachers share all instructional components, often changing roles as they "intuitively or consciously reflect-in-action and try to make the lesson more meaningful to the students" (Dynak et al., 1997, p. 71). See also Welch's chapter in *Inclusive Education* ("Collaboration as a Tool for Inclusion"), which describes how specialists and classroom teachers can work together successfully in a variety of roles from consultation to team-teaching.

# QUESTIONS TO THINK ABOUT

*(These questions can be given to students prior to reading the case or to small groups for review in class before the whole-class discussion.)*

1. How do the participants in the case differ in their perceptions of one another and the situation as a whole? Specifically, how does Joan perceive her role and the reasons she has not been successful? How do Mary, Harold, and John perceive the purpose of Joan's work? In what ways do Joan's and the teachers' perceptions conflict?
2. How do you make sense of the conflict? In what ways do the stated intentions of the participants in the case differ from their actions? What are the unstated concerns and needs of each of the participants?
3. What are the prerequisites for successful collaboration among school professionals? Under what conditions might the teachers have been more receptive to working with Joan? What skills, knowledge, and attitudes do teachers need to work collaboratively?

# THE DISCUSSION OUTLINE

To begin the whole-class case activities, you could follow the discussion structure that has been described for all the previous cases, which consists of three parts: understanding the context and key players, framing the problem, and developing plans of action (these three headings can serve as main headings on the chalkboard or flip chart to record students' comments during the discussion). In this case, plans of action are developed through process drama activities. For students who are familiar with case pedagogies, you may decide that analyses of the context, key players, and problems in the case can be covered during the process drama activities and are therefore not necessary as preliminary discussion items.

What follows is one way to open the discussion, followed by questions you might ask during each segment of the discussion, should you decide to begin with the structured discussion:

The case you have just read involves a reading specialist attempting to work with junior high subject-area teachers in a new role, that of consulting teacher. This role involves collaboration with teachers to provide instructional support to help students with disabilities succeed in the general education classroom where possible, rather than being placed in remedial pull-out programs. However, in this case, the reading specialist, Joan, was not successful as a consulting teacher. Analyzing the case can help us to understand the problems that specialists (or special educators) and classroom teachers may experience as they work together. More broadly, the case illustrates some of the problems any educator may face when attempting to change role expectations and faculty relationships in schools. Let's begin our discussion by talking about the context and the key players in the case.

## A.   Understanding the Context and Key Players

- What are we told about Wellington Junior High School and its students?
- What are we told about Joan?
- Why does each teacher agree to work with Joan? In other words, what are their goals? What do they want her to do for them?
    Mary?
    Harold?
    John?
- How does each teacher see Joan's role? How does Joan see her role?

## B.   Framing the Problem

- What went wrong?
- How would the key players in the case answer this question? How would their answers differ from yours?

## C.   Developing Plans of Action

To help students deepen their engagement with the complex issues of this case *before* they attempt to formulate plans of actions, you might explore the material through a process drama experience (O'Neill, 1995). When this case was piloted at the University of Utah, we began the process drama by involving participants in several ecology-building activities that functioned as a physical, cognitive, and emotional warm-up (a host of such activities can be found in Boal's *Games for actors and non-actors,* 1992):

- Students were asked to pair up with someone who was approximately the same height. They were asked to move back-to-back, lean on each other (shoulder blades to shoulder blades), then step out slowly, putting increasing pressure on each other. Each pair continued to step out until a distant balance was achieved. The exercise was repeated with students facing each other, positioning themselves hand-to-hand, then stepping backward, putting increasing pressure on each others' hands.
- Students were then asked to find new partners and to pick a person who would "go first." These "initiators" were given the line: "I can't believe the way Jessica behaved today." Working simultaneously, these pairs were asked to assume instant roles and to develop their conversations for a minute. (These conversations carried us into teachers' lounges, lunch rooms, hallways, classrooms, etc.) We selected two of these conversations to replay for the group. The exercise was repeated with the other partners opening the conversation with the probe: "I heard what you said about me." Two of these scenes were selected for replaying.
- To help create images of a school's culture, we asked students to form small groups. One person from each group was asked to step forward and strike a pose. These "sculptures" were examined for positive space (i.e., the space occupied by torsos, arms, legs, etc). The remaining members of the small groups were asked to move into their respective sculptures one-by-one, and to fill a bit of the negative space (i.e., holes created by outstretched arms and legs) with the images of pyramids and cones guiding their choices of how to move into the image (to help them choose low, middle, and high levels). We then moved rapidly from small group to small group, assigning various "family names" to each, such as the "athletic family," "computer family," "shy," "sleepy," "athletic," "cheerleader," "teaching veteran," "administrator," etc. Students were then asked to reconfigure their family sculpture without discussion to capture the essence of their name.

At several points in this particular case, strong judgmental comments are voiced by the reading specialist and the teachers. To help students feel the power of judgments, we asked each small group to formulate one statement about one of the family sculptures they had observed. (Several small groups made judgmental comments about cheerleaders, about veteran teachers, etc.) We then reflected about how easily these sorts of comments emerged, and how preconceptions and judgmental comments affected levels of interaction.

Following these ecology-building activities, we asked each of the small groups to personalize their frames of reference by sharing their responses to two guiding questions:

- What do you remember about the treatment of students with special needs in your school experiences?
- How did tracking affect your educational experiences?

We then began the process drama experience with the case. For the opening episode, we asked everyone to assume the role of Joan, and to write a brief journal entry in role that captured a day in Joan's school life before her attempts at coteaching. Following this, we assigned each small group an episode from the case, instructing them not to be bound by gender in their selection of actors, and asked them to create and rehearse their episode for a few minutes:

*Group 1:*  The initial meeting when the principal first discusses coteaching with Joan,

*Group 2:*  The meeting between Joan and the principal when she is asked to develop a presentation for the staff on coteaching,

*Group 3:*  A snippet of Joan's inservice presentation to the faculty,

*Group 4:*  A phone call from Joan to a teacher friend after her meeting with Harold,

*Group 5:*  A scene from John's science class,

*Group 6:*  A meeting between Joan and Mary,

*Group 7:*  A meeting between Joan and John.

These episodes were presented for the class without commentary. The final moment occurred when we asked one of the participants who had played Joan to pack up her belongings and leave "our school" after her meeting with John. The silence at this point was deafening.

The power of process drama comes from participants' engagement as creators and shapers of meaning. As O'Neill (1995) notes: "Participants control significant aspects of what is taking place; they simultaneously experience it and organize it; they evaluate what is happening and make connections with other experiences" (p. 1). If the process drama develops authentically and aesthetically, from inciting incident to climax to denouement, a level of engagement is achieved that is immediate and visceral, but also distancing. That is, in experiencing each others' work, multiple images and multiple layers of meaning surface that are both accessible and assessable.

For the purpose of debriefing after our process drama experience, we invited students to share their perceptions and reflections of what they had seen, heard, and felt. To initiate this crucial component of process drama work, we asked participants to form a circle. We then moved around the circle, asking students to report one thing they remembered seeing or hearing from any of the episodes (e.g., "I saw teachers not paying attention during the inservice presentation" or "I heard a lot of loud talking and interrupting during John's science class"). The intent of this perception activity was to capture key details from the playing, not to evaluate what was played well. This is an important distinction. You may find it necessary to help steer students away from evaluative comments. The focus needs to stay on perceptions.

Once we sensed that sufficient details from the playing of the episodes had been recaptured, we asked students to report one feeling they had that connected them personally to the case: one thing they liked or one thing they were reminded of as they experienced the episodes. This reflection exercise helped us talk about the work. Collectively, these reflections grounded the importance of the work and helped students move beyond the case toward generalizations about practice.

You could conclude the case discussion by having students develop plans of action that might resolve and prevent problems related to school-based collaboration. To accomplish this goal, we had students assume the role of a consulting teacher about to initiate a similar project in a different school. In preparation for this role, students were asked to write about their process drama experience in their journals and to refer back to their answers to question 3 on the "Questions to Think About" discussion sheet. At this point, you might distribute copies of Huefner's (1992) "Commentary," in which Huefner describes the prerequisites to successful implementation of the consulting teacher model. Reading Welch's chapter in *Inclusive Education,* titled "Collaboration as a Tool for Inclusion," and Dynak, Whitten, and Dynak's (1997) "Refining the General Education Student Teaching Experience through the Use of Special Education Collaborative Teaching Models" would also be helpful to students. In small groups, students could then collaborate on answering the following questions:

- How would you recruit teachers initially?
- What would the team's goals be?

- How would the team make decisions and work together? How could the team acquire the necessary skills and processes that can facilitate decision making and collaboration?
- What kinds of organizational support would you need?

To conclude the case discussion, students from each of the small groups could share their plans of action with the whole class.

## FOLLOW-UP ACTIVITIES

This case could serve as a starting point for library research and interviews with school personnel on the topic of collaboration. Students could examine various models for consultation and collaboration among special education and general education teachers and develop a more elaborate plan for implementation in a school.

## REFERENCES

Boal, A. (1992). *Games for actors and non-actors.* New York: Routledge.

Dynak, J., Whitten, E., & Dynak, D. (1997). Refining the general education student teaching experience through the use of special education collaborative teaching models. *Action in Teacher Education, 19*(1), 64–74.

Huefner, D. (1992). Commentary. In J. H. Shulman (Ed.), *Case methods in teacher education* (pp. 106–109). New York: Teachers College Press.

O'Neill, C. (1995). *Dramaworlds: A framework for process drama.* Portsmouth, NH: Heinemann.

# AUTHOR INDEX

## A

American Association for the Advancement of Science (AAAS), 77, 82, 87, 99
American Association of University Women, 34, 46, 195
Apple, M. W., 21, 22

## B

Baldwin, R. S., 105, 123
Ball, D. L., 70, 74
Barnett, C., 54, 74
Bean, T. W., 105, 123
Becker, J., 8, 23
Belenky, M. F., 6, 22
Best, R., 195
Bird, T., 3, 4, 23, 53, 74, 84, 100, 118, 121, 123
Birrell, J. R., 83, 99
Boal, A., 230, 234
Bodroghkozy, A., 188, 195
Bowermaster, D., 31, 46
Boyle, O., 143, 148
Braaten, S., 40, 46
Buchmann, M., 69, 74, 96, 99
Burbules, N., 3n, 4, 6, 8, 22

## C

Cambourne, B., 102, 122
Carger, C. L., 147
Carter, K., 3, 22
Christensen, C. R., 7, 8, 9, 22, 28, 46
Clark, B., 30, 46
Clinchy, B. M., 6, 22
Colbert, J. A., 17, 23
Collier, V., 143, 148
Cook, C., 41, 46
Cooney, J. B., 92, 100
Crawford, J., 147
Cummins, J., 144, 147

## D

Dana, N. F., 96, 99
Dana, T. M., 96, 99
Delpit, L., 33, 34, 46, 62, 63, 74, 133, 137, 144, 147
Dewey, J., 21, 22
Deyhle, D., 152
Diaz-Soto, L., 147
Dillon, D. R., 7, 8, 23
Dmytriw, L., 17, 23
Doyle, W., 84, 99
Dynak, D., 228, 233, 234
Dynak, J., 228, 233, 234

## E

Eisner, E., 121, 122
Elbow, P., 6, 7, 22
Elmore, R. F., 38, 46, 219
Enersen, D. L., 7, 8, 23

## F

Faltis, C., 147
Feiman-Nemser, S., 69, 74, 94, 95, 96, 99
Frederick, P., 7, 11, 12, 13, 22
Freire, P., 4, 7, 8, 23, 123
Friend, M., 41, 46
Fuchs, D., 31, 46
Fuchs, L. S., 31, 46

## G

Garrison, J., 3, 4, 23
Garvin, D., 7, 8, 22
Geist, P., 71, 74
Genesee, F., 147
Gess-Newsome, J., 97, 100
Goldberg, M., 77, 99
Goldberger, N. R., 6, 22
Gore, J., 4, 22
Gormley, K., 97, 100
Graves, B. B., 40, 46

# SUBJECT INDEX